STORRS LECTURES ON JURISPRUDENCE
YALE LAW SCHOOL, 1978

Gifts and Promises

Continental and American Law Compared

John P. Dawson

YALE UNIVERSITY PRESS
New Haven and London
1980

Published with assistance from
the Louis Stern Memorial Fund.

Designed by James J. Johnson
and set in VIP Caledonia type.
Printed in the United States of America.

Published in Great Britain, Europe, Africa, and
Asia (except Japan) by Yale University Press,
Ltd., London. Distributed in Australia and
New Zealand by Book & Film Services, Artarmon,
N.S.W., Australia; and in Japan by Harper & Row,
Publishers, Tokyo Office.

*Library of Congress Cataloging in Publication
Data*

Dawson, John Philip.
    Gifts and promises.

    (Storrs lectures on jurisprudence; 1978)
    Includes index.
    1. Gifts—France. 2. Promise   (Law)—
France. 3. Gifts—Germany, West. 4. Promise
(Law)—Germany, West. I. Title. II. Series.
Law   346′.43′047   79–23034
ISBN 0–300–02446–0

Contents

Preface

The invitation of the Yale Law School faculty to give the Storrs lectures in 1978 was an unexpected honor for which I was unprepared. The Storrs lecture series has been admired for many years and many reasons, mostly for the contribution it has made to the widening of horizons and the opening of new directions, often viewed from high vantage points. Being sure that I am not endowed with the scanning equipment or range-finders needed for such an overview, I concluded that I should take off nearer to ground level. So I have chosen a narrowly defined and familiar theme and propose to follow it closely over a considerable distance in space and time.

As with most comparative legal studies, the main purpose will be to discover whether we have something to learn from the experience of certain foreign systems of law. In order to start on the present inquiry one must first clear away much misinformation that is widely circulated in this country as to the treatment of gratuitous transactions in European countries. To understand why the solutions in those countries are so different from our own, much history will be needed. For me this was an additional reason for choosing the subject. To understand why France and Germany in their treatment of such transactions have come to differ from each other more than they do from us, one must examine some central questions of legal method under codes. My hope is that the differences between the two countries will emerge more clearly because the issues that produce them are mostly drawn from common experience and are relatively simple and familiar.

I am indebted for aid and criticism to my son, Professor Philip Dawson of the history department of Brooklyn College, to Professor W. Burnett Harvey of the Boston University Law School, and to Professor James R. Gordley of the Law School of the University of California at Berkeley. To the Yale Law School faculty and the highly valued friends I have there I want to express again my respect and gratitude.

J. P. D.

Abbreviations

B.G.B.	Bürgerliches Gesetzbuch
B.G.H.Z.	*Entscheidungen des Bundesgerichtshofs in Zivilsachen*
C.	Code (part of Corpus Juris)
D.	Digest (part of Corpus Juris)
D.H.	Recueil hebdomadaire Dalloz
D.P.	Dalloz périodique
J.C.P.	Juris-Classeur périodique (La Semaine juridique)
J.W.	*Juristische Wochenschrift*
J.Z.	*Juristenzeitung*
M.D.R.	*Monatschrift für deutsches Recht*
N.J.W.	*Neue juristische Wochenschrift*
N.R.H.	*Nouvelle Revue historique de droit français et étranger*
O.G.H.Z.	*Entscheidungen des Obersten Gerichtshofes für die Britische Zone in Zivilsachen*
R.G.Z.	*Entscheidungen des Reichsgerichts in Zivilsachen*
S.	Receuil Sirey
Seuff. Arch.	Seufferts Archiv für Entscheidungen der obersten Gerichte in den deutschen Staaten
Warneyer	Warneyers Jahrbuch der Entscheidungen
Z.S.S.	*Zeitschrift der Savigny-Stiftung*

Introduction

The landscape to be examined in this survey has been reported by many observers to include as one of its features a
great gap, a chasm, that divides all legal systems derived from
the English common law from those of the European continent. The gap is revealed by asking a short question: Can a
fully capable person make a binding promise to another to
give or do something for nothing? For countries within the
sphere of influence of the English common law the standard
answer would be no, almost never. For the more civilized
countries of western Europe the standard answer would be
yes, since they have never suffered from the blight that
afflicts countries adhering to the English common law—the
requirement of bargain consideration.

In order to discover whether the gap is in truth so wide,
attention will be directed toward two European legal
systems—those of France and Germany. One reason for
choosing them is the considerable influence both have had
on the law in force elsewhere in western Europe, so that they
can serve in some degree as prototypes. But there are differences between these two "civil law" systems themselves,
not so much in the provisions of their codes, which on these
themes are much alike, as in the results reached by courts in
applying them. These differences will invite comparisons of

another kind—as to the degrees of respect that France and Germany show toward their codes.

Main emphasis will be placed in this account on the law now in force, but the inheritance from the past, especially from Roman law, will have to be described in greater detail than is usually needed in modern comparative studies. There was a contribution also from medieval and early modern, precode experience that gave a new direction but in a strange way confirmed the Roman solutions. This means that attention will not be confined to promises, which historically have been the principal target of the consideration test. The Romans and their followers seldom marked off promises of gift from completed gifts in order to subject them to different treatment. In our own law the starting point is that most promises of gift are wasted words, and it is only their performance that counts, so that the gift is conceived as a one-sided act—a transfer in which the transferor holds all the controls. In western Europe a different way of thinking has come to be a habit. In what might be called the Romanesque tradition, a gift is conceived as a two-sided transaction, a contract which, like any other contract, requires mutual assent and is discussed, if trouble comes, with the vocabulary of the law of contract. At times this has made a difference. One effect has been, in any event, to blur the distinction, which is elementary for us, between promises of gift and completed gifts.

The main target, nevertheless, will continue to be the differences in both past and present in the treatment of gratuitous promises—promises for which, as we would say, there has been and will be no consideration. The effects of the requirement of consideration on contract formation in our law will be for the most part taken for granted and no attempt will be made to assemble all the complaints that have been made against it. Dissatisfaction with the doctrine of consideration has been expressed, in English, in so many ways and for so many reasons that a glossary of quotations is hardly needed. The expressions range from attempts to explain it as an obsolete relic of late medieval English procedure to the charge that it is a sign of cultural retardation. Some of the critics, of course, condemn it altogether and demand that it be abolished. One of the most ardent of the abolitionists, however, was able recently to report some good news: that bargain consideration, produced only a century ago by that odd couple, Christopher Columbus Langdell and Oliver Wendell Holmes, has recently and quietly expired. No active surgery was needed, it seems, merely a denial of life support. For this coincided with the Death of Contract when Contract was consumed by the law of Tort, an event that was celebrated at a festive funeral not quite ten years ago.[1]

To me it has seemed that the account of both deaths was exaggerated. In these essays the premise will be that bargain consideration has been and will remain for a long time to come a central feature of our law of contract, central in the sense that it provides a strong affirmative reason for enforcing promises, the reason that is by a wide margin the most often used, though it is not the only one. The reason is persuasive: the promisor receives or is assured that he will receive the kind of advantage that he in fact desires and has expressly promised to pay for. This reason is persuasive enough so that, in the countries to be surveyed here, means were found long ago to enforce substantially all those exchanges that we too enforce and that comply with our tests of bargain. Actually, this is not the issue on which battle is joined. Even the most embittered critics of bargain consideration do not really object to the enforcement of bargains. The

1. G. Gilmore, *The Death of Contract* (Columbus, Ohio, 1974).

objection has been to its transformation into a formula of denial, a formula that would deny legal effect to most promises for which there is nothing given or received in exchange.

In our own law of course the negation is not complete. Some promises are enforced for other reasons. So two questions arise at the outset; a third lurks around the corner. The first question is whether it is true in fact that in France and Germany greater readiness exists to enforce promises for whose performance there is and is to be no exchange. The second question is whether, if such readiness does exist, Europeans have articulated specific reasons for enforcement that we have overlooked or too hastily discarded, so that from European experience we have something useful to learn. The third question throws the first two questions into reverse by asking: Do we enforce promises for reasons that Europeans do not now accept? Reliance by a promisee would be an example. But the main concern will be to discover whether it is true, as is commonly said, that the range of gratuitous promises that are enforced in France and Germany is much wider than it is with us and whether this points to a deficiency that we should try to correct.

In the comparisons that will be made it will fortunately be possible to disregard entirely much debris that the consideration test has accumulated and that has distracted attention from its central idea—bargain as a ground for enforcing promises. The most harmful distortion of the central idea has come, I believe, through extending it to the discharge or modification of obligations. Another piece of debris that has been picked up is the offer, for which consideration (or in some states a seal) is needed if the offeror desires to make his offer irrevocable. This is a needless hindrance to the processes by which agreement is reached and, being artificial as well as needless, was soon made to look silly, so that a dollar, a hairpin, or a false recital would do. It was not quite so misguided to apply detriment tests to transactions in which the promises exchanged leave wide choice on one side and not on the other, so that the obligations in that sense are not "mutual." Imbalances of this kind raise problems that are real and extremely troublesome, but much too complex to be dealt with through the formal tests of detriment and benefit that consideration can supply. In the European systems that will be discussed, problems raised by issues like these are identified by their proper names. This means that when comparisons are called for, the debris can be disregarded and one can concentrate attention on the central idea of bargained-for exchange in its role in the formation of contracts.

I The Legacy from Roman Law

During the period of more than 1,000 years when the law of Rome was an operating system applied and maintained through the authority of a territorial state, no signs appeared that any need was felt for a generalized restriction on contract formation that resembled in any way the consideration test. This is not surprising, if only because during most of that long stretch of time Roman law did not have what could be called a law of contract. There were various types of contracts, each with its separate cluster of rules. They were formed in different ways, they performed different functions that for the most part did not overlap, and they had come to be recognized at different periods of time. As one author put it, "there had to be strong reasons for any contract being recognized as legally binding and, further, for it being recognized at that particular time and place."[1] Certain types of exchange transactions were made enforceable early—sales of land and goods, leases, various forms of partnership. But evidently no need was felt to design a transaction whose primary function would be to aid the generous in giving away something for nothing. The promise of gift as a distinct contract-type, fully enforceable in undisguised form, was not recognized until very late, near the end of Roman law as an operative system.[2]

1. A. Watson, *Contract of Mandate in Roman Law*, p. 1 (1961).
2. Below, note 44.

From an early time, however, it was possible to make or to promise a gift that was disguised in the very limited sense that it employed one of the forms designed for other approved transactions. If this was done, most of the time and between most people no objection at all would be raised. The most obvious example would be a conveyance made in standard form, perhaps with actual or symbolic physical delivery, as in *mancipatio,* the oldest method of transferring ownership.[3] Or if a donor was not ready to convey yet wished to bind himself by promise, there was the ancient ritual of stipulation, in which the promisee formulated the promise and asked: "Do you promise——?" (stating the terms) and the promisor answered "I promise." The exchange of question and answer was oral, face to face. No witnesses or writings were required, though both were commonly used. In the standard form of stipulation there was only one promisor, and no recitals were called for to describe his motive nor any payment or other return from the promisee. This, the familiar, all-purpose formality of Roman contract law, was as serviceable and as widely used as the sealed instrument in earlier English law. Like the sealed instrument, it could clearly be used to promise payment or some other act for which there was to be no exchange at all.[4]

There was, in addition, one group of fully accredited transactions, each with a separate function but with one common feature: all of them were designed to be, and really

3. *Mancipatio* is described by Buckland, *Textbook of Roman Law,* pp. 238–241, 3d ed. (1973). As he points out, the later texts that described less stereotyped forms of transfer related mainly to gift transactions.

4. The enormous practical importance of the *stipulatio* in all branches of Roman private law and procedure is described by M. Kaser, *Das römische Privatrecht,* 2d ed. (1971), 1: 538. As he says, it was a promise that could be used in conjunction with a variety of other contracts, to modify or to reinforce them. He describes it as "one of the most original and important creations of Roman law."

were supposed to be, entirely unremunerated. Two of them we would call bailments of movables: the deposit (*depositum*), which gave bare custody, and the loan for use (*commodatum*), which gave privileges not only to use but to draw income from the asset loaned. For any net profit the borrower was accountable but otherwise he must pay or give no fee or reward. This absence of any recompense was built into the definition.[5] In truth it was mostly an issue of definition, for if a price was to be paid the transaction would become a lease and in that guise would, as a rule, be fully enforceable. The absence of any payment by the depositee lowered the standard of care required of him in preventing loss or injury, so the question whether any payment had been agreed to could occasionally have some importance. Even though no payment was provided for, the duty to provide safe custody was explained as a product of contract, and in the loan for use, at least, a fixed term for its duration that was agreed to at the outset was enforced against a lender who later changed his mind.[6] In retrospect these forms of gratuitous promise seem important mainly because they serve as clues to the thinking of the Roman jurists, who regularly included them on the list of enforceable contracts while continuing to insist that any such transaction was necessarily gratuitous if it was to fit the type.

More ancient and much more important was the repayable loan, the *mutuum*, usually a loan of money, though

5. Buckland, *Textbook*, pp. 464–469; J. Michel, *Gratuité en Droit Romain*, pp. 56–70, 74–94 (Brussels, 1962). Related to the deposit and loan for use was the pledge. The pledge became highly developed and was much used, but it raised somewhat different issues, which are discussed by Buckland, *Textbook*, pp. 471–476.

6. D.13.6.17.3 is explicit on this as to *commodatum*. As to gratuitous lending of land, Michel (*Gratuité*, pp. 51–53) argued that a provision for a fixed term was similarly enforceable against the lender-owner, but the evidence he offered to support this contention was less convincing.

other fungibles would do. It was called a "loan for consumption" because the borrower was free to spend it and was obligated only to repay an equal sum. Since he was obligated to repay, we would no doubt label this an exchange transaction, but, seen through the lenses of the Roman jurists, it appeared in substance to be gratuitous because the sum to be repaid was an equal sum and no more. It was an essential feature of the *mutuum* that borrowers could not bind themselves to pay more than had been lent. This was not because of hostility to interest or other premiums for the use of money; the permissible rate of interest was long regulated by public legislation, but within the limits so defined, interest was entirely lawful. Indeed, it could be agreed in advance that, as an incident to a loan of money, payment of interest would be promised in the form of a stipulation, the ritual of question and answer being performed on the side. There is evidence from other sources that by classical times this had become common practice. So it seems strange that official sources continued to insist that through the *mutuum* the borrower could not promise any increment whatever beyond exact repayment of the sum or quantity that he had received. The *mutuum* was without doubt an enforceable contract, one of the first to become enforceable. Its function was not to produce gain for the lender but to provide a friend, relative, or one in need with disinterested aid. For this form of service it would be dishonorable to exact a return.[7]

Still more was this true of mandate, the nearest Roman equivalent of our agency. This was a contract to render service to another. Roman law recognized only partially the notion of representation, so that the mandatary (agent) would not be empowered to create rights in his principal, and in relations with third parties would purport to act on his own

7. Buckland, *Textbook*, pp. 462–465; Girard, *Manuel Élémentaire du Droit Romain*, 7th ed. (1924), pp. 516–524; Michel, *Gratuité*, pp. 105–118.

behalf.[8] But even before it became enforceable as a contract (probably in the second century B.C.) the notion of mandate had come to include a very great variety of services rendered to friends and relatives.[9] From the beginning and always it was considered to be gratuitous. Legal sources continued to insist on this, and at the end Justinian reaffirmed it in his Institutes. If compensation was provided for, the transaction might be something else (for example, services could be "leased"), but it could not be a mandate.[10] Such assertions in due course became somewhat unreal, for, by the second century A.D., imperial officials had begun to enforce the payment of salaries promised in return for services rendered, under a special imperial procedure independent of the ordinary courts.[11] But the standard sources of Roman private law continued to insist on the gratuitous nature of this "consensual" contract, for whose formation no specific acts or formalities were needed; to create the relationship a nod would do.[12]

It was surely no great stretch to describe mandate as a contract, as the Romans regularly did. It is true that the mandator (the "principal") could revoke the mandate for any reason if the other party (the "agent") had not yet acted. The mandatary ("agent") also had power to revoke for "just

8. Buckland, *Textbook*, p. 519.
9. Watson, *Mandate*, pp. 11–22, 78–79.
10. Michel, *Gratuité*, pp. 168–170. The statement by Paul in D.17.1.1.4 is a fair sample: "A mandate is a nullity unless it is gratuitous (*mandatum nisi gratuitum nullum est*). For its origin is in duty and friendship. Pay is contrary to duty; if money enters, the affair more resembles a lease."
11. Buckland, *Textbook*, pp. 514–515; E. Rabel, *Grundzüge des römischen Privatrechts*, 2d ed. (1955), p. 112. Michel, *Gratuité*, p. 197, describes the insistence of Justinian's Institutes on the gratuitous nature of mandate as probably an example of "legal archaeology," since the original rule had so long been displaced by the remedies awarded under "extraordinary" procedure.
12. Watson, *Mandate*, p. 61.

cause," and this power was later extended even further. But on either side an express, communicated revocation was required to cancel the rights and duties that arose on the inception of the agreement.[13] The principal duty was that imposed on the mandatary to carry to completion the task he had undertaken and to do this with appropriate diligence and care. He was also required to account for and surrender any gain that might accrue to him.[14] The mandator, on the other hand, owed a duty to indemnify him for any expenditures or losses incurred without his fault through his performance of the task or service. A common form of mandate, for example, was the guaranty of an obligation owed by the mandator to a third person. A duty of the principal debtor to save his surety harmless would be for us, of course, a normal incident of suretyship. Roman lawyers derived it from the contract of mandate, which could thus carry reciprocal obligations. But in their view the service rendered in guaranteeing a debt was entirely gratuitous, and no less so because the one to whom the service was rendered must protect the guarantor (the "agent") against loss.[15]

It seems strange that this attribute—"gratuitousness"—should have seemed to be worth preserving in lawyers' discourse long after the money loan and mandate, transactions of real importance in everyday life, had come to be very commonly used to earn profit or pay. The explanation that appeals to me has been proposed by a Belgian author—that these conceptions originated at a much earlier time in the upper levels of a highly stratified society. For Romans who

13. Ibid., pp. 70–77; Buckland, *Textbook*, p. 518.
14. There could be, in addition, liabilities for departing from the mandator's instructions (Watson, pp. 178–202). As to the tests for liability, Watson concludes (pp. 198–202) that there were too many kinds of mandate for a single rule and that other variables were introduced by distinctions between intentional fault and negligence.
15. Watson, *Mandate*, pp. 154–166.

either occupied or sought to infiltrate these commanding heights, acceptance of payment for personal services was demeaning, even sordid, and income from commerce rather than from landed estates had to be earned under various disguises.[16] The admired posture was that of the generous friend, ready to give aid or render service but finding abhorrent any notion of an agreed, enforceable reward. If the enterprise undertaken because of friendship, mutual respect, or personal honor was left incomplete or was carelessly managed, the compulsion to adhere to high standards of conduct was felt strongly enough so that it was appropriate for courts to intervene and administer correctives. In describing both the standards and the correctives (the argument proceeds) the great jurists of classical times served in high degree as spokesmen for the values and expectations of the very small governing group that was centered in the city of Rome. With this group the jurists themselves had close personal ties.[17] The survival of their conceptions of gratuitous but enforceable contracts could then be explained by the system of values the jurists observed on the high plateau on which Roman society had placed them. Established much earlier, the conceptions that animated them persisted long after the great senatorial families had been obliterated in the civil wars and an imperial government had created entirely new forms of oligarchy. As we shall see, these same ideas persisted much later as a permanent feature in Rome's legacy to the future.

This is of course what concerns us now—the message that these passages were to carry to attentive readers of the Corpus Juris over the centuries that lay ahead. The message of Justinian's code was to require much decoding, but this much at least came through—contracts providing for human services or for the mere use, without alteration, of another's

16. Michel, *Gratuité*, pp. 147–156.
17. Ibid., pp. 580–584.

property do not ordinarily call for remuneration but are enforceable nevertheless. The message might not have come through quite so clearly if it had not been confirmed from another direction, in a back-handed way.

There was in classical law one flat prohibition. It applied to gifts between husband and wife. In Roman sources it is ascribed to "custom," not express legislation. Some modern authors contend that the custom was ancient.[18] The earliest reference to it came from a time when Roman law was approaching full maturity (that is, shortly before the Christian era), and perhaps it originated then.[19] The explanation given for it reflected an ideal conception of marriage at the highest level of mutual devotion and disinterestedness, resting on the belief that "honest love exists only in the spirit" and that marital harmony must not appear to be "procured at a price."[20] The strenuous and determined effort made to maintain these ideals suggests that the motives for marrying were not always so pure.[21] The ease with which marriages could be dissolved in Roman law—by unilateral declaration of either spouse[22]—may have pointed up the need for protecting the vulnerable or unwary. There must have been another reason: much more concern than the surviving sources show over the diversion of assets from one family line to another, enriching the family of the acquisitive spouse. At any rate, stern measures were used. Except for small gifts to mark an-

18. F. Dumont, *Les Donations entre époux en droit romain,* pp. 14–20 (1928).

19. This is suggested by E. Rabel, *Grundzüge,* pp. 193–195. That the prohibition was the product of custom, not legislation, is now agreed. Dumont, *Les Donations,* pp. 14–20; O. Gradenwitz, *Die Ungültigkeit obligatorische Rechtsgeschäfte* (1887), pp. 193–205.

20. D.24.1.3 (Ulpian speaking). Similar explanations, by Ulpian and Paul, appear in D.24.1.1 and D.24.1.2.

21. Gradenwitz, *Die Ungültigkeit,* pp. 205–206.

22. Buckland, *Textbook,* pp. 117–118.

niversaries or for personal adornment, all gifts between husband and wife, made by either spouse, were absolutely void, passed no title; if possession had been surrendered it could be summarily retaken.[23]

It was in this peculiar setting that Roman lawyers were given their principal, almost their only, occasion for analyzing the essential elements of a gift. There were, of course, gratuitous transactions of other kinds that were subject to control or prohibition, such as transfers by a debtor made to obstruct his own creditors or the siphoning off by a guardian of his ward's assets. But for some reason, perhaps through chance that determined which classical texts would survive, attempts made in the extant sources to define the essential elements of a gift almost entirely concentrate on gifts between husband and wife. As one might expect, there emerged from this peculiar setting a conception of gift that was also peculiar. Since it was to shape thought for many centuries to come we should pause to examine it.

To be noted first are the omissions. Services—human action or inaction—of every kind were entirely excluded. Nor was it a gift to permit the use or occupancy by one spouse of assets belonging to the other—land, goods, servants, slaves. The declared purpose of the prohibition was to preserve marriage as an intimate and trusting personal union, free from calculations of economic advantage. While their life together lasted the assets of the marriage partners were treated in effect as a common fund that both were free to use, manage, and enjoy and from which they could even take income.[24] What they could not do was to make transfers that had the double effect of diminishing the "patrimony" owned by one spouse and increasing to a corresponding degree the

23. Girard, *Manuel*, 1000–1001; Dumont, *Les Donations*, pp. 136–147.
24. D.24.1.18 is explicit. Dumont, *Les Donations*, pp. 140–47, collects other examples of shared use of assets in aid of their common life.

"patrimony" of the other.[25] Both impoverishment and enrichment, in this form, were required. If, for example, the use to which the subject matter was put left the donee in the end with no net gain, this would mean that after all no gift had been made.[26] If the net loss and net gain were unequal, there was a gift only to the extent of the lesser amount.[27] Since the

25. The question whether the *patrimonium* of one spouse had been diminished was discussed, for example, in D.24.1.5.13, where a husband had renounced an inheritance with the result that his wife would then inherit it. The conclusion announced was that, though the wife would gain, the husband had not become poorer, since he would be merely abstaining from acquisition and not surrendering an interest that he already owned as part of his *patrimonium*. Similar conclusions on similar facts, that surrenders of inheritances were not gifts, appear in D.24.1.5.14 and D.24.1.31.7.

26. D.24.1.5.8 (land transferred by either husband or wife to the other for use as a burial ground; no gift since the land would then become *locum religiosum* so that the donee would not be enriched); D.24.1.5.12 (land transferred by husband to wife to be used for sacrifices to the gods or to be dedicated to public use; no gift because it would become a sacred place and the donee would not gain.

In these two instances the transfer seemingly imposed a requirement that the land be dedicated to religious or public purposes. In D.24.1.5.17, however, it was not at all clear that payment over to relatives had been made a mandatory term imposed by a husband who paid money to his wife, but since it was in fact paid over to the relatives, the payment was declared by Marcellus not to be a gift to the wife. And in D.24.1.7.1 a wife seemed to be acting of her own volition when she used money, given to her to buy perfume, to pay her husband's debt to a third party. Since she was not in the end enriched, the conclusion was that there had been no gift.

27. In D.24.1.28.3, Paul discusses the case of a wife to whom a husband gave a sum of money described as 10 (sesterces, perhaps) and she used it to buy a slave worth, alternatively, 5 or 15. If the slave was worth 5, this would be the limit on recovery (just as, Paul adds, if the slave died there would be *no* recovery for lack of enrichment). If the slave turned out to be worth 15, on the other hand, recovery would only be 10, since this would be the amount by which the donor was "poorer."

Paul discussed a similar situation in D.24.1.55: a wife gave money to her husband who used it to acquire some other asset, land or movables. Paul concluded again that if the value of the newly acquired asset later rose or fell, the sum used to buy it or its subsequent value, whichever was less, would be a ceiling on the wife's recovery.

declared purpose was to promote the affection and mutual trust on which successful marriage depended, there was good reason to exempt most forms of mutual aid, including the free use of each others' assets, and concentrate on profit-taking that had permanent effects in diminishing the disposable assets owned by one marriage partner and bringing about a net increase in those owned by the other.

The prohibition of gifts between husband and wife was thus read as applying to a severely limited range of transactions, but within that range the jurists enforced it with vigor. Any attempted transfer that was construed to be a gift was totally void.[28] If possession had been surrendered the asset could be summarily recaptured, or if it had been destroyed or consumed its value could be recovered to the extent that the receiver had been "enriched."[29] If the donee had exchanged the asset given for another, the donor spouse was allowed to "trace" and claim ownership of the substituted asset,[30]

28. D.24.1.5.18 discusses a case in which a husband conveyed land to his wife by gift and she built a house on it. The house, Pomponius said, immediately became the husband's by accession, since he had continued to own it, though the suggestion was added that the wife should be reimbursed for her outlay. Conversely, if the subject of the gift was destroyed or consumed, the risk of loss remained with the donor whose ownership had continued. D.24.1.31.2.

29. D.24.1.5.18.

30. In D.24.1.29 the "tracing" extended through three stages: money given by husband to wife was used by her to buy a slave, who was then sold, and with the proceeds another slave was bought. Pomponius concluded that the husband owned the second slave. In D.24.1.28.5 Julian extended this notion to property or even a child later acquired by a slave who had been purchased by the wife with money given by the husband. A case with elements that are still more familiar to American lawyers is one discussed by Paul in D.24.1.55: a wife had given money to her husband, who used it to buy property (Paul was uncertain whether it was land or goods). The husband was insolvent, as the "trustee" so often is in our constructive trust cases. The donor wife was allowed to recover the asset bought, but not more than the value represented by the sum of money she had given since that was the limit of her impoverishment.

though other such examples of what we call the constructive
trust (usually described as an "Anglo-Saxon" aberration)
would be hard to find, early or late, on the continent of
Europe. It was not necessary that there be a recoverable asset; a gift could occur through the extinction of a debt—the
release by one spouse of a debt owed him/her by the other[31]
or payment of a debt owed by one of them to a third person.[32]
A promise by one married person to pay or guarantee the
other's debt to a third person was a promise of gift and was
simply disregarded, since it was wholly void and had no effect on the rights of either creditor or debtor.[33] The prohibition applied only to gifts; it did not extend to exchange transactions, so that contracts of sale between husband and wife
would ordinarily be valid. But what if a discrepancy were to
appear in the values exchanged in such a sale? The relations
of the parties might arouse a suspicion that the extra margin
of value was intended to be a gift to the one who gained.
Concern on this ground could arise only if the parties were
married to each other, for until very late in Roman law no
attempt was made to set limits to the disparities in the values
exchanged in sale transactions; deliberately making them
unequal was an entirely acceptable way of conferring gain on
another.[34] But if the parties to the transaction were husband
and wife, the disguise of sale would be penetrated and to the
extent that a gift was intended the transaction would be
void.[35]

31. D.24.1.5.1; D.24.1.5.5.
32. D.24.1.7.7.
33. D.24.1.5.4. The contrast is greater because ordinarily, where married persons were not involved, promises of sureties were commonly conceived of as contracts of mandate, which to fit that category *must* be
gratuitous (see above, notes 10, 12).
34. Buckland, *Textbook*, p. 483; Girard, *Manuel*, p. 575.
35. Dumont, *Les Donations*, pp. 92–116. As this author points out (pp.
93–99), the usual solution was partial invalidity, though some jurists said

The vigor and vigilance shown by the jurists in policing transactions between husband and wife contrast sharply with the lethargy they showed toward another form of control over gifts, an attempt by earlier legislation to set limits to their size. The legislation, the *lex Cincia,* dates from 204 B.C. Modern authors have surmised that its original purpose was to restrain luxurious living and conspicuous expenditure in a society devastated by recent wars. Some have thought that in later times it served some purpose in reducing the influence of the wealthy over their social and economic inferiors.[36] The legislation remained at least nominally in force throughout the classical period, into the third century A.D., but it seems plain, whatever the motives for it were, that it had no supportive help from the classical jurists. Their writings do not even show how high the ceiling was or what form it took—for

---

that sales at a low price between married persons, with the margin of value intended as gifts, were entirely void. In D.18.1.38, for example, Ulpian says: "If one sells at a low price for the purpose of making a gift, the sale is valid. We do say that an [ostensible] sale is void altogether if the whole transaction is a gift, but if the property is transferred for a low price for the purpose of making a gift there is no doubt that the sale is valid. This is true between most persons, but between husband and wife a sale made at a low price for the purpose of making a gift has no legal effect [*nullius momenti est*]."

In D.24.1.52. pr. Papinian is quoted for the conclusion that "if a husband leases to his wife at a low rent the lease is void." Dumont describes (*Les Donations,* pp. 101–104) husband-wife partnerships that were held to be void because they produced a margin of gain to one spouse and also (pp. 104–108) the scaling down of overpayments made or promised for the performance of some act by the other spouse.

36. These suggestions are made by M. Kaser, *Das römische Privatrecht,* 1: 602–604. The theme is also discussed in the book review by W. Kunkel in 72 *Z.S.S. (röm.)* 470, 478–479. For later interpreters the impression that there was no intelligible purpose may have been enhanced by numerous exceptions that the original legislation contained—for gifts to relatives (some of them not very near relatives, such as cognates to the fifth degree), wards, natural objects of bounty such as those in the donor's *potestas,* persons engaged to marry, or relatives of any degree to whom the donor contributed by way of dowry. Girard, *Manuel,* pp. 989–990.

example, a fixed sum for each gift transaction or a percentage of the donor's estate. The ceiling must have been high, for there is little evidence that repentant donors ever made much use of the statute. If the ceiling was exceeded, the gift was not avoided but was merely scaled down. As the statute was construed by the Roman jurists, completion of the gift by transfer of title and possession made it immune to attack, so that in net effect it merely provided a defense when enforcement was sought of an unperformed promise of gift.[37] Then this defense was itself reduced to a purely personal privilege that could only be exercised by the donor himself and was terminated by his death.[38] The notion that very large gifts should be subjected to special scrutiny was to reappear later in Roman law. In their own time the classical jurists made this antique statute, which attempted to control gifts by a limit on their size, into what has been described as an "imperfect law," almost devoid of sanctions.[39]

In the meantime the variety of contract-types was steadily increasing as promises in new forms were devised and placed on the accredited list. One of these, which was made enforceable by imperial legislation, was plainly marked as a promise of gift—the promise of a citizen to give funds to a city for the construction or rebuilding of public works.[40] The

37. Rabel, *Grundzüge*, pp. 192–193; Buckland, *Textbook*, pp. 254–255; Girard, *Manuel*, pp. 989–992. The author last cited leaves open the possibility that donors might have been able to secure restitution of the excess over the statutory limit.

38. O. Karlowa, *Römische Rechtsgeschichte* (Leipzig, 1901), 2: 587; Girard, *Manuel*, pp. 991–992; Kaser, *Das römische Privatrecht*, cited in note 36.

39. The phrase *lex imperfecta* is used to describe it by Girard, *Manuel*, pp. 994–995.

40. This, the *pollicitatio*, had an antecedent in the promise to give to the temple of a god, which had been enforceable from an early time, without need of legislation. Rabel, *Grundzüge*, pp. 118–119. An element of bargain could be detected in that the promise became at once enforceable if

other innovations were for the most part due to the classical jurists. Traditionalists, carefully preserving the contents and limits of the standard contracts, they nevertheless did not succumb to that occupational disease of lawyers, hardening of the categories. Some of the deviant forms they approved, the "innominate contracts," were clearly bargains, exchanges already half-completed with a promise on only one side—for example, goods delivered in return for a promise of other goods (or of land), money paid for the promise of an act or abstention, an act in return for a promise to pay (if you swear to assume my family name I promise to pay you 100 sesterces).[41] Where a contractual obligation already existed it became possible to make new arrangements and modify their terms through informal "pacts" that were given full legal effect though they brought advantages that were strictly one-sided.[42]

---

the promisor had received or was about to receive an "honor" from the city. Otherwise it became enforceable when the promisor began paying or when the city began construction. Buckland, *Textbook*, p. 454, n. 7; Girard, *Manuel*, pp. 488–489; D.50.12.1–3. The *pollicitatio* was to be considered much more broadly in the later civilian tradition, of which a most interesting account is given by T. B. Smith, "Pollicitatio-Promise and Offer," in *Studies Critical and Comparative*, p. 168 (1962).

41. Many of the "contracts without name" had come to be recognized before the end of the classical period. They are discussed by Buckland, *Textbook*, pp. 518–523 (3d ed.); Girard, *Manuel*, pp. 624–635. The example given, a promise to pay for the adoption of a family name, (D.39.5.19.6) suggests that the Romans could recognize a bargained-for detriment without knowing how to describe it.

42. The most interesting and probably the most important was the *pactum de constituto*, which could fix dates and new terms of payment for the debtor himself or could be used by a third person to assume, in effect, the role of surety. By another form of pact, employed primarily where a claim on one side was disputed or uncertain, the parties could agree to make the oath of one party decisive. Compromise agreements of various kinds and agreements to arbitrate could also take this form. The whole subject is discussed by Buckland, *Textbook*, pp. 524–529 and Girard, *Manuel*, pp. 638–647. Buckland comments that the *pacta* "though in a sense unilateral, had

More important for the general population whose affairs were regulated by Roman law was the shift in later centuries to the use of written documents, as the ancient question-answer ritual of the oral stipulation fell into disuse. It seems that under the late empire, especially in the Greek east, a signed writing in any form came to be accepted as enough to justify enforcement of a promise.[43] But the surviving evidence is scattered and indirect. To attentive readers who searched the rediscovered Corpus Juris in the twelfth and thirteenth centuries this conclusion could not have come through clearly. It was the impression made on them that would determine main directions for centuries thereafter.

From the texts assembled in the Corpus Juris by Justinian's compilers it would have been most difficult to secure an ordered overview of the law of contract. The landscape was cluttered with a profusion of contract forms and types, each stamped with special features that marked it off from the rest. It was evident that the Roman jurists had not felt the need for overarching generalities that could explain and encompass all or most of the law of contract. Still less was there a limitation phrased in general terms that excluded from enforcement promises for which there was to be no return or recompense—no "consideration." On the contrary, there were four transaction-types, two of them (mandate and money loan) well known and important in daily life, of which it was still regularly said that they would be distorted and

---

in general a *quid pro quo*," and that in the *pactum de constituto* this consisted of a "suspension" of the previously existing right of action in the creditor. This, I suggest, was a legal consequence and not an essential feature on which the parties must agree. There surely was nothing like a requirement of a new quid pro quo or "consideration"; there was, in other words, no preexisting duty rule.

43. Kaser, *Das römische Privatrecht*, 2: 373–377 (2d ed.); B. Nicolas, "The Form of the Stipulation in Roman Law," 69 *Law Quarterly Review* 63, 233 (1953).

denatured if a reward or return was provided for. To the question, posed in the abstract, whether gratuitous promises in general should be enforced, Justinian himself was ready, it seems, to give an affirmative answer. A rescript in the Code that had been issued under Justinian's own name stated in brief and cryptic terms that those who promise to make gifts can be compelled to complete them even though the promisors later repent. Justinian confirmed this in another place, declaring that it made no difference whether the gift promise was written or oral.[44] It is hard to believe that he meant all this, and if he did he promptly took some of it back. But for the medieval cryptologists who strove so patiently to decipher and to reconcile the discordant messages of the Corpus Juris, all its words must be accorded equal weight. These statements were certainly included among the messages they considered authentic.

Special restrictions on the making (and promising) of gifts did reappear in late Roman law, taking the form of requirements of public registration. Imperial legislation in the late empire first permitted registration on an optional basis and then for a period of time imposed it as a requirement for all gifts. One main object in imposing this as a requirement

44. The rescript, dated A.D. 531, appears in the Code as C.8.53.35.5. It is indeed, as Buckland described it (*Textbook*, p. 529) "somewhat obscure and imperfect." The novelty of the ideas advanced is greatly diluted by describing the promise of gift as one made in the form of a *stipulatio*, which in classical times would have been fully enforceable by virtue of the form alone. The passage then goes on to say in sweeping terms that the promisor "can be compelled to complete the gift, for he intended a gift and it cannot fail for want of delivery." More impressive is a passage in Justinian's Institutes 2.7.2, which says that inter vivos gifts "are to be carried out when the donor expresses his will, in writing or without writing. And as in a sale, our constitution [the reference, it is usually thought, is to C.8.53.35.5] provides that they carry the necessity of making delivery, and if they are not delivered they have the fullest and perfect force and the necessity of [making] delivery falls on the donor."

seems to have been to facilitate tax collections.[45] But registration of a promise or transfer before a local judge or other public official might have another effect, that of providing authentication and facilitating enforcement. It may be, as some authors have suggested, that with the advent of Christianity public authorities were willing to give active support for private generosity that was directed toward the support of the church and in aid of pious causes.[46]

In imperial legislation of the last two hundred years until the end of the reign of Justinian, there were several changes in the controls over gift transactions, and various compromises were tried. The main trend was clearly toward relaxing the requirement of public registration. Gifts by way of dowry to affianced or married persons were exempted, as were gifts for pious causes, gifts to the emperor, and some others. More important was the exemption of gifts of smaller value. Gifts had to be registered only to the extent that they exceeded a defined limit of value, which was successively raised. Justinian fixed it at a very considerable sum, 500 *solidi*.[47] The reasons for this uneasy compromise can only be

45. Kaser, *Das römische Privatrecht*, 2d ed. (1975), 2: 280–281, speaking of the legislation of Constantine which became effective in the early fourth century A.D.
46. E. F. Bruck, *Uber römisches Recht in Rahmen der Kulturgeschichte*, (1954), pp. 126–130, and R. von Ihering, *Der Zweck im Recht*, 3d ed. (1893), 1: 276–289, are examples. Kaser (n. 45) expresses doubts concerning these views.
47. Buckland, *Textbook*, pp. 255–256; Girard, *Manuel*, pp. 998–99. The legislation of Justinian fixing the figure of 500 *solidi* appears as C.8.53.36.3 and is dated A.D. 531, the same year as the rescript on promises of gift referred to in note 44 above. The text made it clear that where gifts exceeded the ceiling they were void only as to the excess.
The *solidus*, introduced by Constantine, contained 4.48 grams of fine gold (about 5 pounds avoirdupois; *Cambridge Economic History of Europe* [1963] 3: 576). This quantity of gold would probably have sold on the London exchange in February 1979 for about $20,000. Its equivalent in sixth-century Byzantium I would not even try to guess.

guessed at. Reasons familiar to us could have been included, such as a desire to procure more reliable evidence of subject matter and terms and to induce greater deliberation where important economic interests would be affected. Or if the transfers made or promised were large, a watchful authoritarian government might have wished to know when the resources of the wealthy were being diverted from the normal channels of devolution. The impression probably given to readers centuries later was that registration on public records was an appropriate means of scrutinizing and even validating gifts of considerable size but not a central feature in defining the limits of contractual obligation. In most of Europe the requirement that gifts (including promises of gift) be publicly recorded was to come much later, for different reasons.

When the intensive study of Roman law was resumed in twelfth-century Italy, medieval jurists soon discovered that the array of contract forms and types provided in the Corpus Juris left numerous gaps, many consensual transactions that did not fit any one of the types. For a transaction that did not fit they used the phrase *nude pact*. All agreed that if *nude* in this sense, it could not be enforced in secular courts, though it might be a source of "natural" obligation or, as Ulpian had suggested, might support a defense.[48] The glossators showed great interest in the various means by which a pact could be "clothed" (*vestita*) and even some compassion for those that were not supplied with garments and were left to shiver in the cold outside.[49] To some jurists, at least, promises of gift seemed on first glance to be naked, but Justinian's own statement could not be disputed, so the conclusion of the Ac-

48. Ulpian, in D.2.14.7.4, had said: "a nude pact does not support an action, only a defense."

49. Quotations from the early glossators, up to and including Accursius, appear in L. Seuffert, *Zur Geschichte der obligatorischen Verträge* (1881), pp. 39–45.

cursian gloss was that they were clothed "with the aid of the law."[50] Increasingly the notion of "cause" intruded into the secular lawyers' discussions, and the tests for defining nudity in pacts tended to coalesce with those defining absence of "cause." But "cause" as a limit on the power to contract had already acquired, even in Roman law, so many meanings that it had lost any meaning of its own. This became increasingly true as time went on. The notion of cause certainly did not serve, then or later, to mark off promises of gift as especially vulnerable or suspect, for one of the primary meanings of *cause* came to be "purpose" and a promise of gift clearly had a "cause"—its cause (purpose) was make a gift. On the whole, despite the increasing complexity of the arguments they used, the secular jurists, from the early glossators through the great fourteenth-century commentators, Bartolus and Baldus, adhered very closely to the texts of the Corpus Juris in defining the bases of contract liability and agreed that, whatever church courts might do, a "nude" pact could not be enforced in secular courts.[51]

50. Accursius is quoted by Seuffert, in ibid., pp. 42–43: "But this rule that a nude pact does not support an action does not apply in those cases that are found in the laws [citing eight passages in the Corpus Juris, of which the second was Justinian's rescript on promises of gift]. In these instances an action is born of a nude pact but it can be said that this is through the aid of the law."

Earlier, Azo had in effect confessed that the enforcement of gift promises was hard to explain: "If a pact is nude it cannot support an action because of too great frigidity, unless miraculously [*mirabiliter*] it falls within certain situations in which a nude pact supports an action, as with a gift" citing then six other examples, among them *pollicitatio, constituta pecunia; Summa in Primum Librum Codicis*, Rubrica de Pactis, pp. 18a and 19a [Lyon, 1564]). It is not at all clear where Azo thought that a promise of gift could search for and find a garment. As he described the process, every pact was necessarily born naked "but when born it looks before and behind when its eyes are opened to see whether it was preceded or followed or has near at hand any contract whose garment it could wear in order to escape the north wind and the fury of the storm." Quoted by Maitland, Bracton and Azo (Selden Society, (1895), p. 143.

51. A convenient short summary of discussions by the post-glossators is

Strong pressure to expand the range of enforceable promises had come from church authorities, who considered breach of promise to be a sin. Religious sanctions, leading to the ultimate penalty of excommunication, were administered by church courts directly, and canonist lawyers strongly urged that all promises seriously intended should be enforced in secular courts as well.[52] The canonist campaign continued to meet resistance among most secular jurists of the fourteenth and fifteenth centuries, though they spent much effort considering and refuting the canonist arguments.[53] There is no need to follow the irregular course by which the learned men were gradually emancipated from the tyranny of the Roman law texts, and new modes of contract formation—for example, the promissory oath, signed writings—came to be accepted in the ordinary courts of many localities. Both of these processes were well under way by the sixteenth century in Italy, France, and Germany.[54] The Romanized legal systems of western Europe seemed to be moving steadily toward expansion of contract liability and a readiness to enforce all seriously intended promises, including promises of gift.

There were, however, some countervailing forces at work, aimed directly at gift transactions. The attack when it began came, so to speak, from the rear, directed not toward promises to give but toward gifts that had been already executed,

---

given by Seuffert, *Obligatorische Verträge*, pp. 52–66. Related issues are dealt with by C. Karsten, *Die Lehre vom Vertrage bei den italienischen Juristen des Mittelalters* (1882), pp. 116–135; A. Sollner, "Die Causa im Kondiktionen- und Vertragsrecht des Mittelalters," *Zeitschrift der Savigny-Stiftung für Rechtsgeschichte* 77 (röm.): 182, 219–223, 252–253.

52. Seuffert, *Obligatorische Verträge* 45–52, and Karsten, *Die Lehre vom Vertrage*, pp. 136–175, discuss these matters.

53. Seuffert, *Obligatorische Verträge*, pp. 52–86 has references to numerous authors.

54. Ibid., pp. 96–118, 144–157; G. Gorla, *Il Contratto* (1954), pp. 38–48.

often a considerable time before. The ground for attack was the deprivation caused to families of persons since deceased through gifts they had previously made in their lifetimes, especially those made to strangers. The main impulse to extend this form of protection to the interests of families came from sources whose origins were ancient and drew only indirectly on Roman law. This impulse continued to work strongly through much of western Europe. So at this point a detour is required over terrain that for persons accustomed to Anglo-American law will seem most irregular and strange. The course of events in France will be examined first.

II France

1. The Origins of Forced Heirship

In legal systems that have been much influenced by Roman law, a standard feature, often described as forced heirship, is a set of guarantees aiming to ensure that close relatives of every owner will inherit a substantial, predetermined share of his estate on his death. The only comparable provision in English law—a life estate (through dower or curtesy) to the survivor when one of two married persons dies—seems to Europeans to be astonishingly meager. The converse is true. Most persons familiar with Anglo-American law respond to forced heirship with disbelief when they come upon it suddenly. So quite apart from its relevance to the topic here discussed, uncompensated promises, something may be gained by exploring the origins of a divergence that remains so wide. One of the purposes will be to explain how forced heirship owed to classical Roman law not much more than the name, *légitime*, that is commonly used in French to describe the guaranteed share of the forced heir.

The antecedents of these ideas lie far back in the forms of social organization among the races of Germanic origin that came to occupy Europe, including Gaul, as Roman power declined. They had notions of family solidarity and of the subordination of individuals to the decisions of family groups that were no part of the heritage from Rome. For present purposes it is not necessary to enter far into the contentions of some modern scholars that the controls by families were then so intensive as to amount to family ownership, which preceded any recognition of individual ownership.[1] A distinction emerged quite early between assets acquired by inheritance and those acquired by purchase or gifts from outside sources. The evidence is persuasive that in some early Germanic communities no one had any power at all to give away inherited land.[2] After their conversion to Christianity, the church exerted strong pressure to overcome such restrictions, considering gifts for pious causes to be an imperative of religious duty and essential to bliss in afterlife. One solution to this painful dilemma was to secure the assent of all those who would otherwise inherit and who would show their acquiescence by signing the dispositive document. This practice became widespread through much of western and central Europe in the late middle ages.[3] In northern and central France in the twelfth century it was a normal feature of transfers by gift.[4] But relatives who considered any gift excessive for any reason could refuse to sign, and some formula was needed to resolve the resulting disputes. A compromise in the form of a disposable quota gradually emerged in the north and center of France during the decades shortly before and after the year 1200. No attempt was made to control transfers of assets other than land—movables or other forms of property, tangible or intangible—or transfers of land acquired by other means than inheritance (described as *ac-*

1. References to some of the voluminous literature are given by Brissaud, *Histoire générale* (1935), 2: 1125–1126. These themes will be referred to again in chapter 3.

2. Brissaud, *Histoire générale*, 2: 1625–1627.

3. Chénon, *Histoire générale du droit français public et privé des origines à 1815*, 2: 276–279; Brissaud, *Histoire générale*, 2: 1185–1187.

4. F. Olivier Martin, *Histoire de la coutume de la vicomté et prévoté de Paris*, 2: 151–159, 304–305.

quêts or *conquêts*). But as to inherited land (described as a *propre*), the disposable quota was small, only one-fifth in most districts of north and central France, one-third in some. There were differences between local districts, some applying the quota selected only to dispositions by will and some also including gifts inter vivos.[5] These quotas took form as rules of customary law that were fully enforceable in the geographical district to which the local custom applied.

At about the same time there developed another form of control over the disposal of inherited land that should be mentioned at this point, though only to show the force and persistence of family claims. This was the power of the owner's kindred to cancel any sale of inherited land and any conveyance, if one had already been made to the purchaser, and then to recover the land, reimbursing the purchaser for any payments he had made. This power, which came to be called the *retrait lignager*, could be exercised by any relative, even distant collaterals, provided they shared with the seller a common ancestor on the line of inheritance from which the land had come. The time limit was short, a year and a day from the purchaser's entry into possession, but all of an owner's inherited land could be reclaimed in this way by the

---

5. The variations between the districts are described by Chénon, *Histoire générale,* 2: 280–284. In the west of France (Normandy, Brittany, Anjou, Touraine) the restrictions applied to both inter vivos and testamentary gifts but the disposable portion was one-third. In north central France, led by the custom of Paris, the disposable portion was smaller (one-fifth) but the restriction applied only to testamentary gifts.

Olivier Martin, *Coutume de Paris,* pp. 304–319, gives a detailed and interesting account of the progression in the district governed by the custom of Paris. A disposable quota of one-fifth was clearly established in the 1200s, applicable as elsewhere only to inherited land but at the outset setting a ceiling on both inter vivos and testamentary gifts. By the end of the 1300s, however, and for reasons that this distinguished author could not explain, the restrictive quota was made applicable in the Paris custom only to gifts by will, as it continued to be until displaced by the Civil Code of 1804.

kindred, without any exemption of a disposable quota as there was with gifts. Despite all the disruption it produced and its severe effects in obstructing commerce in land, this power to prevent diversion to strangers through the sale of family land had a long career before it. It was formulated through usage and was accepted as a rule of customary law in the northern two-thirds of France in the years shortly before 1200. It was not abolished until 1792.[6]

So it seems necessary to raise the question why English law escaped all this, though it is too soon to describe how grateful we should be that it did. The decisions made on these issues in the two countries coincided closely in time. The rights of kindred to obstruct or to cancel transfers of ancestral land to outsiders faded away in England during the same period, quite short, when they were being defined and confirmed in France. The evidence of a power in the kindred to obstruct had appeared indirectly in England in the same form that it had taken in France and elsewhere in western Europe—signatures by near relatives expressing their consent to the disposal of inherited land. Such signatures appeared as a routine feature in eleventh-century England, as commonly as they did in eleventh-century France.[7] This

6. The account in Olivier Martin, *Coutume de Paris*, 2: 319–353 is excellent. As he there points out, the *retrait* replaced the earlier requirement that an owner must, before selling it, offer it at the price proposed to the kindred of the lineage from which the land had come. The *retrait lignager* is also discussed by Brissaud, *Histoire générale*, 2: 1340–1356; Chénon, *Histoire générale*, 2: 272–278.

7. Pollock and Maitland, *History of English Law*, 2d ed. (1952), 2: 309–312. Problems as to the origins of this practice, expressing acquiescence by the kindred, are still unresolved. Maitland was unwilling to accept the hypothesis that the Anglo-Saxons had brought to and preserved in England communal living arrangements, with controls over the use and disposal of land that were intensive enough to be described as forms of family ownership. Though skeptical toward claims made for "family communities" among other Germanic tribes, he was clear that if they had existed the Anglo-Saxons had in any event "wandered away from the road"

form of indirect evidence, of course, does not answer some crucial questions, such as whether abstention from signing would constitute an effective veto that would nullify a grant and, if nonsigners continued to oppose, whether or how their resistance could be overidden. Many of the problems were eliminated in England when the common law judges abolished outright all wills of land. They thereby sealed off one of the two main avenues by which owners could defeat the expectations of their kindred.[8] Were there limits to the power to make inter vivos gifts? One highly credible twelfth-century author thought that an owner could give only a "reasonable" part of his inherited land and even as to land acquired by other means could not disinherit his heirs entirely, but he defined the restraints no more precisely than this.[9]

In a very short interval, in the years immediately before and after 1200, references to such restraints disappear rapidly. Maitland attributed this to the "high handed" action of the common-law judges, resulting from their strong predilection for simplified, clear-cut rules.[10] It now seems more likely that

the other Germanic races had traveled (ibid., 2: 251–255). But as a more recent writer has pointed out, the Anglo-Saxons developed the device of "bookland," with confirmation by king and witan, in order to free land from such restrictions, and employed it on such a scale as to suggest a strong impulse to escape the restrictions. Scattered evidence from "folkland" transactions also indicates that the rights of "family communities" had to be taken into account. J. Braude, *Die Familiengemeinschaften der Angelsachsen* (Leipzig, 1932).

8. Pollock and Maitland, *History of English Law*, 2: 328–330.

9. Ibid., pp. 308–309, referring to the conclusions in the treatise we know as Glanvill.

10. Ibid., pp. 311–312. Maitland here pointed out that English law had reached a stage where it could readily have accepted the *retrait lignager*, "but above our law at this critical moment stood a high-handed group of professional judges who were all for extreme simplicity." However, Maitland also laid stress on the commitment of the royal judges to primogeniture as the governing principle for inheritance of freehold land. As sole

the fade-out occurred without conscious decision directly addressed by anyone to these issues. This was a time of rapid change in conceptions of tenure of freehold land, especially land from which military service was due, transforming it from tenure for life into full-scale ownership and conferring on the tenant much wider powers of disposition.[11] The restraints on disposal of inherited land, whether by sale or by gift, were still very vaguely defined. If they were taken into account in common law litigation over freehold land, the judgments as to what transfers were "reasonable" for an owner to make were largely entrusted to juries and buried in general verdicts.[12] The machinery at hand certainly did not make it easy to manufacture clear-cut, easily understood rules that could be widely applied, like the "disposable fifth" as the limit on gifts of inherited land that was then taking form under the Custom of Paris. So family claims to family land were allowed to lapse, probably for a reason no more compelling than that for common-law courts with the means they had at hand their enforcement did not seem worth the extra effort required.[13]

heir of such land, the eldest son would be the appropriate person to contest any grant by his ancestor, but if it contained a warranty by the grantor, the eldest son would confront a dilemma, since he would be obligated by his ancestor's warranty to defend the grant against his own challenge. But heirs were often called on for warranties with which their own interests might conflict. Of itself, solicitude for the interests of the eldest son does not seem a sufficient reason.

11. This theme, a major revision of views previously held, is developed by S. E. Thorne, "English Feudalism and Estates in Land," [1959] *Cambridge Law Journal*, pp. 193, 204–209.

12. The difficulties in identifying the issues presented for decision in the cases that were decided in royal courts are described by Milsom, *The Legal Framework of Feudalism* (1976), 121–131. In addition there was a good deal of coming and going between the royal courts and seignorial courts, without many clues as to reasons for seeking or securing royal court intervention.

13. A comment by Milsom (p. 122) on the rules, described by the author Glanvill, giving protection to kindred against disposal of ancestral

Not all residents of the island were impervious to the claims of near relatives to shares in the wealth of family members. Over most of England in the thirteenth century there were customs that applied to assets other than land and set strict limits to the power of owners to disinherit their widows and children. Where the widow and a child (one or more) survived, they were entitled to two-thirds of the decedent's assets other than land; if either a widow or a child survived, she or he was entitled to one-half. These restrictions were well enough known so that they were referred to obliquely in Magna Carta and were asserted occasionally in common-law litigation, rested either on local custom or at times on the "custom of the realm."[14] These occasions became rare, for by 1200 the administration of decedents' estates had been acquired without contest by the courts of the church. Toward the church courts the common law judges showed deep distrust. They often sought to harass and discredit but did not seriously attempt to displace them.

---

land, is that "in the end they perished because they could not well be enforced in the king's courts." He explains the difficulties convincingly. I confess that I am left with the question whether there was not also a subliminal judgment at work, rating these claims of the kindred well down on the scale of those worth the effort needed to organize them.

14. Pollock and Maitland, *History of English Law,* 2: 348–356, discusses the subject fully, with the conclusion that "it is fairly certain that in the twelfth and thirteenth centuries some such scheme . . . was in force all England over." Glanvill and Bracton, as Maitland pointed out, spoke of the restriction as a generally applicable rule, with escape from it allowed only through local custom. Magna Carta (ca. 26 in the 1215 version) merely takes some such restriction for granted, stating that on the death of a tenant-in-chief who owed no debts to the king "then all the chattels fall to the dead man, saving to his wife and children their reasonable shares."

Holdsworth, *History of English Law,* 3: 550–556, reaches the same conclusion: "I cannot doubt that in the twelfth and thirteenth centuries this scheme of succession was the general rule." Holdsworth was willing to date its disappearance, except as highly localized custom, as early as the fourteenth century, though Maitland was more hesitant in fixing terminal dates.

As to the activities of the church courts over the later centuries, very little is known. It seems a fair guess that the claims of widows to guaranteed shares in their husbands' estates were the hardest to fit within Roman-canonist doctrine. They certainly would have been hard to reconcile with the dominant authority assigned by the common law to the husband, including full ownership of assets other than land that had been owned by the wife before marriage.[15] As to the claims of children to guaranteed shares, church courts might not have felt very strongly impelled to enforce a rule that had no basis in any English statute and only sporadic support from common law courts. Their activities on this as on most other topics were not reported and left no impression.

So these rights of the immediate family to inherit substantial shares in decedents' assets other than land disappeared, lost somewhere in the dense fog that surrounded the work of the English church courts.[16] Like the claims of kindred to limit or prevent the disposal of inherited land, they were allowed to fade away. It would be too much to say that in either instance there was evidence of a conscious choice to reject such claims made by persons empowered to make the choice. At most, it seems, there were inadequate means and a lack of incentive to maintain them, though the final result was that the English common law veered away from a course that was to be followed by most other legal systems of the western world.

In France from the thirteenth century onward the claims of the "lineage" on ancestral land, both the quotas on gifts and the *retrait lignager*—the power to retrieve such land

15. This point is made by Holdsworth, *History of English Law*, 3: 555.
16. They survived, however, quite late in London local courts. In the north and in the province of York they were not eliminated until 1692, by statute. Pollock and Maitland, *History of English Law*, 2: 348–356; Holdsworth, *History of English Law*, 3: 550–556.

when sold—certainly did not fade away. The formulas and procedures that were taking form as the century began became well known and soon came to be directly enforced by the courts and discussed by writers on French customary law. As they became well known and better defined their scope was extended in two directions. Annuities payable in money but secured by liens on land (*rentes constituées*) came to be classified for this purpose as interests in land. By the sixteenth century, when this extension occurred, the annuity secured by a lien on land had become a much used form of long-term investment.[17] Also equated with interests in land were royal offices when, in the seventeenth century, they became subjects of private ownership, as saleable and inheritable as land itself.[18]

Thus these restrictions came to apply to the three principal forms of prudent, long-term investment of family resources: land, annuities secured by liens on land, and royal offices. It will be recalled that the fraction of such inherited assets which an owner could dispose of by gift was small, in most districts of northern and central France only one-fifth of their total value. This limit might make owners restive for various reasons. If they had no direct descendants the portion "reserved" would go by intestacy to collateral heirs, with whom they might have had only slight acquaintance. If an owner, not of noble rank, did have living descendants— children, perhaps—they would ordinarily take equal shares.[19] This could be unwelcome for various reasons. Some

17. R. E. Giesey, "Rules of Inheritance and Strategies of Mobility in Pre-revolutionary France," 82 *American Historical Review* 271, 273–274, 279–280 (1977).

18. Ibid., pp. 281–284.

19. If the decedent was of noble rank, however, primogeniture was in force in most of the *pays de coutumes* and would usually give the eldest-born son a two-thirds share. On all such issues the customs of different districts varied greatly in details. Chénon, *Histoire générale*, 2: 247–257.

children might be in greater need or might be favored over the others, or there could be a purpose that worked strongly on many owners, to keep family resources concentrated in particular descendants in order to maintain or augment the family's influence and power.[20] The controls, it is true, could be evaded. Inherited interests could be sold or exchanged for other assets which, being newly acquired, would be exempt from the restriction. In numerous customs of northern France, controls over gifts applied only to transfers at death so that inter vivos gifts could be made without restriction. But a recent study has shown how the "family possessiveness" that was promoted by these patterns of inheritance contributed much to the continuity and stability of families. It also immobilized a large share of the capital available for investment[21] and greatly narrowed the incentives to growth and change in French society under the ancien régime. But leaders of thought who regarded strong families as "pillars of the state" could praise these controls over the devolution of family assets for their effect in preserving "the strength and glory of the family."[22]

It seems unlikely that this set of limited and leaky controls would have survived the searching scrutiny of a revolution if there had not been at work a different idea that had been moving up from the south. For France had been di-

20. One of the recurring themes in the study by Giesey is that patterns of ownership and inheritance developed under the ancien régime gave incentives to the middle class as well as the nobility to compete for honors and rewards, especially through tenure of royal offices. Then, to sustain the costs of a career in royal office, it was often necessary for families to concentrate their resources and prevent undue fragmentation among numerous heirs. As he points out (pp. 274–277), the equality of treatment provided in most of the customs for non-noble tenures inspired much maneuvering by heads of families to produce inequalities, even though the purpose was still to promote ambitions of the lineage.

21. Giesey, "Rules of Inheritance," pp. 278–281.

22. Ibid., pp. 285–289.

vided since the early middle ages into the "country of customs," stretching all the way across the north and center and comprising about two-thirds of the land area of modern France, and the "country of the written law" in the south. The "written law" was, of course, Roman law that had survived in simplified, streamlined forms and had been accepted, with many local variations, as the private law of the southern lands. Included in this legacy was a set of rules for what was called in French the heir's *légitime* or "legitimate part." This requires another, very short excursion.

Roman law from an early time had adopted the premise that the power of fully capable persons to dispose of their assets by will should be essentially unlimited. So the problems of finding redress for the disinherited were approached in an extremely roundabout way. It began to seem after much time had passed that the exclusion from a will of some near relative (say, a son) with whom the testator had retained close ties was abnormal enough to call for explanation. A special procedure was organized before a special tribunal of leading citizens (*centumviri*). They were asked the question whether the testator had been insane when he made the will; an affirmative answer would make the will wholly void. Under late, postclassical law, the proceedings were transferred to the ordinary courts, the classes of omitted heirs who could complain were more clearly defined, and the share to which they were entitled (their "legitimate part") was fixed by arithmetic at one-fourth the share that the person or persons excluded would have taken through intestacy.[23] As originally devised and as it functioned throughout the classical period, the inquest was addressed only to gifts by will. Under the late empire there were a few instances of inter vivos gifts that were set aside because their disproportionate

23. Buckland, *Textbook*, pp. 324–329; Girard, *Manuel*, pp. 913–921.

size or some other evidence showed a purpose to frustrate indirectly claims of relatives to inherit that could otherwise have been asserted against the donor's estate.[24]

The *légitime* had some clear attractions when compared with the controls over disposal of inherited land that the customs of northern France had defined. It concentrated attention on those blood relatives for whom the personal attachment of the decedent should be deepest and his sense of personal responsibility the strongest: his own children and their descendants, his parents and other ancestors in the direct line (brothers and sisters were included only in one special case).[25] Descendants and ascendants in the direct line would also be (together, perhaps, with a surviving spouse) the ones most likely to depend on the decedent's resources if they were to prosper or perhaps even to survive. Even in the northern "country of customs" special measures had been taken quite early to protect needy dependents who stood in close relations to the deceased where he had little or no inherited land but had other assets that could be reached.[26] There were also two other ways in which the *légitime* dif-

24. The usual remedy of the disinherited was described as the "complaint of undutiful will" (*querela inofficiosi testamenti*). In Justinian's Code there is a short section (C.3.29) entitled "Concerning Undutiful Gifts," which includes nine imperial rescripts, dated between A.D. 245 and 294, authorizing the cutting back of inter vivos gifts made by certain individual donors if it was found that they were excessive or that their purpose had been to evade the controls over "undutiful" wills. To these rescripts in the Code should be added D.31.87.3, which mentions an authorization of the Emperor Alexander to scale down an inter vivos gift by half if it was made to escape the restrictions on disinheritance by will. Buckland, *Textbook,* p. 329, and Girard, *Manuel,* pp. 920–921, discuss this theme further.

25. Siblings of the decedent could assert a claim only if some asset would otherwise go to a "base" (*turpis*) person. Buckland, *Textbook,* p. 325.

26. Brissaud, *Histoire générale,* 2: 1635–1636.

fered from the controls over gifts of inherited land: (1) The fractions guaranteed were much smaller, one-fourth of the intestate share of each heir in the protected group as against four-fifths of the land in the "reserve." But (2) the guarantees applied to the decedent's whole estate, not merely to inherited land and those assets (annuities and offices) that were equated with land.

The *légitime,* essentially as defined in late Roman law, was well established in most districts of southern France by the year 1100.[27] As knowledge of Roman law was diffused more widely in the north, the *légitime* received much praise from late medieval authors and became well known.[28] It was not until the middle of the sixteenth century that a real break-through came, when the Parlement of Paris, the leading royal appellate court with a jurisdiction that extended widely over northern France, declared that the *légitime* had been accepted as a part of local usage and incorporated in the Custom of Paris. This conclusion was formally ratified some thirty years later when an assembly of the three estates of the Paris area included the *légitime* in the revised text of the Custom of Paris, which was promulgated in 1580. It was somewhat more than a century later, in 1688, that in the Custom of Paris the protection of the heir's "legitimate part" was definitively extended beyond wills to inter vivos gifts.

Throughout most of the customary districts of northern France the *légitime* was adopted by similar means, a combination of court decisions and revision by local assemblies of the texts of the published customs. There were variations between the districts as to the classes of heirs protected (for example, only descendants in the Custom of Paris) and as to

27. Chénon, *Histoire générale,* 2:286–287; Brissaud, *Histoire générale,* 2: 1634–1637.
28. Chénon, *Histoire générale,* 2: 287–290.

the shares guaranteed (in the Custom of Paris one-half of the intestate share, in other customs one-fourth).[29] In many districts these restrictions were carried back to include not only gifts by last will but those made by owners in their lifetimes, as had been true from the beginning with the restrictions on gifts of inherited land. The two types of restriction persisted side by side, overlapping and reinforcing each other. Certainly by the seventeenth century the *légitime,* as a limitation on the power to disinherit close relatives, was conceived by most persons to have a secure place in that ideal construct, the "common law of the customs" of France. When, after the Revolution, the minds of many turned toward the drafting of a national code, this form of limitation was accepted without question as part of the national heritage.

Royal legislation in the meantime had erected an entirely different kind of protective barrier against thoughtless generosity. This legislation, repeatedly reenacted, required that all inter vivos gifts of any kind be registered either on the records of a court at the donor's place of residence or else by a notary public. The framers of royal policy seem in retrospect to have been obsessed with this theme. This is the more remarkable because throughout the history of the ancien régime the central government, which found ways to intrude in and obstruct most forms of human activity in France, showed massive indifference and intervened very

29. Much the best account of developments under the Custom of Paris is that of Olivier Martin, *Coutume de Paris,* pp. 360–366. In this as in many other matters, the Custom of Paris led the way for the other districts of northern France. Chénon, *Histoire générale,* 2: 288–291, is also most helpful.

A general survey of the literature, court decisions, and texts of the customs on the *légitime,* filled with praise for its conformity to natural law, is provided by F. Bourjon, *Le Droit commun de la France* (1770), 1: 868–885. A much fuller account is given by J. M. Ricard, *Traité des donations* (Paris, 1783) 1: 661–727.

rarely on issues that were concerned only with private law.[30] The legislation concerning gifts began with an ordinance of 1539 which declared void any gift that had not been registered on the records of a court sitting in the district in which the donor resided.[31] This or an equivalent form of registration by a public official was required by royal legislation that was repeated five more times, the last time in 1731 as part of an extensive royal ordinance which explicitly included not only promises of gift but executed gifts in any form, with only two exceptions.[32]

The motives of royal officialdom for their preoccupation with this theme were not stated. One may have been to aid in collecting royal taxes on gifts.[33] Authors of the time surmised that the framers of royal policy sought to prevent clandestine gifts in order to protect both creditors and heirs of donors.[34]

30. This theme is developed further by Dawson, "The Codification of the French Customs," 38 *Michigan Law Review* 765, 791–795 (1940).

31. Isambert, *Receuil général des anciennes lois françaises,* 12: 627, registration in this form being described at the time as *insinuation.* It was required (art. 133) for the donee's acceptance as well as for the donor's act of transfer.

32. Ordonnances and édits of February, 1566 (ibid., 14: 204–205); May, 1645 (ibid. 17: 51); November, 1690 (ibid., 20: 113); December, 1703 (ibid., p. 438). In the ordonnance of 1731, public registration in one of the forms specified was prescribed in articles 1, 2, 26, 27, 28 (ibid., 21: 343–350).

The ordonnance of 1731, art. 22, expressly exempted from public registration (though not from notarization) gifts of movables that had been manually delivered to the donee or whose value was less than £1000. Gifts to couples recently or about-to-be married were also regularly exempted, as in the ordonnance of 1731, arts. 13, 17, 19 (ibid., 21: 348).

33. This was described as a leading motive for the ordonnance of 1731 by H. Regnault, *Les Ordonnances civiles du Chancelier Daguesseau* (1929), pp. 269–271.

34. This was the explanation of F. Bourjon, *Le Droit commun de la France* (1770), 2: 126. Duplessis, "Traité des Donations," in *Oeuvres* (1778), 2: 195, argued for the need to set such limits on the power of owners to dispose by gift "to the end that there be conserved at least a part of their property to their heirs and also to the end that families be maintained

Concern for the interests of heirs, I suggest, was probably high on the scale. Decisions by courts that imposed other and stricter requirements for inter vivos gifts[35] have been explained by modern French authors as inspired by the same motive: to prevent the dissipation of family resources.[36] There must have been many who fully approved the high barriers erected by royal legislation to the making of gifts. For one other phenomenon needs to be explained: the acquiescence shown by the high appellate courts, the nine (eventually thirteen) Parlements, that had in effect a power of veto, each for its own district, by refusing to register royal legislation. Among the numerous edicts that were nullified in this way were some that would have imposed similar requirements of form on exchange transactions; these edicts were made unenforceable for extended periods of time over much of France by the refusal of Parlements to register them.[37] The royal controls over private gifts inspired no such resistance.[38] Indeed, their central feature, a requirement of

---

in their splendor and cannot be ruined by excessive gifts they might make." Ricard, *Traité des donations*, 1: 230, argued for a requirement that the subject of the gift be physically surrendered, "so that individuals cannot succeed so easily in depriving their heirs of their property by so facile a contract."

35. The requirements of delivery and of complete surrender by donors of all powers of use or control were tightened, the gift *causa mortis* was eliminated. Olivier Martin, *Coutume de Paris*, 2: 482–489.

36. The conservation of property within families was suggested as the principal motive for the changes by Olivier Martin, in the passage cited in the preceding note; also by R. Martinée-Baranger, *Bourjon et le Code Civil* (1971), pp. 86–87, 100–104.

37. Olivier Martin, *Coutume de Paris*, 2: 486.

38. The willing acceptance of the gift ordonnance of 1731 must have been due in part also to the foresight and care with which Chancellor Daguesseau, proponent of the ordonnance (also of its counterpart, an ordonnance on wills) prepared the way with questionnaires addressed to the Parlements and extensive exchanges of views back and forth, negotiating the terms to be included. These measures are described fully by Regnault, *Les Ordonnances civiles*, and give a useful corrective to the image of "absolute" monarchy that supposedly existed in the eighteenth century.

public registration for substantially all gifts, large and small, seemed so much a part of the order of things that it was maintained in force throughout a revolution and then, without contest, preserved for the future by being securely lodged in a Civil Code.

For the other controls over the transmission of wealth that had been invented under the old regime there was to be no such easy transition. Their troubled history in the fifteen years between the Revolution and the Civil Code must be briefly described, since the result was a swing in a new direction. During most of that time, the most divisive of all private law issues and the cause of the most intense debate were the controls over the transmission of wealth after death. The main target was the power to dispose by will. Revolutionary leaders such as Mirabeau and Robespierre urged that in principle all control by an owner should end with his death. Being not quite ready to abolish wills altogether, they proposed that an owner should have no power to dispose by will of more than one-tenth of his estate. In the discussions that followed, the old distinctions between types of property (movables and land, land inherited and land acquired otherwise) disappeared. After several experiments, the legislature in 1794 adopted the solution that had been so strongly urged, a disposable quota of one-tenth of the decedent's whole estate; this restriction was even made retroactive to July 14, 1789.[39]

The purpose of the legislature was directly opposed to that pursued by the framers of policy under the old regime. It was not to conserve but to break up aggregations of wealth, to

39. P. Sagnac, *La Législation civile de la révolution française* (1898), pp. 220–239; G. Aron, "Étude sur les lois successorales de la révolution," *N.R.H.* (1901), pp. 444, 478–485, 585, 593–614; Chénon, *Histoire générale*, 2: 1637–1638. There is an account of these events in English by J. Dainow, "Forced Heirship in French Law," 2 *Louisiana Law Review* 669, 675–678 (1940).

prevent concentrations in individual family members. Success in this, it was hoped, would not only bring a wide dispersal of ownership but would also promote another cause that stirred at least as much passion—equality of treatment for all eligible heirs. The abolition of privilege and equality for all were mandates of the Revolution, organizing principles of the new social order.[40] It was also urged that a mandate for equality would reduce the destructive and authoritarian powers of heads of families, who had been able to exercise control by threats to grant or deny rewards to potential receivers of their bounty. This last objective did not have the same appeal for all. Some contended (as Napoleon was later to do) that parental discipline was good and much needed. Indeed, on other issues also there was passionate dissent, strong enough to induce deputies from the south to threaten at one point to secede from the legislature. For a decade at least these issues tapped deep springs of emotion and severely tested ultimate beliefs in the future of French society.

As protest and debate continued, it became more apparent that, even if there had been agreement on ultimate aims, the means chosen would not achieve the end in view—a major reordering of society—merely by dispersing accumulations of family wealth more widely within the same families. A much less ambitious though related purpose began to replace it, the purpose essentially of the *légitime*: to ensure that each owner's wealth was distributed fairly and equally among those immediate relatives whose blood ties were closest and whose claims were strongest—children and other

40. Equality in successions between heirs of the same rank had been required by decrees of April 8, 1791 and March 7, 1793. Sagnac, *La Législation civile,* pp. 219–220; Aron, "Étude sur les lois successorales," *N.R.H.* (1901), pp. 585, 590. As Aron put it, equality in inheritance had become a fundamental principle of "almost constitutional dimensions" (ibid., pp. 444, 474–478, 585–593).

descendants, parents and other ascendants in the direct genetic line. The idea was familiar enough, for, as I have said, such guarantees to the nearest of kin had been working their way into the law in force in most localities in France over the previous two hundred years. The legislature in 1800 reverted to this idea. Instead of the Roman device of a "legitimate part" for each forced heir (a fraction of his share by intestacy) the statute adopted a formula that had long been in use in limiting the disposal of inherited land. It defined a reserve, a percentage of his total estate that a decedent could *not* give away and that must pass by intestacy. The reserve varied with the number and kinds of forced heirs that survived— one-half of the estate if there were no children, three-fourths if there were three or fewer children, four-fifths if there were four, and so on.[41]

The draftsmen of the Civil Code took this as their basic pattern when serious work on the Code began. In the successive stages of discussion, amendment, and approval of the text, these forms of control and the purposes they served were likewise accepted without debate. Not a whisper was heard of any of the great ambitions that had been expressed so recently, to remake society by these means. On the other hand, no question was raised as to the duty of parents to assure to their own children "a suitable portion of their patrimonies." Imposing this as a duty should inspire no complaint by parents since it would conform to their "presumed affection," and in nature there is no love more "constant" and "general" than that of a father for his children. In any case, this duty is part of the responsibility assumed when children are brought into the world and it rests on natural

41. If the decedent had no descendants who survived him but only siblings or ascendants, he could dispose of one-half his estate; if he had three or fewer children, one-fourth; if four, one-fifth; if five, one-sixth. Aron, "Étude," pp. 672, 713–719.

law.[42] All the participants likewise agreed, though with a conviction that seemed to be felt less intensely, that the duties were reciprocal and were owed in equal degree by children to their parents.[43] There was much dispute over the claims of siblings to guaranteed shares. In the end the conclusion was that claims of brothers and sisters were not strong enough to justify an added restriction on an owner's power to dispose of his own property.[44] There was much dispute also over the size of the reserve, that is, the fractional shares of their estates that owners could *not* give away, under varying hypotheses as to the numbers and kinds of descendants who survived.[45] But it was taken for granted without debate that if the guarantees were to be effective they could not be restricted to testamentary gifts, as they had been in classical Roman law, but must be carried back to inter vivos gifts that brought the owner's total gifts above the disposable quota.[46]

The Civil Code when it took effect in 1804 defined the

42. These were the main points made by Bigot-Préameneu when presenting this section of a draft of the Code to the Conseil d'État. P. Fenet, *Receuil complet des travaux préparatoires du Code Civil*, (Paris, 1827), 12: 244–248. The course of the discussions at the successive stages in reviewing the draft of the Code are well described by Dainow, "Forced Heirship in French Law," 2 *Louisiana Law Review* 669, 679–682 (1940). He, too, reports finding "not a single opinion expressed against the limitation of a parent's power of disposition" (ibid., p. 679).

43. Fenet, *Receuil complet*, 12: 248–251.

44. Ibid., pp. 444–445, 470.

45. Ibid., pp. 254–319.

46. The first draft of the Code that was presented for review by the Conseil d'État had included both testamentary and inter vivos gifts in calculating the disposable quotas, with provisions for cancellation or reduction of those in excess of the quotas (ibid., p. 299). The necessity for including inter vivos gifts for both purposes was explained to the Corps Législatif by Bigot-Préameneu, who gave much credit to the 1731 ordonnance on gifts (art. 31) for employing a method that the Code adopted by which excessive inter vivos gifts were cancelled or reduced in reverse order to that in which they had been made. (Fenet, *Receuil complet*, 12: 540).

reserve of which an owner cannot dispose by way of gift as one-half of his entire estate if one legitimate child survived, two-thirds if two, three-fourths if three or more survived.[47] If no descendants at all survived but one or more ancestors did, parents or grandparents took one-half or one-fourth, depending on their number.[48] Gifts could also be cancelled or scaled down for the quite different reason that they produced unequal shares for heirs of equal rank. The principle of equality, so ardently pursued during the French Revolution, was accepted as a dictate of elementary justice by the framers of the Civil Code,[49] though they qualified it in one respect—by allowing the owner's disposable quota to be used to give preferred treatment to one or more heirs over others.[50] From reports of litigation in France since the Code it seems that inequality of treatment between coheirs is a more common ground for assailing gifts than the claim that the total of the decedent's gifts exceeded the disposable quota.

47. Art. 913. "Child" is defined to include the descendants of a deceased child, who take by representation and are entitled only to the share of that child.

48. Art. 914 provides for a reserve of one-half the decedent's assets if there were one or more living ancestors on both sides, one-fourth if only on one side. Art. 915 introduces another wrinkle, where there are one or more ascendants and one or more illegitimate children.

49. The proposed draft of the Code provisions on *rapport* (return) by heirs of gifts that gave them larger shares than those received by other heirs was discussed fully in the preparatory stages, with unanimity on the purposes pursued. At some of the sessions Napoleon and some of his ardent supporters were participants. Fenet, *Receuil complet,* 12: 62–75, 201–209.

50. Art. 843 requires that the donor in an inter vivos gift must expressly declare that he intends to treat his heirs unequally for his disposable quota to be used in this way. As a result of an amendment of 1898, such a statement is not needed for testamentary gifts, an intent to produce inequality being inferred. The return (*rapport*) by heirs of inter vivos gifts is regulated in the twenty-seven articles that follow, with many details that are of no interest here.

The estate that is subjected to these controls includes all the "giveable" property that the decedent ever owned if it was disposed of by way of gift at any time in his life. There is not even a cut-off point in this retrospective overhaul, such as the ten-year limit which, as we shall see, is imposed by the German Code. So before the value of a decedent's estate can be known, this postaudit requires a listing and appraisal of all the assets previously owned and then given away.[51] Then if the gifts by will and inter vivos, all taken together, exceed the decedent's disposable quota, the testamentary gifts are cut back first, the lifetime gifts being, if possible, left intact. If, after the testamentary gifts have all been cancelled, the disposable quota is still exceeded, then the inter vivos gifts are "reduced" or "returned" one by one in reverse order, starting with the gift most recently made and moving backward in time, with no time limit provided.[52]

To persons accustomed to Anglo-American law it must seem strange that a set of controls so far-reaching and so unpredictable in their consequences should have survived in a modern society. I have suggested earlier that in the history of English law the claims of families to share the wealth of their individual members were simply allowed to fade away for reasons no more persuasive than that they were difficult to administer through the procedural mechanisms of the early common law. This meant that the controls exercised by family groups in England depended almost entirely on private arrangements made by their leading members. Those familiar with the strict family settlements that were organized in

51. Art. 922 provides that in order to enforce "reduction" (where the disposable quota has been exceeded), the assets owned at death will first be assembled and "reunited fictionally" (*fictivement*) with all assets previously owned and then disposed of by inter vivos gift, being appraised according to their "state and value" at the times the gifts were made.

52. Art. 923.

England, relying especially on the mechanism of the express trust, will agree that the controls they produced could be strict and long-lasting indeed. But except for the rights of lifetime use of land (dower and curtesy) that were assigned to the surviving spouse, there were to be in English law no rights in the property of the dead, no guaranteed shares in inheritance administered by the courts, with quotas.

In France the conception of the guaranteed family share remained familiar in two forms, one derived from early Germanic notions of family solidarity and the other borrowed from the Romans. Then, in the upheaval and optimism generated by the Revolution, an equalized distribution within families, enforced by law, seemed to promise a general reordering of French society. In the succeeding period of reappraisal, the controls at first imposed were sharply cut back by enlarging somewhat the shares of which owners could dispose, and much more by narrowing greatly the protected family group to include only those on the direct genetic line, the line of transmission by which life itself had been given and received.

In France it seems clear that forced heirship as the Code now defines it has had continuing and widespread support. The legislature has amended the Code provisions on this topic seldom and only in minor ways, though the provisions on some nearly related topics, such as gifts between husband and wife,[53] have been vigorously debated and often revised.

---

53. The Roman law prohibition of gifts between husband and wife had been maintained in the intermediate centuries with the purpose clearly manifested, as it had not been in Roman law, of preventing the diversion of property owned by either to inheritance by the family of the other. Excepted from the prohibition was the *don mutuel,* the grant by both spouses of a lifetime usufruct for the survivor in assets other than inherited land (Olivier Martin, *Coutume de Paris,* 2: 288–298). Under the Code different solutions have been tried, with complicated quotas that varied with the number of children of the marriage or that either spouse had produced by a

The courts have shown for the forced heirship provisions a degree of respect that is by no means typical of their attitudes toward the Code itself. There have been a few French critics who have complained that forced heirship has had some undesirable consequences, but their proposals for change have made no impression. There seems to be no doubt that the solutions now in force express convictions that are widely and firmly held in France.[54]

And it is not only in France that this is true. In all of western Europe—west of what we have come to call the iron curtain—also through most of Latin America and even in our own state of Louisiana, shares in inheritance are guaranteed to those in the direct genetic line.[55] So a glimpse of the workings of this strange device, so widespread in the western world but so far outside our own experience, will have some

---

prior marriage. The definitions of gifts are more strict than those commonly used, the sanctions more severe, and much debate and continued tinkering by the legislature have ensued. Planiol et Ripert, *Traité pratique*, vol. 5, secs. 139–160, give a detailed account.

54. Planiol et Ripert, *Traité pratique*, vol. 5, secs. 22 and 23, give a persuasive statement of this point of view. The authors review the criticisms and counterproposals that have been made and that have proved unacceptable, as does Dainow, "Forced Heirship in French Law," 2 *Louisiana Law Review* 669, 687–692 (1940). The criticism most often and insistently made is that forced heirship produces undue fragmentation of estates, especially holdings of farmland, thus driving the young into the cities, and also (some say) reducing the incentive to have children and impairing parental authority. On these issues not much evidence is offered for either side.

55. The provisions of the Louisiana Code are described in a comment, "Forced Heirs, the Légitime and Loss of the Légitime in Louisiana," 37 *Tulane Law Review* 710 (1963). As is pointed out there (pp. 722–723), forced heirship provisions drawn on the model of the French *légitime* were in force in Texas for a time (ten years) but in 1856 were eliminated. They are not likely to be eliminated in Louisiana, whose state constitution still forbids the legislature to abolish forced heirship. In Appendix 1 is a brief survey of the provisions on forced heirship in some other European and Western Hemisphere countries.

interest of its own. At any rate, I think that without such a glimpse it would be difficult to understand how antique Roman conceptions of gifts between husband and wife have been used in modern law to engineer a major compromise. They have become the means for ensuring to owners during their lifetimes free management and enjoyment of the assets they own, while ensuring that their close blood relatives will inherit generous shares of these assets, whose permanent and transmissible value is preserved by controls over gifts to others. Other ideas that were also found in Roman law have been used in aid of this compromise, by excluding as not even potential subjects of gift a wide variety of activities, privileges, and advantages that may be saleable to others but that subtract nothing from the estate that can be transmitted at death. This narrowed range of the "giveable" will be the next topic considered.

In addition to the safeguards for the interests of close relatives, the French Code sets up two other forms of control over gifts. One of them, notarization, is framed in sweeping terms. It applies to all gift transactions, not merely promises of gift. It will require much attention at a later stage, not because it is important in daily life but because of the bizarre measures that have been taken by the courts to circumvent it. The other type of control, the donor's power to revoke, will occasionally appear in the later discussion. There are three grounds stated by the Code, all of them derived from Roman law: the donee's "ingratitude," the donee's failure to perform an express condition, and the subsequent acquisition of a child by a previously childless donor.[56] If one could judge by

56. Art. 953, with elaboration of these themes in the thirteen articles that follow. The ingratitude of the donee that will justify revocation is defined (art. 955) as an attempt on the life of the donor, "cruelty and grave wrongs or injuries," and refusal of support. The Roman law antecedents of these ideas are described by Buckland, *Textbook*, pp. 253–254.

the evidence provided by the law reports, revocation by donors would seem not at all common, though it does have some effect in making gift transactions vulnerable to attack in one more way.

2. What Is Giveable

The French Code wastes no words in defining the interest that can be the subject of a gift. It is a "thing" of which the donor "divests himself . . . in favor of the donee."[1] For an interest to become a subject of gift, therefore, it must already have been reduced to an ownership that the gift can "divest" and then transfer. It is evident that this definition leaves out about as much as it includes—privileges, satisfactions, advantages, and rewards that can be conferred through human interaction in a multitude of ways. Elsewhere in the Code there is a broader conception of the "contract of benefaction," defined as one "in which one of the parties procures for the other a purely gratuitous advantage."[2] It is thus made to appear that the gift as the Code defines it is merely one of a larger group of transactions that presumably have some legal effect and confer a one-sided advantage but nevertheless are not gifts.

A catalogue listing of some of these transactions appears in the Code, described in terms that bear the marks of antiquity: deposit, loan for use, loan for consumption, and

1. Art. 894: "The *inter vivos* gift is an act by which the donor divests himself actually and irrevocably of the thing (*chose*) given in favor of the donee who accepts." An earlier draft of the article that became 894 made this more explicit by defining gift as an act that divests "the ownership of the thing given." "Ownership" was struck out at a late stage on the chance that it might be read to require transfer of full, not merely partial, ownership. M. Boitard, *Les Contrats des services gratuits* (1941), p. 109.

2. Art. 1105.

mandate.[3] It is characteristic of this group of transactions, as it is of contracts for unpaid services of other kinds, that where they are in fact gratuitous, the legal connections they establish are "fragile," that is, very easily dissolved.[4] Another characteristic is that the levels of duty they impose are distinctly lower than in similar transactions in which compensation of some kind is provided.[5] They clearly can generate incidental duties, so that, for example, an unpaid employee should be liable for disclosing trade secrets learned during the course of his employment.[6] The one rendering gratuitous

3. As to deposit, the Code says (art. 1917) that "properly speaking, it is essentially gratuitous." The loan for use is also described (art. 1876) as "essentially gratuitous." Mandate is (art. 1986) "gratuitous unless otherwise agreed." The loan for consumption, which includes the ordinary loan of money, is first described in the Code as one in which no interest is charged and the borrower's obligation is simply to repay the precise sum lent (arts. 1892–1904). The loan with interest comes in the next chapter (arts. 1905 ff.).

4. A good discussion of the "fragility" of the ties of obligation in such "contracts of benefaction" is that of Boitard, *Les Contrats,* pp. 284–294. For example, as he points out, the owner in a deposit can reclaim the object deposited at any time even though he had fixed a term for it. This is not true of the loan for use, but there the owner can recover the object lent if he can show "a pressing and unforeseen need for it." Mandate can be dissolved by either party at any time, though the mandatory (agent) must reimburse the mandator (principal) if a premature termination increases the principal's loss (art. 2007).

5. Most of the litigation has been concerned with injuries inflicted in the supplying of free medical services and free transportation. A full account is given by Boitard, *Les Contrats,* pp. 79–83, 83–87, 220–233, 242–259. Liability will usually be heavier when some element of self-interest is added, even though the services are primarily "benevolent." Ibid., 145–150; Dupeyroux, *L'Acte à titre gratuit,* pp. 82–86.

An interesting comparative survey of the reduced liabilities in mandate, deposit, and other gratuitous transactions in French, German, and American law is given by Gorla, *Il Contratto,* pp. 372–384.

6. This suggestion was made by A. Rouast in "La Prestation gratuite de travail," in *Études de droit civil à la memoire de Henri Capitant* (1937), pp. 695, 705.

services by agreement will normally be entitled, as in older times, to reimbursement for necessary expenditures made or losses reasonably incurred. If his own performance when rendered fails to comply with minimum standards of attention and care, he himself will probably be liable for losses thereby caused. There may even be a duty to complete action once begun if abandonment would cause foreseeable loss. Whether liability of either type depends on tort or contract is a matter of labels on which as a rule not much depends. There could be a question, which only a foreigner would be likely to ask, as to whether a legal system gains much by this minimal intervention to enforce these mini-contracts, even though the effort required is also minimal. In French law it is entirely proper to call such transactions contracts. If intended and taken seriously, there is no inhibition of any kind that prevents the enforcement, even full-scale specific enforcement, of such one-sided promises, unrecompensed though they be.[7]

7. In Dalloz.1846.2.219 (Colmar, 1845), the defendant, owner of a hotel, promised to set aside space in his hotel and to permit occupancy of this space by the plaintiff without charge if he would resume operation of a transport service between the cities of Belfort and Thann. Plaintiff had previously used this space when he operated a transportation service along the same route, but had given up the enterprise and taken work with the postal authorities. Defendant promised that if plaintiff cancelled his connection with the postal system and reinstated his own transport service, defendant would again make the space available without charge. Plaintiff did both but defendant rejected his demand for the space. The court pointed out that defendant would derive an advantage in having plaintiff's passengers, potential hotel customers, deposited in the hotel. It described the transaction as a kind of loan for use (*commodat*) and directed the trial court to put plaintiff into occupancy of the space promised by whatever measures of constraint were necessary.

The court did not mention as a reason for enforcing the promise the reliance by the plaintiff in abandoning his connection with the postal service and setting up his own transport business. Did this reliance have some influence nevertheless? In our own law, if proved, such reliance

Then if the advantage is wholly one-sided, why is it not a gift? The answer was composed some two thousand years ago. To make a gift the donor must deprive himself of some enduring and transmissible portion of his assets; this does not occur when services are rendered to another person.[8] Likewise, there is no correlative enrichment of the type required—a lasting addition to the receiver's estate—if the only result is that services were rendered or the use of property was permitted without charge. It is true that if the receiver of this kind of benefaction wanted it badly enough to pay for it, receiving it free would be a benefit, an expenditure saved. But this kind of argument is hazardous, for it can be transposed: if the same assumption were made, it could be contended that the benefactor on his side was impoverished by foregoing a gain, the payment that he might have been able to exact. If the claim were one for restitution of an unjust enrichment these contentions would almost certainly prevail. If, for example, performance of a contract were broken off for some good reason (such as fraud or substantial breach) and the one not at fault had supplied services or the use of physical assets to the party at fault, the advantage conferred would clearly be a gain requested by and recoverable from the receiver.[9]

Then why cannot saleable advantages of this kind be the subject of gifts? A few French authors now say they can. Most French courts, almost though not quite all of the time, resist this suggestion firmly. So do most French authors. When pressed for reasons, they can mention that safeguarding formalities such as notarization are much less needed here and would be hard to organize around a "gift" that took

should nowadays be enough to justify enforcing the promise, even though the plaintiff was to pay nothing.

8. Rouallt, "La Prestation gratuite," pp. 695, 704 (see note 6).

9. Planiol et Ripert, *Traité pratique,* vol. 7, secs. 754, 764.

the abstract form of profit foregone or expenditure saved. Most emphasized, however, is the antiquity of the notion that a gift is a transfer between "patrimonies" and does not include human services rendered or a mere use of physical assets that leaves their substance intact. This notion has prevailed a very long time and good reason should be given to change it.[10]

The right of which a donor "divests" himself does not need, of course, to be embodied in some physical object. A right to payment of a sum of money can be assigned by way of gift.[11] Payment of a debt owed by a debtor to a third person can constitute a gift to the debtor.[12] Likewise, a release by a

10. A standard formulation of the "diminution of patrimony" test appears in ibid., vol. 5, sec. 9. A very good review of the issues and the authors, including the dissenters, is that of Boitard, *Les Contrats*, pp. 106–118. Boitard then cites (pp. 118–121) several cases in which benefactions of this kind were ordered "returned" because they had produced inequalities between the "donor's" children. Boitard does suggest (pp. 106–118) that both overreaching and ill-considered sacrifices are less likely where services and the use of property are involved so that safeguarding formalities might be less needed. But his argument mostly rests on the antiquity and widespread acceptance of the "diminution of patrimony" test, rooted in Roman law and adhered to ever since.

Gino Gorla likewise contended that the restriction of gifts to transfers of property must be explained as a survival from the past which might be considered obsolete in a modern society that is "founded on labor." But, he concluded, the rules concerning gifts have a connection with the need to protect the heir's *légitime* and, formulated as they are, do have a function in "protecting the donor and his family against hasty decisions." Gorla, *Il Contratto*, pp. 84–94.

11. The payee's endorsement of a promissory note with physical delivery to the donee would be sufficient. A 1922 statute introduced a requirement for all transfers of negotiable paper, that the price paid by the transferee be disclosed. But as the next section will make more clear, the remedy would be for a nonexistent price to be recited, so that the gift would be disguised as a sale. Planiol et Ripert, *Traité pratique*, vol. 4 secs. 3333–3335; vol. 5, sec. 416.

12. J.C.P. 1943, p. 2283 (Tribunal de Limoges, 1943); Planiol et Ripert,

creditor of his own debtor, made without any payment by the
debtor, would fall within the category of gift, though to forestall any question whether it should be notarized it would be
a wise precaution to recite, however falsely, that the debtor
had paid something.[13]

Renunciations of other kinds of rights (for example, to
some present or prospective share in a decedent's estate, or
an easement in another's land) can also constitute gifts to
those who are thereby enabled to acquire some valuable
interest or secure permanent relief from a burden. Some authors contend that a "renunciation" is not a transfer but the
surrender of a right, so that the resulting gain is nothing more
than an incidental consequence. But where the one who
"renounced" has revealed a clear donative purpose, courts
have been entirely ready to call such transactions gifts.[14]

The necessary transfer between "patrimonies," with subtraction from one and increment to the other, can occur by

Traité pratique, vol. 5, sec. 414. D.P.1913.1.203 (1913) and S.1850.1.510
(1850) require return (*rapport*) of the amount so paid to the extent that the
payment gave the debtor a larger share than his coheirs.

13. D.1850.2.194 (Lyon, 1848), D.1863.1.454 (1862) and D.1882.1.477
(1881) all held, however, that unnotarized releases which the creditors in
fact intended as "liberalities" to the debtors were effective a gifts, though
in the case first cited the gift had to be "returned" (*rapporté*) because it
had produced an inequality in their inheritance as between coheirs. False
recitals and other "disguises" will be discussed in the next section.

14. Planiol et Ripert, *Traité pratique*, vol. 1, secs. 327, 419–420, summarize the issues. Where such transactions are described as gifts, the chief
result is to require acceptance by the donee. Notarization is not required
for reasons that are left unclear; perhaps the gifts are thought to be well
enough "disguised" or else they are considered to be fully executed, as
though by hand delivery. The arguments that renunciations are "abdica-
tive" and not "translative," so that they do not produce gifts, are developed
at length by P. Raynaud, "La Rénonciation à un droit," *Revue Trimestrielle
de Droit Civil* (1936), p. 736; M. Lessona, "Théorie générale de la rénonciation en droit civil," *Revue Trimestrielle de Droit Civil* (1912), p. 361; A.
Ponsard, *Donations indirectes* (1946), pp. 133–142.

other roundabout means. An intermediary, for example, can be used and the increment can reach the ultimate receiver in a quite different form. A common type of so-called "indirect" gift is purchase by the benefactor of some asset owned by a third party who, after he has been paid by the benefactor, conveys it to the donee. Such transactions are at times described as "disguised" gifts. They can, of course, be clandestine and may delude outsiders, including tax collectors, by being broken into separate parts. But they do not have the usual feature of the "disguised" gift which, as we shall soon see, involves deliberate misstatement of terms. Perhaps the success achieved by plausible falsehood in circumventing the requirement of notarization helped to ensure that "indirect" gifts likewise did not need to be notarized. But for all the other relevant purposes (donor's revocation, calculation of disposable quotas) "indirect" gifts are undoubtedly gifts.[15]

In determining what is "giveable" the policies and purposes behind the Code's controls have been most crucially

15. In J.C.P. 1943, p. 2283 (Tribunal de Limoges, 1943) the court held that notarization was not needed for such a three-cornered transaction, in which shares of stock were paid for by a father and delivered by the seller to his sons. The court held this delivery gave title to the sons, good against claims of subsequent creditors of the father. A valuable note by Carbonnier follows the report.

Similar three-cornered purchases of land were held effective as gifts and therefore subject to revocation for donees' ingratitude in J.C.P. 1946.2.3050 (Nîmes, 1945); J.C.P. 1947.2.3719 (Cassation, 1947). Similarly, "reduction" was ordered because payments encroached on forced heirs' guaranteed shares (D.1859.1.503) and cancellation was ordered because the gifts were between husband and wife (D.C.1942,6; D.1951, 617, followed by an instructive note). In the more recent cases the payment to and transfer by a third person were held to be "indivisible" parts of a single transaction, so that a donor entitled to restitution recovers, not the money he had paid, but the asset purchased if its value had risen in the interval (as successive inflations have made likely). These and other problems raised by indirect gifts are discussed by Planiol et Ripert, *Traité pratique*, vol. 5, secs. 114 quater, 415; vol. 4, sec. 2358; Ponsard, *Donations indirectes*, pp. 179–183.

tested by gifts of "fruits and revenues." The simplest example of such a gift would be a conveyance of land to a donee who, placed in possession, is authorized to extract its income. Here the Civil Code itself has an explicit provision. Even if the conveyance to him is set aside because it exceeded the donor's disposable quota, the Code provides expressly that the donee needs to account only for the revenues realized after the donor's death.[16] The Code has nothing to say about a lease of land by parent to son at a rent far below the known rental value for the purpose, understood by both, of providing a benefaction to the son-lessee. But no Code provision is needed. Any claim for the margin of income gained would be met by a showing that the estate of the lessor-owner was in no way diminished if on his death the land was restored intact.[17] The same argument applies with equal force when the donee, a son, is given no interest at all in the land and is simply authorized to collect rent due from tenants under leases to them by the owner-father; the son has subtracted nothing from the land by merely collecting its "fruits and revenues."[18] Then why not extend the same argument to the case where the benefactor collects the income himself and pays out equivalent sums, either to the recipient of his bounty or to some third party for his account? An example would be an insurance policy in which the insured pays regular premiums in amounts no more than (presumably much less than) his current income, the policy being payable to another whom we would call a "donee beneficiary" because

16. Art. 928. In Art. 856 there is a similar provision for instances of return (*rapport*) by the heir who has, through an inter vivos gift, received more than his share in the succession.

17. Sirey1866.2.486 (Montpellier 1863), involving a lease by a father to his son at a rent much less than rental value.

18. D.1921.1.21 (1917), where a son had for 17 years with his father's approval collected a total of 204,000 francs from buildings owned by the father in Paris.

he or she contributes nothing. A series of court decisions starting about 1900 held such premium payments not to be gifts, even though their purpose was to create a capital fund payable on the insured's death to the named beneficiary in one lump sum.[19]

Benefactions in instalments stretched out over time merely reveal in aggravated form the hardships and dilemmas created by the controls over gifts that require their recall after years—often many years—have elapsed. The French Code, as I have said, imposes no time limit at all (unlike the German, which goes back only ten years) on the retroactive recall of gifts that exceed the disposable quotas or that bring unjustified inequalities as between coheirs.[20] Where a gift is "reduced" for exceeding the decedent's disposable quota, the asset must, wherever possible, be restored *in specie* and intact, though where the ground is unjustified inequality as between coheirs, the normal remedy now is an accounting for the value when it was received.[21] Reasonable expenditures to preserve or improve the asset can be recovered,[22] but

19. Planiol et Ripert, *Traité pratique*, vol. 5, sec. 325. In 1930, legislation expressly exempted from inclusion, as part of the insured's estate, of premiums that had been paid on policies insuring his own life if not "manifestly excessive" having regard to the insured's "capacities" (*facultés*).

20. The rent collections in the case referred to in note 18 above had, for example, been made for seventeen years, though fortunately the court concluded that the son could keep them. In S.1862.1.716 (1861) the payments had been made for thirty-one years.

21. That "reduction" of gifts must whenever possible take the form of specific restitution is the main thesis, demonstrated convincingly and at length, of F. Jeantet, *Le Droit à la réserve en nature* (1939). Until amendments to the Code in 1938, this was the normal solution in *rapport* also, but as to land an option is now provided between specific and money restitution. Art. 358, 360.

22. Compensation is allowed for improvements to the extent of the value they add (art. 861), and for expenditures "necessary" to conserve the subject of the gift (art. 862). The donee is liable, of course, for "deteriorations" due to his fault or negligence (art. 863).

otherwise, so far as I can discover, no account whatever is taken of any reliance by the donee, including any expenditures inspired by the delusion that his resources had been permanently increased. One response might be that reliance by the receivers on gratuitous transfers is in any case and at all times imprudent. It is not so much that any such gift is subject to revocation by the donor, since two of the three grounds for revocation depend on shortcomings of the donee which he should have means to prevent.[23] But he cannot control, seldom could he even estimate in advance, the extent of the risk that the gift will be assailed by the heirs of the donor after his death. To estimate this risk the donee would need to know the value of the assets that the donor had already given away and would give away later in his lifetime, the value of the estate that the donor would leave on the uncertain day when his turn would come to die, and what heirs would survive with enforceable claims to the recall of lifetime gifts.

It seems that uncertainties of this kind are part of the price that must be paid for guarantees to heirs that encompass inter vivos gifts but can operate only after the donor's death. If reliance by donees could prevent the recall of gifts that transgress the limits, the guarantees would be considerably undermined. So to some it has seemed much better to approach the problem of gifts made in instalments from the opposite direction and to say that gifts of "fruits and revenues" simply are not gifts, that they are exempted not only from notarization but also do not count as gifts in figuring disposable quotas and equalizing the shares of coheirs. How could this be done? The Court of Cassation found a way. The provisions that were said to require this I have already men-

23. These two are the donee's "ingratitude" and his failure to perform an express condition to the gift. The third, subsequent birth of a child to a donor who at the time of the gift had no living descendants, should not represent a high risk to most donees.

tioned. They were addressed to the donee who had been given both title to and possession of the subject of the gift and from it had extracted "fruits and revenues." The Code provision assumed that the gift was to be "reduced" or "returned" but declared that in that event the donee needed to account only for the income received after the donor's death, the point at which a duty to restore would arise. It was a considerable leap to say that this provision applied by analogy to a case in which the benefactor had retained full ownership and control of all his assets throughout, had received regular income from them, and had paid out in periodic "liberalities" sums equal to or less than the income received from the property that he continued to own. A simple illustration would be a grant of a lifetime annuity in a fixed amount per year by parents to a daughter. When the parents die, should the sums received be "reduced" (if their total brings the decedents' gifts above their disposable quota) or "returned" (if the payments produce inequality between coheirs)? The answer given in this case was no—the parents' "holdings" had not been diminished by periodic payments that did not exceed their income.[24]

24. D.1922.2.181 (Nîmes, 1921). In the instrument granting the annuity of 3,000 francs a year there had been a recital that this sum "represented" their regular revenue. The court declared that the case was governed by Code article 856, which allowed the donee who had been put into possession to retain "fruits and revenues" received before he became subject to an enforceable duty to restore the subject matter.

In the extensive recent literature on gifts of "fruits and revenues" it is difficult to find anyone who considers that article 856 (or its counterpart, art. 928) can carry so heavy a load. R. LeBalle, "Du Rapport et de la réduction des liberalités portant sur les fruits et revenus," 46 *Revue critique de la législation et Jurisprudence* 541 (1926); P. Esmein, "Les Donations de Fruits et Revenus," *Répertoire général, pratique du notariat,* 1934, art. 23958, p. 637, and art. 23987, p. 677; Planiol et Ripert, *Traité pratique,* vol. 5, sec. 323; Dupeyroux, *L'Acte à titre gratuit,* pp. 387–403. A fully developed argument that income received by owners should be spendable in any way they please and without any accountability by their donees, is

There was much to be said for this conclusion, though the Civil Code did not say it. Anyone nourished on American law would be first of all concerned over the effects of such gifts, received in instalments, on the recipients' behavior. The bounty conferred, periodically in scaled-down amounts, would probably be absorbed into current revenue and currently spent. If it then turns out on the benefactor's death, several or perhaps many years later, that the instalments must all be added up and restored in one lump sum, the burden on the donee could be sudden and heavy, especially if the resources with which to make the payment have been dispersed or dissipated. But in France, so far as I can learn, this sort of argument has not been heard. The arguments mostly used have come from a different direction and center on the purpose of controls over gifts. There are different kinds of such controls—notarization, revocation for specified reasons—but the primary purpose is to conserve the capital resources of families by limiting their disposal without equivalent return. So the question becomes: Why should quotas be imposed if the benefactions are made in instalments, over an extended time?[25] If they are divided up and "periodic," the amount of the instalments is likely to coin-

---

presented by H. Desbois, "Des donations de fruits et revenus," *Semaine juridique* (1929), p. 939.

25. The "periodicity" required could take any one of three different forms: instalments of income and outgo roughly matched in timing and amount; periodic payments that are intended to produce a single capital fund (e.g., premiums paid on life insurance); or an initial charge on a capital asset that will produce periodic payments stretched out over time (e.g., a rent charge on income-producing land). A full account of the variations is given by Desbois ("Des donations de fruits et revenus," *Semaine juridique* [1929], p. 939), who is himself a strong advocate of these judicial inventions but concedes (p. 940) that "periodicity" in some form is essential, so that a transfer in one lump sum directly from donor to donee would not be exempt even though the sum transferred was entirely derived from income.

cide with income currently received from other sources. Some authors and perhaps some courts would insist that this correlation must be shown to exist.[26] If it does, one can argue that the income as it accrued would probably have been spent in some other way, so no one loses if it is simply given away. It has even been urged that the "fruits and revenues" that are exempt from controls over gifts should include, not only income itself as it is received, but also its traceable product—assets or interests that income was used to acquire.[27] French courts have not yet been willing to take this last long step, and on these issues generally prediction is even more difficult than it usually is in French case law. One can only say that benefactions in "periodic" instalments that do not exceed the benefactor's current income have a good chance of being considered not gifts for any purpose.[28]

The ingenious Romans who invented so long ago this peculiar conception of what is not "giveable" would be surprised, no doubt, if they could now revisit their former province of Gaul. They invented it, they said, in order to preserve high levels of mutual trust between Roman wives and husbands, undefiled by mercenary motives. To accomplish this laudable and affirmative purpose, they devised a formula that would negate transactions of a particular kind, those that

26. The decisions, starting in 1913, that started the main series of modern decisions exempting gifts of "fruits and revenues" relied primarily on article 856, Civil Code. D.1917.1.58 (1913); D.1921.1.21 (1917); D.1922.2.181 (Nîmes, 1921). But the two cases last cited also used the argument quoted, that the "holdings" of the benefactors had not been diminished since the payments did not exceed income.

27. This sweeping proposal to eliminate income and all its traceable products from controls over gifts made an impression because it was proposed in that form by a distinguished scholar, Paul Esmein, in two articles in the *Répertoire général, pratique du notariat* (1934), arts. 23958 and 23987.

28. An excellent review of more recent decisions and discussions is supplied by Dupeyroux, *L'Acte à titre gratuit*, pp. 387–403.

would have the twofold effect of both depleting the capital resources of one and augmenting those of the other. This formula was prominent enough in Roman law sources so that it would no doubt have survived in any event, but in later centuries another, very different purpose emerged, a purpose it has served most effectively. As transferred into modern law, the purpose was to ensure that the close blood-relatives of every owner of transmissible wealth would inherit on his death a generous share of all that he had ever owned and given away. This was a purpose whose consequences reached far beyond the result at which the inventors had aimed—to prevent married persons, overly fond or overpersuaded, from giving too much to each other. Now it was to be used to fix limits, expressed in the form of quotas, to the power of all owners to make gifts of what they owned. These quotas varied with the numbers and kinds of blood relatives that survived. Gifts exceeding the quotas were not set aside until after the donors had died, so there would be for them no added discomfort. It would be their intended donees that would incur distress and disruption when required to surrender the subject of the gift, some time and perhaps many years later. But the percentages that were "reserved," of which owners could not dispose, were ordinarily high, high enough to operate as a major deterrent to the making of gifts outside the owner's bloodline.

When guarantees to the surviving kindred moved to the forefront among the reasons for special controls over gifts, the Roman law tests for husband-wife gifts had great attraction, mostly for their omissions. Services—personal action or inaction of any kind—would be wholly exempt from post-audit, no matter how beneficial to others they might be. Likewise the use of physical property or any other facility that left its permanent features unimpaired. So owners of transmissible wealth could retain maximum control during their own lifetimes over its management and use and the disposal of its income, both by themselves and by others they selected as objects of their bounty. The only limitation was that the owners must not impair that percentage of its enduring and transmissible value that they were required to hold intact for their nearest of kin. My own surmise is that if some accommodation like that provided by the Roman law tests had not been found or invented, forced heirship would not have retained the widespread support that it continues to have.

3. *Escape from Notarization—The Two Main Routes*

The requirements of form that had been imposed by royal legislation in 1731 applied not only to promises of gift but to gift transactions of every kind. If not registered or notarized they were declared wholly void. This legislation remained in force between 1789 and 1804, the effective date of the Civil Code, without audible protest from any source. It seems likely that these requirements were welcome to many as a form of deterrence, and especially welcome to those who would have liked if they could to abolish altogether or restrict severely the power to dispose by will. The need for notarization for all forms of inter vivos gifts was taken for granted. In the Conseil d'État, for example, in the preliminary stages of legislative approval of the Civil Code, this requirement was accepted without discussion.[1]

   In fact, in the Code as finally adopted the requirements of form were made more severe. The main requirement was

---

   1. Fenet, *Receuil complet*, 12: 353–355. In this and later sections the themes will intersect with those discussed in the pioneering article by Arthur von Mehren, "Civil Law Analogues to Consideration," 72 *Harvard Law Review* 1009 (1959). I have made more use of this article than specific citations will indicate. This is in part because it deals with a number of related themes with which this study is not directly concerned.

that the donor must appear before "notaries" to authenticate the document that expressed the transfer or promise, and that a copy of this document must be kept, all of this "on pain of nullity."[2] Acceptance by the donee had been mentioned before as a needed expression of assent, but the Code made this more explicit—the transaction would be void until the donee's acceptance had itself been notarized and was actually transmitted to the donor.[3] When the Code spoke of authentication before "notaries" this is what it meant, for *two* notaries were required, and if only one could be found, then two other unlicensed persons must replace the missing notary to serve as witnesses.[4] The donor and normally the donee would also be present. After the terms of the transaction had all been written down, one of the notaries must read the whole document "aloud" to the group and all were required to sign. The only thing missing was an indication whether the meeting must open and close with prayer.

The first step will be to describe the means by which the requirement of notarization has been successfully nullified.

2. Art. 931, Civil Code: "All acts constituting *inter vivos* gifts must be adopted [*passés*] before notaries in the ordinary form of contracts and a copy retained, on pain of nullity." Art. 1339 reinforces this by providing that a gift void for defect of form cannot be made effective by any subsequent act or declaration of the donor and that it is necessary for him to redo it "in lawful form."

3. Arts. 932 and 933. Special indulgence is provided in Code articles that follow for acceptance by other means on behalf of minors, deaf mutes, and charities. The first of the royal ordinances (that of 1539, art. 133) had required notarization of the donee's acceptance, but this requirement was omitted in later royal legislation. The requirement of an express acceptance was read in by courts, simply on the ground that gifts were contracts. Ricard, *Traité des donations,* 1: 212–224, 228; Bourjon, *Le Droit commun de la France,* 2: 159.

4. Even before the Revolution these had been the statutory requirements for notarization generally. Legislation of 1843 reduced the requirement to a single notary for other transactions but has retained the original requirement of two notaries (or one plus two laymen) for gifts. Planiol, Ripert, et Boulanger, *Traité pratique de droit civil,* vol. 4, sec. 3268.

The difficulties in presenting the account are simply the usual difficulties that any reader must encounter in deciphering the reasons for French court decisions, though the difficulties do increase as one moves back in time. The legislation that in 1790 set up a high court of review (the Tribunal of Cassation, after 1795 called the Court of Cassation) produced for France a striking innovation. It required the new court to disclose its reasons for decision. In complying with this mandate the court soon developed a stereotyped and laconic style whose main purpose seemed to be to demonstrate the court's dutiful submission to the legislature. The high courts of the old regime had succeeded in establishing a veto power over legislation that had enabled them, among their other achievements, to launch a revolution.[5] Legislation in future was to carry the endorsement, not merely of a king, but of an elected legislature, which at once asserted vigorously some very wide powers. For the new high court to claim continuing powers to veto legislation would have been most unwise; a posture of deference was called for. But a posture does not alter habits of mind that had been set long before. Under the old regime judges, especially judges in the highest courts, had been very free indeed to map their own way, to wander off on paths they discovered for themselves. So very early after the Code appeared the high court set off along two avenues that it mapped out by itself, one a major detour around the Code and the other a broad boulevard directly through the middle.

A. *The Manual Gift*

Actually, for the detour around the Code there was a good deal to be said, although there was nothing in the Code that

5. These topics are discussed by Dawson, *The Oracles of the Law* (1968), pp. 375–385.

said it. The detour was the so-called *don manuel*, the gift of a movable object by delivery from hand to hand. In the comprehensive royal ordinance of 1731 gifts of movables through physical delivery had been treated in a somewhat equivocal way. They had been expressly exempted from the requirement of public recording, but as to the alternative, notarization, no exemption for hand-delivered gifts was mentioned.[6] After the Code took effect, the conclusion that physical delivery with donative intent produced a valid gift was not reached by the Court of Cassation until 1815, eleven years later. It has been uniformly followed ever since in court decisions too numerous to count. It has been approved emphatically by most authors,[7] though a few have admitted some suppressed uneasiness, since the Code provision is sweeping: "All acts that constitute gifts must be confirmed before notaries in the ordinary form of contracts and a record must be kept, on pain of nullity."[8] Gifts by hand delivery are referred to by the Code in one other place, but in such a way as to suggest—very strongly, I would say—that even though the subject of a gift could be transferred readily from hand to hand, notarization was still required, for a reason that was clearly persuasive to the draftsmen of the Code: that written

6. Ordonnance of 1731, art. 22 (Isambert *Receuil général*, 21: 349). Chancellor d'Aguesseau, the leading sponsor of the ordinance, expressed in a private letter his own opinion that the ordinance did not require notarization for gifts completed by "actual transfer" of movable property. Quoted by A. von Mehren and J. Gordley, *The Civil Law System* (1977), p. 905.

7. Planiol et Ripert, *Traité pratique*, vol. 5, secs. 378–379, give references.

8. Art. 931. One argument that has been used to justify enforcement of *dons manuels*, is that this clause used the word *actes* in defining the requirement of notarization and *actes* meant "documents," which would not be used if manual delivery was the method employed. It is true that, like *deed* in English, *acte* is often used to describe a piece of paper, but it is also often used to mean a human act, as is pointed out by Planiol et Ripert, *Traité pratique*, vol. 5, sec. 379, who reject this suggestion.

records were needed to protect the guaranteed shares of the donor's forced heirs.[9]

One must look to the authors for explanations of the *don manuel*, since here as elsewhere the high court keeps its own secrets well. The explanations are various. The one that has reappeared most frequently is that physical delivery provides adequate warning to the donor of the deprivation he is about to incur, also corroborative evidence and an external stamp of authenticity, and thus performs the functions of a transactional formality as well as a notary could do through his presence and his records—or at any rate performs them well enough. Another explanation amounted to nothing more than a counsel of despair: there was no way of preventing owners from picking up and handing to others objects that they could easily pick up and hand over, so why try?[10] But as time marched on and French legal writers learned about and acquired an interest in the case law that courts had been making, the *don manuel* seemed to some receptive minds to be one of the numerous and original creations produced by French courts "through and beyond" the Code. Some critics thought these creations had served an important and much broader purpose in showing that there were limits to the "plenitude of power" attributed to the legislator and that so-

9. Art. 948 is the only other clause in the Code sections on inter vivos gifts that refers explicitly to gifts of movables. It provides that such gifts will be valid only as to those movables that are listed on an appraisal sheet (*état estimatif*) that has been signed by both donor and donee and then "attached to the record of the gift." This clause was inserted by the Code drafting commission after one member pointed out that without this precaution it would not be possible to determine the *légitime* of the donor's children (Pacilly, *Le Don Manuel* (1936), pp. 177–178; strangely enough, Pacilly then proceeds to read *acte* as meaning "document" and concludes that the Code draftsmen simply had nothing to say about *dons manuels*).

10. This was the main burden of what Professor l'Abbé had to say in his note in Sirey 1883.2.241.

ciety itself does and must have means to generate law other
than the logically ordered abstractions of written law.[11] Or if
one preferred to remain at lower levels of criticism where the
atmosphere is not so rarefied, one could say almost the same
thing much more briefly: that the manual gift had become
"an autonomous institution of customary origin . . . parallel
to that of the notarized gift."[12]

Judicial decisions have steadily expanded the scope and
usefulness of the *don manuel*. Rights in intangibles can be
transferred by gift through hand delivery of a document
whose production is normally needed for enforcement, as
our own courts enforce the gift of a "documented" chose in
action.[13] The donor can reserve a "usufruct," the use and income for life.[14] A manual gift can be subject to a charge that
will require the donee to use or dispose of the gift for a purpose or in a manner defined, including the provision of some
advantage to third persons.[15] But if the effect of the manual
gift is to deplete the reserve that the donor is required to hold
intact at his death—the guaranteed shares of his descendants
or ancestors—the inter vivos manual gift will be counted as

11. Pacilly, *Le Don manuel*, pp. 179–182, invokes the spirit of Gény for
this purpose.

12. Planiol et Ripert, *Traité pratique*, vol. 5, sec. 379.

13. Delivery by gift of certificates of stock or debtors' bonds:
D.1875.2.6 (Cour de Nancy, 1873); D.1875.2.187 (Cour de Rouen, 1874);
D.1882.1.67 (1881); negotiable instruments: D.1892.1.510 (1891); Gazette
des Tribunaux, 1928.2.588 (Tribunal Civil des Alpes Maritimes, 1928);
Planiol et Ripert, *Traité pratique*, vol. 5, sec. 385.

In S.1947.2.83 (Cour de Rennes, 1946) a depositor in writing directed
the bank with which he had an account to pay 200,000 francs to his fiancée,
and she wrote a check on the bank in that amount. The bank paid the
check. This was held to be a "novation" and also an irrevocable gift "in
modern form."

14. D.P. 1880.1.461 (1880); D.1936.1.29 (1935).

15. Planiol et Ripert, *Traité pratique*, vol. 5, sec. 402, and Pacilly, *Le
Don manuel*, pp. 222–237 provide examples.

part of his total estate at death and will be "reduced" like any other gift if this proves to be necessary.[16] So the net result is that any subject of ownership that can be delivered by hand can be transferred by way of gift. There still is debate as to the effect of this innovation, whether it enables owners to concentrate their resources in fewer hands so as to magnify the influence of their families or induces them to promote social equality by distributing wealth more widely.[17] The high court judges give no clue to their own motives in opening up this avenue, but enough good reasons can be surmised so that no one seems to worry that it is not authorized, indeed is forbidden, by the Code.

B. *The Disguised Gift*

The other invention, however, can only be described as bizarre. This is the so-called disguised gift or sham, which wears the trappings of an exchange transaction. Credit for its invention belongs, I believe, exclusively to France. There was nothing like the disguised gift in Roman law. There a transaction that was understood by the parties to be a gift but that was drafted to appear as a sale, was not a sale, though if the "vendor" then conveyed the asset involved, the conveyance would effectuate the gift.[18] In prerevolutionary

16. D.1895.2.278 (Cour de Paris, 1894), where the deceased in his lifetime had given large sums of money to four donees with the deliberate object, known to them, of disinheriting his children. The court ordered the gifts "reduced," that is, that the excess over the amount of which he was free to dispose was to be paid back to a court-appointed conservator. The court thus rejected the more drastic solution adopted in an earlier case which held that the gift was not merely "reducible" but wholly void because of the purpose to evade the heirs' guarantee, a purpose known to both parties. D.P. 1856.2.149 (Cour de Bastia, 1855).

17. Pacilly, *Le Don manuel*, pp. 188–194, argues enthusiastically for the latter view.

18. The topic is fully discussed by J. Partsch, "Die Lehre vom Scheingeschäft im römischen Rechte," 42 Z.S.S. *(röm.)* 227 (1921). There

France most sources, including the law reports, are entirely silent on the subject, though two writers have been discovered who asserted that disguised gifts, though unnotarized, were valid.[19] Very shortly after the Revolution and before the drafting of a civil code had even begun, the new high court was confronted with a rash of pretended sales that were in truth disguised gifts prepared by donors in the troubled years of the early 1790s. This was a time when property left behind in France by the émigrés was subject to summary seizure and severe restrictions on the power to dispose by will were being considered or had already been imposed on all French citizens by the revolutionary assemblies. Donors of all political persuasions may well have heard that such restrictions would soon be extended to include all gift transactions.

The legislation that applied to these transactions was, of course, the royal ordinance of 1731 on gifts. The new Court

---

were several texts in both Digest and Code, and their net result was clear, as in D.18.1.36: "when in a sale one provides that for the purpose of a gift the price of the thing will not be demanded, he is not considered to have made a sale." There were, however, a few texts that were ambiguous enough for some French authors to read them the opposite way.

To be distinguished from the disguised or sham transaction, in which the terms are falsely stated, is the "imitative" use of a standard transaction to accomplish a purpose for which it was not originally designed: a conveyance by way of sale is used to secure a loan, a *mancipatio* is used to free a slave. Numerous examples taken from both classical and medieval sources are given by E. Rabel, "Nachgeformte Rechtsgeschäfte," 27 Z.S.S. (*röm.*) 290 (1906), 28 ibid. 311, 372–379 (1907).

19. One author, Baron Jean Grenier, stated that gifts dressed in other "legal forms" could only be attacked if they were evasions of the law. Danty, *Traité de la preuve par témoins en matière civile*, 6th ed. (1869), pp. 182–183, declared that in general the parties to such a disguised transaction could not show that it was simulated, though third parties could if they were prejudiced. Pothier declared void a gift that was disguised as a sale, but the well-informed lawyer and writer Merlin argued before the Court of Cassation in 1800 that such transactions were clearly valid. Y. Jolivet, *La Validation des donations déguisées et ses consequences en jurisprudence* (1941), pp. 40–43.

of Cassation held in several unreported cases that pretended sales, which were in fact disguised gifts, were void for want of the formalities required by this legislation. Then came a case that was fully reported in which the judges were evenly divided and the tie was broken only by the appointment of five new judges to the court. The decision, rendered in 1800 by a margin of one vote, held that the gift, disguised by false recitals as a sale, was valid.[20] For more than two decades the issue continued to divide the court. The separate sections into which the high court was split took opposing views, though with vacillation back and forth. Finally in 1824 the sections united in upholding disguised gifts, overrode the sustained opposition to this by lower courts, and adhered to this position thereafter.[21]

It was necessary, of course, to make it appear that this transparent evasion of the Code was required by the Code. This was accomplished by invoking two Code provisions which dealt with gifts (1) to incapable persons and (2) between married persons in excess of the quotas permitted. These provisions both expressly declared that such gifts would be void even though disguised.[22] The argument then went into reverse: disguised gifts of only two kinds were declared by the Code to be void so all the rest must be valid, despite the sweeping pronouncement already quoted that "all acts constituting *inter vivos* gifts must be passed before

20. The decision is reported in Sirey 1802.3.1.20. and Sirey 1791, An XII–1–746 (1800) in a remarkably full and discursive opinion, not as yet beaten down into strings of "whereas" clauses. In the opinion for which a majority vote was finally mobilized, the argument mainly rests on Roman law texts which were carefully selected for their ambiguity. The report is most unusual—so far as I know, unique—in disclosing the fact that the vote of the judges was split.

21. This series of events is described in detail in the excellent account by Jolivet, *La Validation des donations*, pp. 21–25.

22. Arts. 911 and 1099.

notaries . . . on pain of nullity."[23] When this argument was tried out on the German Reichsgericht in a case arising in 1880 from Baden, which at the time was governed by the French Civil Code, the German high court refused to follow the reading given the French Code by the French high court or to allow German courts to be deluded by external forms that were known by the German participants to be shams.[24] The disguised gift is also rejected in Italy, though the French solutions are accepted in Belgium.[25] It seems safe

23. Art. 931, quoted above, note 2.

24. 8 *R.G.Z.* 307 (1883), followed on similar facts in 27 *R.G.Z.* 308 (1890).

25. In Italy it has been held in a series of cases that simulation by falsification of terms is wholly ineffective, so that, for example, if a gift (unnotarized) is falsely described as a sale with the recital of a price paid or promised, the transaction is still a gift, void because not notarized: Foro Italiano, 1950, 1: 537 (Court of Cassation); Foro Italiano, 1939, "Donazione," nos. 50–51; Foro Italiano 1942, "Donazione," no. 17; and numerous other cases cited by L. Contursi, *Le donazioni* (1967), pp. 108–115, 138–140, and B. Biondi, *Le donazione* (1961), pp. 579–585, 917–925. In the discussions of the subject by both courts and authors, there has been a constant struggle to keep clear the distinction between the simulated gift, in which the disguise (falsification of terms) is ineffective, and the indirect gift, in which the terms are stated truthfully and gain to some third person is simply an inescapable consequence. The indirect gift is usually valid, as the authors cited indicate. An example would be a case in which a parent with his own money buys a house that the seller is then to convey to the buyer's son.

The German Code of 1900 is explicit (art. 117) that a "declaration of will" is void if it is made to another with the agreement of both that it is merely a "pretense" (*Schein*), but if it disguises another transaction, "the rules for the hidden transaction govern." In the few reported cases since the Code on disguised gifts, this provision has been applied strictly: Seuff. Arch., 69, no. 121 (Reichsgericht, hereafter cited as R.G., 1913), promise of gift disguised as a loan; 80 *R.G.Z.* 135 (1912), disguised as a sale; 87 *R.G.Z.* 301 (1915), gift to wife disguised as creation of community property. Compare Seuff. Arch., 78, no. 11 (R.G., 1922), which was the converse, an exchange disguised as a gift.

In Louisiana likewise, a disguise in the form of an exchange transaction (e.g., a sale) will be penetrated and if it is in fact a gift, it will be void if not

to conclude that this invention—better described as an aberration—is peculiarly French.

Judicial approval of both the disguised gift and the *don manuel* can only be read as attempts to escape the elaborate and burdensome requirements of form that the Code had carried over from the past.[26] French courts under the old regime had been unruly enough in many ways but they had acquiesced in these restrictions on gifts. The puzzle comes in trying to discover why the breakaway came when it did. By 1800 there were some high court judges (in the Court of Cassation a majority of one) who were ready even before the Code took effect to permit the use of transparent camouflage in order to facilitate gifts. The judges then became locked in a debate that was utterly sterile but that had a bearing on some larger issues on which public opinion was still sharply divided and new solutions were still being sought. Then, after the final defeat and expulsion of Napoleon in 1815, the émigrés who returned to judicial office viewed the Civil Code as "the consecration of the work of spoliation that had ruined them."[27] There was no strong impulse to demonstrate

notarized: Smelley v. Ricks, 174 La. 734, 141 So. 445 (1932). Where disguises have been held effective, it has been in order to protect third parties who have purchased from the ostensible buyer (donee) in reliance on his title as it appears on the public record. Comment, "Disguised Donations, Donations Omnium Bonorum and the Public Records Doctrine," 51 *Tulane Law Review* 299 (1977).

Belgium is the only country in western Europe, so far as I know, that follows France in making a disguise in the form of a sham exchange a substitute for notarization: Pasicrisie Belge, 1867.1.159 (Cass., 1867); Pasicrisie Belge, 1932.2.109 (Brussels, 1931); Pasicrisie Belge (1950); and numerous decisions cited and discussed by De Page, *Traité élémentaire de droit civil belge* (1944), vol. 8, pt. 1, secs. 508–515, pp. 598–612.

26. This is suggested also by a thoughtful author, who confesses that it leaves the reasons for the sudden change by courts in their own attitudes as obscure as ever. Jolivet, *La Validation des donations*, pp. 41–43.

27. E. Meynial, "Les Recueils des arrêts et les arrêtistes," *Livre du Centenaire du Code Civil*, 1: 175, 184, who used the phrase I have quoted

their respect for Napoleon's Code, as was shown by numerous other independent courses of action which the courts of this time pursued. The disguised gift would help to undermine the Code and had the added virtue—it must have seemed a virtue—of freeing owners from an obstructive and overbuilt restriction on their power to make gifts.

Trying to guess what might have been is usually unprofitable. There is at least a question whether, if the timing had been slightly different, French courts would have given their solemn approval to a device so far-fetched and bizarre as the disguised gift. Even before the Code the judges of the new high court, very recently created, had become locked in a contest over this issue, and the line-up of opposing sides within the court continued. If the *don manuel* had come up very early (it was not approved until 1815), it would have provided an intermediate solution, a less controversial escape from formalism. France might then have moved in the direction eventually taken by the German Code of 1900, requiring solemnities only for *promises* of gift and giving full effect to gift transfers if made in the modes that are sufficient for transfers of other kinds. These solutions, as we shall see, have in Germany inspired no revolts or roundabout detours. The disguised gift is an evasion of the Code so cynical and transparent that it may well have served to stimulate the search for other ways to circumvent it, a search that, as we shall see, has fanned out in all directions.

The disguised gift enables private donors to manufacture their own formalities, but there is one limit—the disguise must be good, the mask must be well designed. A much-used form of disguise, for example, is the contract of sale with a false recital that a named price has been paid, or where a price is promised with an assurance given by the "seller,"

in the text. The thesis of Meynial as to the impact of the returning émigrés is further discussed by Dawson, Oracles of the Law, pp. 385–386.

separately and privately, that he will never collect it.[28] But a
lease, a loan, a rent charge, or a partnership can also serve as
a disguise.[29] Also very common are acknowledgments of imaginary debts or promises to pay specified sums of money in
exchange for nothing. It is essential for the signer to recite
that he has received or has been promised something for
which a legal obligation to pay could arise. Construction of
the document to ascertain whether the recitals are convincing is a question of law for the court. The recitals do not need
to be precise: money can be promised for "the care given,"[30]
but if the recital is "in gratitude for the care given" it will be
on its face a promise of gift.[31] If the reason for the promise is
declared to be to reimburse for injury caused by the misconduct of someone else, and it appears on the face of document
that from this misconduct no liability arose, the promise will
be void.[32]

There are advantages to be achieved by disguising gifts
other than escape from the costs and inconveniences of
notarization. Informed observers have testified that one of

28. S.1813.1.330 (1813) is an early and often-cited case with a false recital that the price had been paid. Many more cases of simulated sales are
cited by Planiol et Ripert, *Traité pratique*, vol. 5, sec. 425 bis. See also
Jolivet, *La Validation des donations*, pp. 48–51, 61.

29. Planiol et Ripert, *Traité pratique*, vol. 5, sec. 424.

30. S.1896.1.69 (1896), aunt acknowledges debt of 10,000 francs to
nephew for "the care given." Cf. S.1927.1.15 (1925), settlement of accounts
between lawyer and client reciting that legal services (not described) had
been rendered. In both cases the Court of Cassation held the disguises
perfect and reversed lower court findings of gift.

31. D.P.1901.1.68 (1898); D.P. 1870.1.327 (1870). These cases are hard
to fit with a later case in which the promise, held enforceable, was to pay a
pension to a retiring employee "to thank him for his faithful and loyal collaboration." D.P. 1936.2.6 (Lyon, 1933). Cases both ways on such ambiguous recitals are discussed by Jolivet, *La Validation des donations*, pp.
90–97.

32. D.1854.1.411 (1954); S.1885.2.60 (Bourges, 1884); D.P. 1889.1.479
(1898).

the leading motives has been to escape the tax on inter vivos gifts which for long was much heavier than the tax on succession at death.[33] This motive must have been exposed to view in the course of much ordinary litigation, but if so, courts have made nothing of it and have apparently assumed the object of escaping taxes to be so normal and natural that the tax collectors could not expect ordinary courts to help them. But the ordinary courts do not economize their efforts in the same way at all where litigation before them discloses that the purpose of a sham disguise is to defeat the guaranteed shares of the donor's own children or to give a hidden preference to one of several coheirs. The reaction to such evidence for a time was strong: if the receiver of the gift so disguised was aware of the donor's purpose, the transaction would be declared void for concerted "fraud." A milder reaction later set in. If a disguised gift now exceeds the decedent's disposable quota, the transaction will be valid but the gift will be "reduced"—cut back as though there had been no disguise. The same will be true if an undeclared preference for one coheir requires him to "return" the excess to the other coheirs.[34]

The conclusion can be stated in more general terms: that

33. Planiol, Ripert, et Boulanger, *Traité pratique,* vol. 4, secs. 3217–3218, pointing out that until 1942 the tax was 52 percent of the value of the gift. They also point out (vol. 4, sec. 3301) that the same motive has been prominent in resort to manual gifts and that the legislation of 1942 that reduced the tax rate required all manual gifts to be reported to the tax authorities. The authors comment: "This fiscal provision would interfere with the practice of making manual gifts if it had to be obeyed but it is very likely that it will not be. . . . These new requirements will permit penalties to be assessed if an undeclared manual gift is discovered; the duty is imposed only to be violated. But these penalties will justify a sanction against anyone who by imprudence or clumsiness allows himself to be caught. This is doubtless what the legislator desired."

34. The course of decision and the conflicting arguments are fully reviewed by Jolivet, *La Validation des donations,* pp. 185–192 ("reduction"), 169–185 (*rapport*).

the main avenues of escape devised by the courts—delivery by hand and well-designed shams—provide escape from only one control, the ceremonial of notarization that was required by the Code for all forms of gifts. In this respect, the liberation has been almost complete. The requirement, with nullity as its sanction, is still contained in the Civil Code, but two leading and highly reliable authors testify that except where useful to maintain family records the notarized gift has in fact disappeared.[35] The requirement as it still appears in the Code serves mostly as a trap for the unwary. If any care at all is taken in arranging hand delivery or a well-designed disguise, there is no need to notarize because for the purpose of the requirement of notarization there has been no gift. For every other purpose the transaction *is* a gift. As to the donor's powers of revocation, one could argue that by using these solemn forms the donor showed his own deliberate purpose to make the benefaction irreversible, to cut off his own power to revoke. Not so. For this purpose a gift no matter how well disguised is still a gift.[36] It is still more clear (it has never been questioned) that disguised or manual gifts will be treated like other gifts if they encroach on guaranteed shares of the donor's heirs or produce the kinds of inequalities to

35. Planiol, Ripert, et Boulanger, *Traité pratique,* vol. 4, sec. 3261 (1959). They qualify this only by mentioning the use of notaries to record property disbursements within families, especially where two families gather to bargain out marriage portions for newlyweds. Elsewhere the same authors describe notarization of gifts as an ineffective and outworn formality, "a costly luxury." Planiol et Ripert, *Traité pratique,* (1957), vol. 5, sec. 342. That many jurists and "men of affairs" no longer see any utility in the Code provisions on notarization of gifts is asserted also by Ponsard, *Donations indirectes,* p. 106.

36. D.P. 1893.2.340 (Riom, 1892) and D.P.1893.1.598 (1893) (gift disguised as 25-year lease, revocation allowed for donee's ingratitude); S.1903.2.13 and D.P.1891.1.284 (1895) (subsequent birth of child to donor). More decisions are cited by Jolivet, *La Validation des donations,* pp. 202–208.

which coheirs can object. The Code's guarantees on these topics, enforceable by his heirs after a donor's death, are a safeguard for the stability of families that cannot be circumvented by *any* disguise. So the same transaction can present two aspects and thinking about it can be split. If anyone asks whether it is a nongift or a gift, the answer will depend on why the question is asked.

4. Onerosity

In the salvo of definitions with which the French Code opens its treatment of contracts, there appear juxtaposed, so as to mark a contrast, the "contract of benefaction," in which one party confers on the other an advantage that is "purely gratuitous," and the "commutative" contract in which each party "undertakes to give or do something." Another adjective, *onerous*, is also used shortly thereafter to describe the contract that requires both parties to "give or do something." The first adjective, *commutative*, vaguely suggests some kind of reciprocity or interconnection, which is further implied by the descriptive statement that what each party gives or does is "regarded as the equivalent" of what the other gives or does.[1] But in order to "regard" them as equivalents it would not be at all essential that one should be intended to induce or call forth the other, as would be required, for example, if it were said that the "something" of one party is to be given or done "in order to secure" or "in exchange for" the something of the other. Onerosity, the feature that prevents a transaction from being classified as a gift, does not depend at all on a finding that the giving or doing by either

1. Art. 1104: "It [the contract] is commutative when each of the parties undertakes to give or do something which is regarded as the equivalent of what the other gives him or does for him." Art. 1106: "An onerous contract is that which requires both parties to give or do something."

one is an object of desire for the other, that there is thus in-cluded some element of agreed exchange for which one or both parties have "bargained." There is nothing in the Code to require such a finding. French courts have not from their own experience discovered the notion of bargain or the uses to which it might be put. One purpose now will be to find out whether they are better off as a result.

A. *The Requirement of Altruism*

If the advantage to be conferred is "giveable," whether the transaction that will confer it is onerous or a gift will there-fore depend, not on whether there is to be some return or recompense, but on whether the motive for conferring it is altruistic. The question is often clothed in short Latin dress: is the dominant motive an *animus donandi*? For this test the language of the Civil Code provides no warrant whatever. Its Latin garb vaguely hints at an origin in Roman law, but there is no reason to think that classical Roman lawyers used the phrase at all. The evidence is persuasive that it was smug-gled into many passages of the Corpus Juris by its Greek compilers.[2] In the Corpus Juris it appeared often enough so that the phrase itself and the psychological checklists that it carried with it entered into the common learning of western Europe after the medieval rediscovery of Roman law. They survived into the Pandectist system in nineteenth-century

2. F. Pringsheim, "Animus Donandi," 55 Z.S.S. 273 (1921). The au-thor connected the compilers' garbling of the classical texts on gifts with their large-scale injection in many other passages of highly subjective no-tions of intent and motive and ethical standards that reflected strong influ-ences from religion and philosophy. The same author later carried this analysis much further, in a comprehensive survey showing the penetration of Byzantine ethical and psychological tests "into the most remote cor-ners" of the Roman legal system through the search for *animus*, the inner (often unexpressed) intention. idem, "Animus in Roman Law," 93 *Law Quarterly Review* 43, 95 ibid. 379 (1933).

Germany, where they drifted about as distracting and discordant themes until the German Code of 1900 which, as we shall see, eliminated them altogether.

The ideas for which *animus donandi* is a shorthand expression have continued to circulate actively among French authors. They are phrased in various ways. A gift, it is said, is characterized by a desire of the donor to "gratify" another, by a complete absence of self-interest, by generosity, altruism or "the preference of another over oneself." Motives like these, it is conceded, are distinctly abnormal in a society that makes the pursuit of private profit both a main motive force and an organizing principle for society itself. But this gives all the more reason for praising and rewarding unmixed altruism where it can be found. The praise at times becomes fervid.[3] One author has declared that the attaching of importance to such motives is the mark of a superior civilization and that French law has been "spiritualized" by taking account of the "generous intent" of donors, unlike German law which considers only the "brutal" facts as to the economic values exchanged.[4] The irony of this is that if unadulterated generosity, an overriding desire to make a sacrifice for another, can turn an "onerous" transaction into a gift, altruism would be rewarded by making the transaction void unless notarized and subjecting it both to revocation by the donor and to recall by the donor's heirs. In only one type of transaction, so far as

3. Rouast, "La Prestation gratuite de travail," in *Études de Droit Civil à la Memoire de Henri Capitant,* (1937), pp. 695, 710. After praising service to others and describing mutual aid as based on a maxim of the law of nature: "Our contemporaries are greatly inspired by this maxim, for the honor of modern civilization. The law cannot disregard this noble practice of mutual aid, any more than any other manifestations of the social spirit." A more moderate statement in which the element of self-abnegation is described as a normal and expected element in gifts though not strictly required, appears in Planiol et Ripert, *Traité pratique,* vol. 5, secs. 313–314.

4. A. Ponsard, *Donations indirectes,* pp. 52–55.

I know, have courts paid a tribute to self-abnegation in this back-handed way.[5]

The encomiums for altruism have had, most of the time, an exactly opposite purpose. It is pure altruism that is so rare and is for that reason so much admired. But regrettably, human nature being what it is, it is much more common for altruism to be somewhat impure. So what if an unmixed benefit has been conferred but the motives of the one who confers it are mixed, because he also seeks to secure some advantage for himself? The standard answer is: the mixture makes the transaction "onerous" and therefore not a gift. As one writer put it, "From the moment that the author of the transaction had acted in his own interest, there is not the smallest fissure through which gratuitousness can intrude." He gives as an example of an onerous transaction a conveyance by a co-owner of a building of his interest in the building, receiving nothing at all in return and desiring only to escape the cost of sharing in its repair.[6] This motive is selfish, therefore the transfer is not a gift. Another example offered is that of a painter who has turned over one of his paintings to a city-owned gallery in the hope that some wealthy visitor will see it and out of admiration for his work contribute to the painter's support.[7]

These are the voices to which the courts listen. They do not speak in Greek, as did the original authors of these ideas who gave them prominence in their garbling of the Corpus Juris. Nor can even the slightest hint of these ideas be found

5. Loans of money from parents to sons, though repayable with interest, have been held to be gifts to the sons because the motive of the loans was to help the sons through financial difficulties. D.1843.1.491 (1842); S.1867.2.8 (Nîmes, 1866); D.1890.1.435 (1890); S.1914.1.366 (1913). Dupeyroux, *L'Acte à titre gratuit,* pp. 76–78, discusses such cases.

6. Louis Josserand, *Les Mobiles dans les actes juridiques du droit privé* (Paris, 1928), no. 261.

7. Demogue, *Traité des obligations,* 2: 897.

in the French Civil Code. For courts this version of "onerosity" has proved most useful, though only for one limited purpose. It has enabled them to sustain and enforce gifts already made or more often merely promised, by holding that they are *not* gifts. If the results seem to be topsy-turvy, almost as outlandish as the disguised gift, this should not occasion great surprise, because the main purpose is the same—to escape the need for notarization.

It may be that as early as 1829 the Court of Cassation had picked up the central idea that a benefaction, however one-sided, would not be a gift if some advantage accrued from it to the benefactor himself.[8] By 1863 the court's grip on this notion was firm. In the case before it, the administrative managers of a local church had contracted with an iron founder who agreed to restore the ancient bell-tower of the church and install in it three new bells. Bardet, a native son who had evidently made good, heard about this and decided to help. He promised in writing both the iron founder and the church that he would pay the cost of one bell if it were made into a duplicate of a bell in the old bell-tower that he dimly remembered from the days of his youth. The bell was made to his specifications but then Bardet died. His widow, when sued by the church to collect on Bardet's promise, contended that the promise was one of gift and void because not notarized. Not so, said the Court of Cassation. It was a com-

8. The 1829 case is reported very cryptically in Dalloz, Jurisprudence Générale, *Dispositions entre vifs,* n. 1300. One Reverchon had signed a written promise to pay 3,000 francs in instalments over the next five years. The promise was made to the mayor of his village as a subscription to a fund to be used to build a new church. Reverchon died, having paid nothing, and his widow, when sued, set up as her first defense that the promise was one of gift and that it had not been accepted in the lifetime of the donor-promisor. The court was even more laconic than usual: this was not a promise of gift but a commutative contract which served the promisor's own interest, so acceptance was not needed.

mutative contract in which Bardet received an equivalent for the money he promised to pay. The lower court had pointed out that the cost of the bell was much increased by complying with Bardet's terms. The high court did not mention this but spoke instead of onerous conditions that Bardet, "a man of considerable fortune" had imposed "for the sole purpose of satisfying his caprice, his fantasy or his vanity." By this formulation the spotlight was removed from the expenditure that Bardet had sought and secured from the promisees in producing a much more costly bell and was focused instead on Bardet and the satisfaction he achieved for his private whims, capricious and fanciful though they were thought to be.[9]

Onerosity can be found where the purposes of the benefactor are much less eccentric than Bardet's longing to relive his boyhood through the bell of his dreams. The advantage being pursued can be strictly mundane, such as an expected increase in the value of an owner's nearby land; this was enough to make "onerous" his promise to convey land as a site for a church.[10] But it is not merely the wretch concentered all in self who can be classified as a self-seeker. A widow, in promising to contribute to the cost of rebuilding a church, would be promoting her own felicity where her purposes were to be able to go to mass more often and have added space to pray at her husband's tomb.[11] Or the contribu-

9. D.P.1863.1.402 (1863). It is suggested by Dupeyroux, *L'Acte à titre gratuit*, p. 154, that there was a much more persuasive ground for decision in the Bardet case. This was the effect of Bardet's promise in altering the conduct of the promisees and causing a considerable "sacrifice" by them, which Bardet's request aimed to induce and which he had expressed his willingness to pay for.

10. D.P. 1895.1.125 (1894).

11. D.P. 1875.5.188 (1875). The question here was not whether notarization was needed but whether the contribution was subject to the tax on gifts. The answer was no: to be a gift, the widow "would have to prefer the town [the payee] over herself" and it was her own advantage that was being served.

tion of a married couple to the maintenance of a chapel would also be self-interested if it would give "satisfaction to their religious sentiments, to their artistic tastes and to the desire they showed to give to the city of Tours" a monument to an illustrious bishop. Their agreement to contribute, which gave them such rich rewards, was therefore a bilateral "onerous" contract and their promise was not one of gift.[12] One could reduce the paradox to its simplest form, without much distortion, by saying that the more deeply felt the moral ideal, the more selfish it was to pursue it.

When the moral values served by the transaction are somewhat less exalted, the search for a selfish purpose that will make the transaction "onerous" encounters fewer difficulties. Indeed, human nature being what it is, the simplest course may be simply to presume that the pursuit of self-interest is its strongest impulse. This distrustful view of human motivations enabled Court of Cassation to find the solution to a troublesome problem that arose out of a transaction in 1853 involving the emperor Napoleon III and the city of Marseilles. The emperor had earlier given his personal support for some land acquisitions by the city from which the city had secured a large profit. The city proposed to the emperor that it convey to him some city-owned land as a suitable site for an imperial palace. The emperor agreed to accept it and the land was conveyed, the only motives expressed by the city being "homage and gratitude" to the sovereign. The emperor built himself a palace on the land conveyed, but in 1871 he was deposed. In 1873 he died. Then in 1880 the city sued the Empress Eugénie, his widow and heir, to recover the land, contending that its deed was a gift and, being unnotarized, was void.

12. D.P.1922.1.76, note (decision of the Cour d'Appel of Orleans, 1911), cited by M. Bouyssou, *Les Libéralités avec charges en droit français* (1945), p. 163. The cases here mentioned are discussed and sharply criticized in this excellent book, pp. 161–172.

The land that the city sought to retake was by that stage
adorned with a palace whose construction the city had itself
proposed and whose cost must have exceeded by far the
value of the land conveyed. From a result so outrageous
some escape route must be found. This was easy; it was already mapped out. This had not been a gift, the court said,
but an onerous contract. For the city there were "natural advantages which must result from the residence, even occasional, of the sovereign in Marseilles." The only motives that
the city had mentioned were its own homage and gratitude to
the sovereign, but this meant only that its motives were
mixed and, the court said, where motives are mixed "the
preponderant element absorbs the other and it would be to
deny human nature if one did not attribute preponderance to
the element of self-interest."[13] There was one old French
word, *estoppel,* that the court might have mentioned, but this
has dropped out of the modern French vocabulary and in
French sources, so far as I know, there is no other word that
can be used to describe harmful and foreseeable reliance. So
in the emperor's case, "onerosity" had to carry the load.

After about a century it gradually became apparent that
this reading of "onerosity" would make almost all gifts, including promises of gift, into "onerous" contracts.[14] It took so

13. D.P. 1883.2.245 (Aix, 1882). After this decision, in 1884, the empress decided after all to convey the land-with-palace to the city, which
promised her to pay any tax that might be due on the original grant to the
emperor in 1853. The city then reversed its position and contended that
the grant had been a gift (in this instance the gift tax would have been
lower). Its dispute with the tax authorities reached the Court of Cassation,
which concluded that the transaction was a bilateral and therefore onerous
contract for a reason that would have been a good one if it had been true:
that the emperor had promised the city to build a palace in return for its
promise to convey the land.

14. The criticisms of the trial court in a 1913 case were pointed. The
case before it was one in which a considerable sum had been given for the
construction of a church building, which was then taken over by the city of

long to discover this because no one had minded in the least. In all the earlier cases, with one exception, the issue was whether the promise or transfer must be notarized; in the one exceptional case the reasoning used enabled the benefactor to escape the higher tax on gifts. For a contract to be "onerous" or "commutative" the Code required that each party must "give or do something." It was transparent misreading to say that a contract was nevertheless onerous although only one party was to "give or do" but his giving or doing produced an advantage, pleasure, or self-satisfaction that he desired for himself. As a misreading of the Code it is no more bizarre than the other escape routes that have been described already and that are much more actively used—the gift by hand delivery and the "disguised" gift. One can expect, though it is too soon to be perfectly sure, that this additional route will be confined, as the others are, to escaping from notarization and from higher taxes. If Bardet's payment for the bell of his boyhood, for example, were to encroach on the shares in his estate that were guaranteed to his sons on his death, his promise would almost certainly have been considered to be a promise of gift and accordingly "reduced."

The impulse to escape from notarization has worked just as strongly, perhaps more strongly, with other forms of benefaction that serve a broader public interest. In the early

---

Paris as a communal welfare center. The donor, seeking restitution of the sum he had paid, was met by the contention that the contract was commutative because of the satisfaction of his own sense of piety by having the local parishioners worship at the church. The court's comment was that if this were so, "there never would be a gift, since the fact of giving for a work of charity or for any enterprise whatever would always create for the one who makes the gift an advantage at a moral level, an intimate satisfaction because of a generous action." D.1914.2.53 (Tribunal Civil de la Seine, 1913). More recent critics who reject these tests vigorously are Bouyssou, *Les Libéralités,* pp. 172–175, and Dupeyroux, *L'Acte à titre gratuit,* pp. 109–115. Both cite other authors who line up on both sides of these issues.

months of the First World War, for example, one Bailly, a
member of the city council of Nancy, promised to pay the
council a substantial sum to be used for the benefit of neces-
sitous families whose wage-earners had been mobilized and
had gone off to war. The council accepted the "benefaction"
with thanks to the "donor." Bailly then tried to change his
mind but soon learned that he could not. As to his claim that
his promise was one of gift, not notarized, the court conceded
that as to the needy families this was a contract of "benefaction," but asserted that as to the "organizer" (presumably
meaning the city council) the contract was "commutative,"
so that no formality of any kind was needed.[15] In the extensive discussion that the case inspired all authors have agreed
that, for such "subscriptions" by numerous contributors, to
retain a requirement of notarization would be to destroy any
hope for concerted private action to meet current social
needs. So the most favored solution is the one sketched out
by the court in the Bailly case, by which "subscriptions"
were called "commutative" contracts between the individual
subscribers and the "organizer," who undertakes to spend
the funds in the manner specified. They have also been described as third-party beneficiary contracts, either to reinforce, or as an alternative to, this suggestion.[16] No one looked

15. D.P.1923.1.20 (1923). The intermediate court of appeal, which had
reached a similar conclusion, (D.P.1920.2.65), added that Bailly had secured an advantage through having city officials made available to distribute the funds and by publicity given to his generosity "in the most flatter-
ing way." A much more persuasive reason to an American reader was the
fact mentioned though not stressed by the Court of Cassation: that the city
council had already relied on the promise by distributing to the needy
families more than the total promised by subscribers.

16. This argument was developed fully by Charles Claro in a note in
D.P.1903.2.121 and was supported by R. Morel in his comment in
D.1923.1.20. More recent suggestions by others are discussed and the un-
reality (as well as the laudable purpose) of the whole effort described by
Dupeyroux, *Acte à titre gratuit,* pp. 42–48.

closely to see whether these lines of analysis had any basis in fact. Again one should ask a question that apparently has not yet arisen: what if it were found on the subscriber's death that the "subscription" encroached on the guaranteed shares of his nearest of kin? Two distinguished authors are clear that the maneuvers used to escape notarization of "subscriptions" should not and would not be used to invade the *légitime*. [17]

There is nothing in French law to preclude a court from slipping into another way of thinking on these topics. This, in fact, occurred in a case arising out of a sailing regatta, one of a series put on annually by the city of Nice. In the races held in 1883, the starting signal was given in an irregular way but the managing committee did not call the race off and allowed it to go through to a finish. The two yachtsmen who crossed the line first and second sued for the first and second prizes that had been advertised. The court of appeal decided, first, that the race committee, having allowed the race to be completed, could not refuse to pay merely because the starting signal had been defective. The court then faced the contention of the defendant committee that its promise was one of gift, not notarized and therefore void. The standard analysis would have called on the court to depict how much the city and its population had gained from having the crowds come to the races, from observing the bright costumes of the elegant ladies and the white sails on the deep blue sea. But how much of all this reached the committee, who were presumably scattered at posts around the course? And in any case would these be reasons for having to pay the two winners?

17. Planiol et Ripert, *Traité pratique,* vol. 5, sec. 315. Bouyssou, *Les Libéralités,* pp. 179–182, is herself perfectly clear that any thought of requiring notarization should be dismissed, quoting another author who asserted that it would be "disastrous." She would accomplish this by calling subscriptions, not commutative contracts, but collaboration in the "public service" and therefore governed by administrative law.

So another reason was found for concluding that there was a "commutative" contract—namely, that the payment was due to the winners "in exchange for the sacrifices of the winning contestants in completing the race at their own costs and risks."[18] At this distance it does not seem that the winners could have incurred much pain or deprivation. The court may have meant to say, and this should have been enough, that the winners had performed the very acts that the committee had expressed its desire to bring about and also its willingness to pay for.

It is not likely, however, that such ideas have any real future in France even though they have the wholly commendable result of dispensing with the need for notarization. That they are not standard equipment, readily available for routine use, is suggested by a vendetta between two newspapers whose managements were bitter enemies. The *Action française* rewrote a news report that had first appeared in a newspaper in Geneva, Switzerland. This news report contained a typographical error that greatly changed its meaning and that the Geneva paper itself corrected in its later editions. The corrected version was delivered in France to *La Vie catholique,* which published an account of the episode, denounced the *Action française* for a deliberate and harmful falsehood, and offered it 1,000,000 francs (the equivalent at that time of about $40,000) if it produced a copy of the Geneva paper showing that it had had a basis for its false account. This the *Action française* readily did, handing over

18. D.1887.1.55 (1886). The reference to the "exchange for the sacrifices" was made by the intermediate court of appeal. After its decision, the case then went on to the Court of Cassation, which agreed with the result but gave as its reason that the committee and the racers had assumed "reciprocal obligations." There was nothing in the case to suggest that the racers were obligated in any way. It is especially unlikely that before the race they had promised to win it.

a copy. It then demanded the 1,000,000 francs and sued when payment was refused.

The court before which the suit was brought was puzzled. What could this be? It was clearly not a wager. Handing over an old newspaper involved even less of a "sacrifice" than had been incurred by the winning sailors in the Nice regatta. It could have been argued that *La Vie catholique* wanted the paper in order to ascertain some facts that were vital to the warfare it was waging, though it had certainly hoped that the story it would tell would be the opposite of the one it did. The *Action française* had given *La Vie catholique* precisely what it had asked for and had expressed its willingness to pay for. For the hard-pressed court these ways of thinking did not exist. It concluded that since the arrangement was not a wager, there was only one other thing it could be—a promise of gift and, not being notarized, it was void.[19]

So far as I have discovered, only one French author has criticized in a searching way the tests of "onerosity" that have so far prevailed or has formulated an alternative. His criticism is aimed in particular at the formula that requires a finding of undiluted altruism so that a transaction becomes an "onerous" contract, not a gift, whenever a selfish motive can be detected and the spirit of benevolence is not quite pure. The cluster of psychological tests, to determine the degree to which the benefactor "preferred another to himself," he condemned as unworkable and illusory guides and in any case irrelevant. The alternative test he proposed would make the result depend on whether there was a "sacrifice" by or "prejudice" to each party that was in fact sought by the other,

19. The *Revue trimestrielle de droit civil* (1931), p. 61 reports the case with comment by Professor Henri Savatier. He protests strongly against calling this a promise of gift: an essential requirement for a gift, he said, is a generous motive, an intent to please and gratify, and this cannot exist between bitter enemies.

so as to produce an agreed exchange. This, he argued, is the essential index of an onerous or commutative contract, distinguishing it from a gift.[20] To readers who reside across the Atlantic the argument is persuasive. The only modification that I could suggest is that *sacrifice*, and even *prejudice*, imply a costly deprivation, more costly than should be needed, and that a more neutral word, like *detriment*, would be better. But any such suggestions are not likely to help, since this author's argument has made not the slightest impression either on French courts or other authors. It seems unlikely that it will.

B. *Natural Obligations*

The concept of natural obligation provides another convenient means of classifying a transaction as onerous, therefore not a gift, though it requires an approach from the opposite direction. Instead of a finding that the altruism essential for a gift was in the particular instance impure, it calls for a finding that the sole motive for making the proposed sacrifice was steadfast adherence to moral duty. So it is not the impurity but the purity of the motive that makes the transaction onerous. The critical question therefore becomes: how wide is the range of moral duties that are deemed capable of generating such high-principled responses? It is wide and not easily defined.

The premise from which the argument starts is solid. If the duty discharged had been legally enforceable at the time the performance was rendered or promised, no one, even for a moment, would think of it as a gift. If money were paid

---

20. Dupeyroux, *L'Acte a titre gratuit*, refers to this thesis repeatedly throughout a most interesting book. He develops it particularly on pp. 153–163 and 272–279. Emphatic repudiation of the subjective tests— presence or absence of self-interest in the benefactor—also appears throughout, but especially on pages 19–30, 80–101, and 169–178.

there would be, in "Anglo-Saxon" terms, an exchange—
money paid to secure a release. The definition of onerosity in
the French Code would likewise apply, since each party
would "give or do" something: the debtor would give
money, the creditor by accepting it would cancel the debt,
whether he said so or not. So it seemed very easy to trans-
pose all this to the discharge of "natural" (that is, unenforceable) obligations. The only difficulty, which could be
troublesome if one allowed it to be, is that with the "natural"
obligation the creditor in truth has nothing to give.

There is one provision of the French Code that has given
great help, though it could have been used to hinder. This is
an article that in general terms authorizes restitution of
money paid that was "not due," but then proceeds to exclude
restitution if the payments, even though not "due," were of
"natural obligations that were voluntarily discharged."[21] This
left unprovided for the *promise* to perform a natural obligation. But the argument that has prevailed almost everywhere
is that if the performance already rendered cannot be assailed, it follows that a person subject to a natural obligation
must be enabled also to promise to perform it. The conclusion is not inevitable. The argument *expressio unius* (the expression of one excludes the rest) would be equally available
to produce the opposite conclusion, but the one French author who has used it has made an impression only in Germany, none in France.[22]

The standard example with which the discussion usually
starts is the promise to perform a previously enforceable contract to whose enforcement a protective barrier has been
interposed—as by lapse of time or discharge by reason of

21. Art. 1235.
22. R. Schmidt, "Die rechtliche Wirkung der Befolgung sittlicher
Pflichten," in *Die Reichsgerichts Praxis im deutschen Rechtsleben* (1928),
pp. 25, 30–31. The French author was Laurent.

insolvency—without casting any doubt on the merit of the original claim. By ancient tradition the enforceability of a new promise in such cases is explained by the "natural" obligation that maintains a ghostly existence, but more mundane ideas such as waiver can be used, as they sometimes are with us, to explain the power of obligors to reinstate by their own unilateral action the sanctions that for the obligor's own protection had been suspended.[23]

Another possible source of "natural" obligation which we too have sporadically recognized is the impulse to express gratitude by undertaking to make some return for benefits received in the past, even though they were received under such circumstances that any legal liability was excluded. Under the Code, French courts showed readiness from an early date to enforce unnotarized promises that were intended to be "remunerative." They may have taken some comfort in the thought that the amount of the benefit received in the past could be used to set limits to the obligation assumed. The standard case was the promise of a former employer of an annuity to a retired employee for services rendered in the past, usually in his household. Though all prior obligations had been discharged, such promises were said to be not promises of gift but fully enforceable contracts.[24] Courts were usually careful to say that the extra rewards must be reasonable in the light of the value of the services rendered and the promisor's own resources; if the amounts promised were considered excessive, French courts felt free

23. Planiol et Ripert, *Traité pratique*, vol. 7, secs. 992–994; M. Gobert, *Essai sur le role de l'obligation naturelle* (1957), pp. 15–43; G. Ripert, *La Règle morale dans les obligations civiles*, 4th ed. (1949), pp. 363–379.

24. S.1811.2.478 (Colmar, 1809); D.1846.1.159 (1846); S.1894.2.191 (Paris, 1892); Planiol et Ripert, *Traité pratique*, sec. 316, pp. 433–435. These and other "natural obligation" cases are reviewed by von Mehren, "Civil Law Analogues to Consideration," 72 *Harvard Law Review* 1009, 1038–1043.

to scale them down.[25] The natural obligation to remunerate was even considered transferable in the sense that a promise made by another, usually a near relative, after the death of the person to whom the services were rendered, would also be enforceable.[26] And the principle was not limited to services. If a gain were realized in another way—for example, in the management of another's property, though with no showing of any misconduct by the manager—a promise based on a "scruple of conscience" to restore the gain received would be an "onerous" and enforceable contract.[27]

One wanders further afield where the source of the "natural" obligation is found in some personal tie of family relationship or past friendship. The clearest example would be the father of an illegitimate child who promises to provide for the child's support.[28] Some thought of remuneration for past services may also be at work if the promise is to provide for the support of a former concubine, but the moral duty is at any rate strong enough to make the promise enforceable.[29] The duty of a wealthy man to provide for his impecunious sisters is at least equally strong.[30] It can even extend to a

25. D.1855.2.162 (Caen, 1854); Gazette du Palais, 1945.1.115. In the latter case, a 2,000-franc monthly annuity was scaled down to 1,200 francs because the promisor had subsequently remarried, acquired a new child, and had been wounded by a bombardment in 1944.

26. S.1809.2.161 (Colmar, 1808), services to ancestor; S.1835.2.412 (Bordeaux 1835), services to dead aunt; D.1849.2.239 (Douai, 1847), nursing care of wife in her last illness. But in D.1967.J.584 (1967), the Court of Cassation accepted a lower-court finding that a president of a corporation owed no natural obligation to remunerate a corporate employee for services to the corporation, so that his promise to remunerate was void.

27. D.1913.1.404 (1911).

28. D.1862.1.208 (1862); D.1873.1.180 (1873).

29. J.C.P.1946.2.3036 (Paris, 1946). The contrary result in D.1925, 656 (Paris, 1925) may be explained by the fact that after generous provision had already been made for her, the bereft female made a rich marriage that eliminated all further needs.

30. *Semaine juridique*, 1932, p. 607 (Paris, 1932), holding that the

mother-in-law.[31] Beyond that, who can say? Do parents have a natural obligation to provide dowries for their daughters, so that unnotarized promises to do so can be enforced? If they have expressed approval of the marriage, they probably do. To say more than that would be hazardous.[32]

The elements that generate such duties of conscience can be mixed in various combinations. A common case is the heir who attends the deathbed of an elderly relative and promises to apply some of the inheritance he will receive in carrying out last-minute oral instructions of the one about to die. Is it because of the enrichment the heir receives that he is bound by this promise or is it because of the obedience he owes to an ancestor's wishes?[33] The intended recipient of this last-minute bounty might also have moral claims on the ancestor that a younger relative should respect.[34] It is very hard to say how far such duties of family loyalty are transmissible enough to provide support for promises. That they can descend through successive generations is suggested by one

transaction was "onerous" enough to exclude not only any need for notarization but also revocation, on the ground that the "donor" later acquired offspring.

31. Gazette du Palais, 1946.1.115 (Tribunal de Béziers, 1945).

32. The uncertainties are fully described by Savatier in a note to the decision in D.1923.2.121 (Poitiers, 1923). His own conclusion is that there is no natural obligation to provide dowries but that notarization of a promise is nevertheless not needed.

33. S.1861.2.1 (Nîmes, 1860); D.1878.1.376 (1876); D.1894.2.15 (Montpellier, 1893).

34. S.1809.2.161 (Colmar, 1808); D.1885.2.101 (Pau, 1884); D.1904.2.439 (Amiens, 1903), and D.1905.1.47 (1905). In these cases the element added was meritorious service to the decedent by the intended recipient, which would probably have sufficed to create a natural obligation in the decedent himself. That veneration for the ancestor's wishes is expected of the heir is suggested by the first of the cases cited, which described the heirs' promise to provide for an aged servitor as the performance of "a moral debt which the contracting parties regarded as sacred."

case in which funds had been given in 1819 to found a church school. The school was closed by legislation of 1886 whose aim was separation of church and state. The heirs of the donor thus became entitled to restitution of the property acquired with the funds given, on the ground of failure of purpose. Instead the heirs assigned their rights to three persons who undertook in return to open on the property another school of a type permitted by the legislation. Having repented of this, the donor's heirs then sued to recover the assets transferred, claiming the transaction was an unnotarized gift. Not at all, the court concluded. It was true that the assignors had derived from the transaction no material advantage whatever. But because of their relations with the residents of the town and their acquaintance with local opinion, they felt bound to maintain the school that their ancestor had founded eighty years before and the town could no longer maintain. This moral obligation the transferees undertook to perform on their behalf, so the transfer was not a gift.[35]

The main service rendered by the concept of natural obligation has been to permit the enforcement of informal promises that are otherwise unrecompensed. So the question that recurs again is whether it has any consequence other than to dispense with the need for notarization. Would a promise or transfer made in response to natural obligation be revocable for a donee's "ingratitude" or a donor's acquisition of an after-born child? Perhaps not. But the sensitive conscience of the promisor would quite certainly not be a good enough reason for depriving his heirs of their patrimony.

35. D.P.1900.2.422 (Tribunal Civil de Langres, 1900). In the course of the argument, however, the court indicated that it did not insist on a proof of idealism at so high a level. The motive could be ensuring performance of a natural obligation, or it could just as well be "a simple satisfaction of vanity or amour propre."

One can be confident that if the performance promised would encroach on the reserve guaranteed to a protected heir, it would be considered a gift and would be "reduced."[36]

5. Mixed Gifts

Some of the transactions so far discussed could properly be described as mixed gifts—mixed both in motives and in consequences. By their terms some of them purported to confer a net gain, but also aimed at some unrelated purpose, the two elements serving as interdependent parts of a single transaction. One way to frame such a composite transaction is to express it as gift with charge. Another way would be to adopt the form of an exchange transaction in which the values exchanged are made unequal with the deliberate purpose of conferring a gift. The dividing lines between these forms can become very blurred, but each presents problems of its own.

A. Gifts with Charge

In the French Civil Code the conditional gift appears only once, in a clause that allows a donor to revoke a gift if the

36. In the case reported in J.C.P.1946.2.3036 (Paris, 1946), the gift was disguised (as an issue of stock in a newly formed corporation), but the donor made it as remuneration for long association with the donee as a concubine which led to the birth of an illegitimate son. The court declared these elements were clearly sufficient to produce a natural obligation but proceeded to "reduce" the gift insofar as it encroached on the reserve of the donor's daughter.

In a case whose result was approved by Savatier, "return" (*rapport*) was ordered of gifts made to one of three daughters so as to produce inequality between them, despite long and attentive nursing care by the daughter thus rewarded—care that for other purposes would quite surely have produced a natural obligation. *Revue trimestrielle de droit civil*, 1954, p. 338.

Planiol et Ripert, *Traité pratique*, vol, 1, sec. 316, are clear that the shares of forced heirs must be protected against "remunerative liberalities."

donee does not perform an express condition.[1] This phrasing has been taken to include both the "suspensive" condition (some act or event that must occur if the gift is to "vest") and the "resolutory" condition (whose effect, when it occurs, is to "divest" the right acquired).[2] The word *charge* had not been mentioned in the Code, but a need was soon felt for an additional word of this kind that would describe a common phenomenon, a transfer described as a gift but calling for an extended course of action by the transferee, often with a contribution of his own. If the transferor showed an intent to require this course of action and make it the subject of an affirmative duty, with a sanction more effective than revocation of the gift, there was no place to look other than the law of contract. Some authors, at least, were ready from an early time to invoke the law of contract and draw the inference that acceptance of a gift containing such a charge would amount to a promise to perform it.[3]

There has been much debate as to how much of a contract is produced in this way and how it should be enforced. If the duty imposed by the charge is "to do or not to do," affirmative specific performance is expressly excluded by the Civil Code, any such duty being "resolved in damages."[4] For the kinds of activities called for in most instances, damages would be extremely hard to figure. The difficulties multiply

1. Art. 953, with further details in arts. 954 and 956.
2. A good summary of the discussions on these themes is given by Bouyssou, *Les Libéralités*, pp. 67–82.
3. Ibid., pp. 278–281 and Ripert et Boulanger, *Traité pratique*, vol. 4, sec. 3695, cite numerous authors who support these conclusions.
4. Art. 1142, Civil Code. The nearest approach to specific performance in these situations appeared in a case in 1855 (D.1855.1.297) in which a children's home, after defaulting on its "charge" of providing care for orphans who resided in the town of Belleville, was ordered to make periodic money payments to the town officers of Belleville, who undertook to provide for the orphans. The case is discussed by Bouyssou, *Les Libéralités*, pp. 289–292.

where the charges are for the benefit of third persons or are intended to augment the working resources of the donees themselves, so that in either case default would cause the donors no loss. Damage remedies, in short, are seldom workable and seldom sought. The contributions made by contract doctrine have been two: (1) to dispense with the need for notarization, and (2) to provide an alternative ground for cancellation when the charge is not performed or its purpose has failed. The Code provision most often invoked is that allowing rescission for substantial breach of contract.[5]

An "onerous" contract is most readily conjured up when the interest served by the charge on the gift is solely that of the donor himself. The action or inaction it calls for may involve very little "sacrifice" or "prejudice" for the donee. Though the transaction is described as a gift and though the disparity in economic values is very wide, if the conduct that is the subject of the charge was desired by the donor, it is readily described as an onerous contract. The charge can be that the donee, a former mistress, leave the locality and not return;[6] that the donee refrain from challenging an accounting that was rendered by the donor as a guardian;[7] that the

5. Art. 1184, Civil Code.

6. D.1905.2.305 (Rennes, 1904), finding "reciprocal" obligations, so that the defendant's promise to pay her 150 francs a month was not a promise of gift and did not need to be notarized.

7. D.P.1869.1.528 (1867). The accounting that the donee was not to challenge had been rendered by the donor, her mother and guardian, as to assets in which the daughter might have had an inherited interest. The charge was expressed as a condition to the gift, and by the Code it was illegal because exacted by one in a fiduciary role. If treated as a gift, the condition would be void and simply disappear, leaving the transfer intact. It was held instead to be a "mixed" commutative contract and gift, so that the mother could rescind for the daughter's substantial breach in challenging the accounting. Similar cases then came in a series with similar results: D.P.1869.2.203 (Pau, 1869); D.P.1870.1.308 (1869); Gazette du Palais, 1888.1.727 (Douai, 1888).

donee adopt and use the donor's name, erect a monument to his memory, or live in a particular house for a specified time.[8] Still more clearly will the transaction be held to be an onerous contract, even though it was labeled a gift, if a substantial outlay or effort by the donee is called for, such as money payments for the benefit of the "donor"[9] or supplying the donor with housing, support, or personal care.[10]

When such services are to extend over uncertain stretches of time, such as the lifetime of the transferor, the "onerosity" of the charge becomes more clear because of uncertainties producing risk, even though the events that might increase the real cost did not in fact occur.[11] Psychological probes are entirely dispensed with where appraisal in economic terms is feasible and the appraisal reveals that the outlay required by the charge is substantial as compared with the value of the asset "given." One does not find courts in

8. The three examples listed last are not strictly apposite because the charges were imposed on testamentary gifts, but it seems clear that the result would be the same with inter vivos gifts. These instances and others like them are described by Bouyssou, *Les Libéralités*, p. 49.

9. In the case reported in S.1939.1.55 (1938), a transfer of land from father to son, though described by the father as a gift, was held to produce an onerous contract so that the transfer did not produce inequality between coheirs, where the charge imposed required the son to pay debts of the father which added up to more than the value of the land.

10. S.1845.2.599 (Douai, 1844); D.P.1851.5.180 (Colmar, 1845). Both these cases involved "gifts" with charges of lifetime care and support for the "donors," the risks being that they might live long and have costly illnesses.

11. This was pointed out in D.P.1874.2.84 (Pau, 1873) where the charge was for the transferee to live with the transferors and cook for them for life, but a clause of the "gift" provided that the transferee would receive nothing if she died before the transferors, and this clause, the court said, added to the "onerosity" of the charge. Conversely, in D.P.1882.2.105 (Paris, 1881), where a nun with whose support the transferee was "charged" developed infantile paralysis so that her care became much more costly, a hindsight test was used to transform the transaction, labeled gift, into a fully accredited "onerous" contract.

such cases measuring on a Richter scale the force of the "donor's" impulse to be generous and examining his background and emotional ties in order to determine the degree to which he was gripped by an *animus donandi,* for the transaction is then judged by an objective test.[12] Even if altruism were found to be the dominant motive, it would not take much selfishness, as we have seen, to produce an onerous contract. This would be true, at any rate, if the only issue in dispute were whether notarization was needed. One should expect more searching inquiries if the result was to produce a clear net gain that encroached on guaranteed shares of the "donor's" heirs.

This matching method, comparing the outlays needed on either side, has even been proposed where the only effect of the charge would be to increase the benefits or advantages of the donee himself.[13] There is one French decision that seems to point in that direction,[14] but it surely points the wrong way. If the city of Marseilles, for example, had been so tact-

12. D.1841.2.229 (Caen, 1841); D.1851.2.133 (Douai, 1850); D.1888.1.256 (1887). Numerous other decisions, some going back to earliest post-Code days, are cited by Bouyssou, *Les Libéralités,* pp. 182–191, and Dupeyroux, *L'Acte à titre gratuit,* pp. 25–30. Such cases have been described with some irony as "onerous contracts disguised under the form of a donation." Planiol et Boulanger, *Traité pratique,* vol. 4, sec. 3667.

13. Gaston Jèze, *Les Principes Généraux du droit administratif,* 3d ed. (1936), 3: 467 whose views are described and rejected by Bouyssou, *Les Libéralités,* pp. 177–179.

14. D.P.1872.2.165 (Paris, 1871). The widow of Balzac had granted to Dutacq a license to publish her husband's *Contes drolatiques* if they included illustrations by Doré. In an injunction suit brought by other publishers against Dutacq's assignee the widow intervened, claiming the license she had granted Dutacq was a gift and void because not notarized. The court rejected her claim: whatever gain the license might bring would probably be offset by "the considerable expenses inherent in a publication of that kind." A note following the case purports to summarize its message: "Gratuitousness is an essential characteristic of the *inter vivos* gift and one must consider onerous every liberality whose charges exceed or equal the value given."

less as to impose on its grant to the emperor a charge requiring him to build a palace on the land conveyed, this analysis would mean that spending his own money (as much as or more than the land was worth) to build a palace would produce an "onerous" contract. In gifts with charge, the matching of outlays on either side gives a quick and easy way of escaping notarization. It has the even greater virtue of dispensing with probes by the amateur psychologists who wear black robes, attempting to rate the generosity of the moving party and decide *how much* altruism was at work. But this formula seems to be misapplied when it produces "onerosity" through expenditures by the receiver that merely augment his own gain.[15]

Harder problems arise when the charge or directive attached to the gift can advance only the interests of outsiders—individuals, groups, institutions, or causes that serve larger purposes. The charge may require that the named donee employ the whole gift for some such outside purpose and retain nothing for him- or itself. The absence of net enrichment or other measurable advantage for the donee has led some authors to contend that such transactions are not gifts.[16] This contention is reinforced where the charge

15. This point was made long ago by Marcel Planiol in a much quoted comment in D.P.1891.2.113. He there gave as an illustration a contribution of 500 francs made to enable the payee, a friend, to take a trip whose total cost would be 1,000 francs. He pointed out that the payment would not cease to be a gift when the payee later contributed 500 francs of his own to the purchase of a ticket. Support for this conclusion is widespread among the authors. Bouyssou, *Les Libéralités,* p. 176.

16. One particularly troublesome case that has led to much dispute among the authors has been the grant to a "foundation" already established, that serves in effect as a medium to distribute funds received, devoting them to the activities in which it was already engaged. Bouyssou, *Les Libéralités,* pp. 207–215, describes the vacillations that have occurred and concludes (p. 215) that courts have been willing "to risk the reproach of incoherence."

imposed calls for a contribution from the receiver's own funds, so that a matching-of-outlays test can again be employed to erase, in effect, the label gift and escape again into contract.

On how broad a front this escape will occur is most uncertain. If the motive is to make notarization unnecessary, the avenue is wide open. Another good reason would be that the donee had been prevented, through no fault of his own, from performing the charge—being precluded, for example, by supervening legislation—and a change in the label of the transaction will enable a court to cancel the "contract" because of failure of its purpose.[17] A donor who wished to revoke—let us say, because of the subsequent birth of a child—ought, I should think, to meet a cool reception. But what if the gift-with-charge infringed the guarantees given to the donor's heirs by exceeding the disposable quota or producing inequality between them? The receiver could still argue that there was no enrichment for it or for him if the

17. D.P.1891.2.113 (Nîmes, 1890) involved this issue. Here the property in dispute had been conveyed in a document described as a "gift" to a town on condition that it be used for a school, with a provision revesting title in the donor if the school for any reason ceased to be maintained. Legislation of 1886 then prohibited the maintenance of the school by the town. The immediate difficulty came from another provision, Article 900 of the Civil Code, which stated that conditions in gifts becoming "impossible" or illegal would be simply eliminated ("reputed to be not written"). If this provision applied the town would keep the land. So the transaction was held to be, not a gift, but an "engagement" with burdens on each party that would serve a common purpose. An instructive note by Marcel Planiol discussed the difficulties in finding solutions in the Code for such situations where the "charge" had to be abandoned because of impossibility due to change of law. These problems arose very frequently as a result of successive statutes aimed at the "separation of church and state" and at the secularizing of schools, hospitals, and other institutions that had accumulated funds through private gift. Another route, intermingling notions of revocation of gift and breach of contract where the "charge" had been a "determinative" element in the gift, was developed by the courts and is more commonly used. Bouyssou, *Les Libéralités*, pp. 258–269, 298–318.

value of the outlays required by the charge would equal or exceed the value "given." If the receiver still had the money, my own guess is that it would have to be restored. If the money had been spent for the designated purpose and beyond recall, the record of French courts inspires confidence that they would find a tactful way to say that it was by then too late.

B. Unequal Exchanges

One other standard form of "mixed" gift is the exchange in which a disparity in values is deliberately arranged for the purpose of producing net gain on one side only. The approach to such transactions has been influenced somewhat by the Code provision that does allow rescission of unequal exchanges but only in one special case: where the loser in the exchange was an owner of land who sold it for five-sixteenths or less of its value.[18] The Code is most explicit that between adults with full legal capacity this is only the type of transaction in which this ground for attack can be recognized.[19] Should it make a difference that the parties were fully aware of the discrepancy in values and planned to produce it? The standard answer to a question put that way would be that, since the transaction is in one aspect at least an authentic exchange, it should make no difference that an element of benefaction is mingled with it.

If the courts had been convinced that the legislative controls over gifts were wise and beneficial, they could have asked a different question: why should a transaction that was

18. Civil Code, arts. 1674–1685 provide to vendors in such cases an election to rescind.

19. Art. 1313. There has been a considerable amount of special legislation setting controls over certain prices and wages. It is discussed with further comment by Planiol et Ripert, *Traité pratique*, vol. 6, secs. 213–214.

understood by the parties to contain a partial gift be exempt, merely because the parties mixed it up with something else? This question could be asked over the whole range of conglomerate transactions, including gifts with charge. The question itself presupposes that the component parts can be disentangled, so the first question would then be whether the gift element could be identified and separated from the rest. This might at times be difficult—perhaps too difficult—as in a gift with a charge that called for conduct by the donee over an extended and uncertain time. But in France the objection that has been raised most strongly, even where a split-up would not be hard at all, is that a split-up would defeat the purpose of the parties who framed and intended a single, composite transaction.[20]

This objection is strong but by no means overpowering if one concedes that controls over gifts have precisely this function: to defeat the intent of one party, at least—often the intent of both. In Germany, as we shall see, courts undertake this kind of surgery cheerfully. In France it is rejected with vigor by the authors who have thought of it; it is not even mentioned by the courts. The result for mixed gifts, then, is supposedly clear: they are either full-scale gifts or else full-scale contracts. Which they are may well depend in any particular case on why the question is asked, but the answer must be unequivocal, one or the other. Having thus narrowed their choices to two, the French found that they needed another, so they invented a third choice—a nothing that is neither.

20. A vigorous argument against any attempt to break up such composite transactions, mainly addressed to gifts-with-charge but cast in general terms, is presented by Bouyssou, *Les Libéralités*, pp. 216–227 and 270–274. Her argument is concurred in by Dupeyroux, *Acte à titre gratuit*, pp. 165–66 and was anticipated by Jean Champeaux, *Étude sur la notion juridique de l'acte à titre gratuit* (1931), pp. 255–269.

The stimulus to invent came from a type of transaction that was very common: a transfer of land in return for money or support to be supplied to the grantor, usually for life. Even though framed and described as a sale, the money or the service to be eventually supplied was uncertain, so the Code provision allowing rescission for inadequacy of price could not be used. But there was another clause in the section on sales requiring that for a sale the price must be "fixed and stated" by the parties.[21] In a series of cases, beginning as early as 1806, courts encountered situations in which annuity payments were less than the income of the land that the "seller" was to convey. The Court of Cassation concluded that the Code provision requiring a price to be stated meant a "real" or "serious" price and that the annuities called for in such cases were illusory and unreal, so no sale at all resulted.[22] They were, therefore, entirely void and could not even be salvaged by a subsequent affirmance.[23]

There were good reasons for subjecting to special scrutiny some of the transactions that were cast in this format, the sale or transfer of property in return for a promise of an annuity for life. The transferors were mostly elderly persons who aimed to provide in this way for their remaining years. Occasionally there was evidence of pressure exerted on per-

21. Art. 1591.

22. D.1849.1.245 (1849); D.1911.1.353 (1911); D.H.1933, 4 (Cass., 1932), and other cases cited by Planiol et Ripert, *Traité pratique*, vol. 10, sec. 42; Jolivet, *La Validation des donations*, pp. 104–110; and J. Rousseau, *Essai sur la notion juridique de simulation* (1937), pp. 30–32. Other references and further discussion are supplied by H. Savatier in his comment in the *Répertoire générale du notariat* (1937), art. 24911.

23. D.1911.1.353 (1911); D.H.1933, 4 (Cass., 1932). In both these cases it was held that the ten-year prescriptive period on rescission of voidable transactions did not apply. In the first case, the court also decided that a subsequent ratification by the "vendor" was wholly ineffective and that no title passed, so that the "purchaser" must pay over with interest the sums he received through a subsequent taking under eminent domain.

sons whose mental or physical disabilities made them excep-
tionally vulnerable—"undue influence" we would call it.[24]
But the original formula purported to provide an externalized
test, the disparity between the instalment payments and the
income earned by the asset sold. It was later held that the
asset did not need to be an income-producer, since the prevailing rate of interest on its capital value could provide a
substitute measure of disparity in determining whether the
annuity promised was a "real price."[25] Ill health that made
likely an early death of the annuitant could mean that an annuity payable for the vendor's life was not a "real" or "serious" price.[26] Or if, instead of money payments, lifetime care
and support were promised, their total cost could be estimated and, again, if the estimate proved to be less than the
prospective income of the asset sold, the "sale" would lack a
price and be void.[27] Then the comparison of prospective income and outgo was applied to some leases at very low
rents[28] and even, in one case, to the sale of a retail store at a
price one-tenth of its income during the previous ten years.[29]

There thus developed a miniature system of price control
for a limited group of exchange transactions in which the ex-

24. D.1893.2.341 (Riom, 1892); D.1919.1.29 (1913); Gazette du Palais,
1931.1.441 (1931).
25. D.1893.1.359 (1893); D.H.1925.1.137 (1925); S.1925.1.80 (1925).
26. D.1903.2.54 (Chambéry, 1901); D.1919.1.129 (1913); Gazette du
Palais, 1931.1.441 (1931); and cases cited by Jolivet, *La Validation des donations,* pp. 110–118.
27. D.1908.1.480 (1908); D.H.1925,133 (Cass., 1925).
28. D.1892.2.340 (Riom, 1892); S.1935.1.63 (1934); J.C.P. 1955, 9300
(Cass. 1955). In D.1882.2.49 (Caen, 1880), a lease of land with an annual
revenue of 3,170 francs was leased for 2,000 francs a year. It was "reduced"
because it encroached on an heir's guaranteed share and one-half the tract
was excluded from the lease.
29. S.1922.1.310 (1922), the price being described again as "not serious." And in D.1910.2.100 (Lyon, 1908), a surrender of an inheritance, disguised as a sale with a recital that one franc had been paid, was held to be
not a sale for lack of a "serious" price and an ineffective disguise for a gift.

change was manifestly unequal. They were often described as "disguised" gifts, but this was a complete misnomer.[30] If the price had only been falsified as a large lump sum or as an annuity or rent at a high rate, there would have been no trouble at all. The trouble arose because the terms had been stated truthfully.

The message that emerges from this dark corner is extremely cloudy. It seems to be that if exchanges become unequal *enough,* French courts can nullify them altogether and actually do so now and then.

6. *A Cluttered Landscape*

A complete overview of a landscape so cluttered would be too much to attempt. But it may be useful to summarize briefly some of the confusion and disarray that have been described and remind the reader of their principal sources.

In the preceding account there has been no mention of one idea—that of "cause"—which in the view of some authors has brought unity to the French law of contract and performs functions similar to that of consideration in selecting the promises that should be enforced. Cause has not

---

30. The question has arisen, for example, whether a gift could be effectively disguised as a sale if the price in the cover document was stated as a life annuity in an amount less than the land's revenue. D.1893.1.359 (1893) held the disguise ineffective, since in the absence of a "serious" price the gift appeared "without any veil." A similar conclusion was reached in D.1910.2.100 (Lyon, 1908), where one franc was recited as the price paid. A decision of the Court of Appeal of Montpellier (J.C.P.1955.2.8536) suggested that a price that was not "serious" should serve as a disguise just as well as a false recital of the price. This was protested by Professor Savatier in the *Revue trimestrielle de droit civil,* 1955, p. 350. He argued that an effective disguise must carry the external signs of a valid transaction and that to use the truth as means of disguising gifts would undermine the whole system of disguises, which requires the parties not only to lie but to "lie adroitly."

been mentioned because it performs none of these functions and in truth has no meaningful functions at all. The word was much used in Roman law and became still more prominent in later centuries. It served as a catch-word in the long campaign, led by the canonists, to expand the range of enforceable promises. More and more insistently it was urged by them, with reinforcement from the social philosophers, that every promise that had been seriously made and that had a cause (in the sense of reason or purpose) should be enforced. In the gallery of ideas that have helped to liberate thought it therefore deserves a small corner located out in a distant wing.[1] The French Civil Code pays it this kind of tribute, listing a "cause," along with capacity and consent of the parties, among the ingredients of an enforceable contract.[2]

Authors writing in English have probably done most to preserve the legend that in French law "cause" is a meaningful guide in contract formation. In France a few authors have fought a losing rear-guard action in its defense, but to most it has long been clear that the Code provision means nothing more than that a contract should have a purpose.[3] With this

1. The earlier history is reviewed by A. Sollner, "Die Causa im Kondiktionen- und Vertragsrecht des Mittelalters," 77 Z.S.S. 182 (1960); G. Chevrier, *Essai sur l'histoire de la cause dans les obligations* (Paris, 1929); J. L. Barton, "Causa Promissionis Again," 34 *Tijdschrift voor Rechtsgeshiedenis* 41 (1966).

2. Art. 1108, requiring, for a valid contract, consent and capacity in the person obligated, a definite object (*un objet certain*), and a "licit" cause; art. 1131, declaring that an obligation "without cause" or with a wrongful or illicit cause has no legal effect.

3. A fair statement, not wholly unsympathetic to the idea of "cause," is given by Planiol et Ripert, *Traité pratique*, vol. 6, secs. 252–253, 260. R. Demogue, *Des obligations en général* (1904), 2: 540, shows greater fervor: "An obligation should not be enforced if it is manifestly useless for the one who assumes it. It is useless when it is not explained by the current desires of mankind: first, one of the most intense, such as the desire to secure an existing or future object, a risky opportunity or a precarious advantage

proposition it is very hard to disagree; indeed, if a contract has no ascertainable purpose the parties to it should probably not be left at large. A promise to make a gift has a cause or purpose—the purpose is to make a gift. In French court decisions the absence of cause has been used in a random way to invalidate a very small number of freakish transactions when better reasons could not be found.[4] Most of the American writers who have labored to find in it some distinct meaning have ended by confessing defeat,[5] though their work has not

---

through use or possession; in addition, since avidity for gain is not everything, the obligation is useless if it is not explained by an unselfish sentiment of gratitude, piety, love, all that makes for grandeur in mankind. If it is demonstrated that these explanations are lacking, that the obligor has become bound without sufficient reason, in return for an impossible promise without serious result, then the transaction has no cause, no object that is legally protected, it is void."

4. A situation that has recurred surprisingly often, and that was hard to fit anywhere, has involved genealogists who discovered that particular individuals had inherited shares in decedents' estates and undertook to disclose the previously unknown facts to the individuals in return for a promise of a percentage of the inheritance. Where the information was readily available and would probably have been discovered by the heir in any event such agreements are held void for lack of "cause." D.P. 1899.2.95 (Bordeaux, 1896); D.P. 1910.2.167 (Rouen, 1909); D.H. 1953, 403 (Cass. 1953). But where the information was not readily available and the genealogist had to invest time and effort in discovering it, sufficient cause has been found to exist and recovery followed. D.P.1866.1.247 (Cassation, 1866); S.1894.2.150 (Paris, 1894); S.1912.2.243 (Lyon, 1911); Gazette du Palais, 1950.2.221 (Riom, 1950). These cases are discussed by von Mehren, 72 *Harvard Law Review* 1009, 1072–1073.

Promissory notes signed by employees under their employer's threat of dismissal were held to lack cause, though the real ground was no doubt duress. D.P.1893.2.359 (Bastia, 1892), discussed by Mason, "The Utility of Consideration—A Comparative View," 41 *Columbia Law Review* 825, 829–830 (1941). Similarly, where courts have hesitated to invoke mistake because it appeared in an unusual form, they have shifted to want of cause. Planiol et Ripert, *Traité pratique*, vol. 6, sec. 262.

5. The most sustained effort is that of A. Schiller, "The Counterpart of Consideration in Foreign Legal Systems," *Report of the New York Law Revision Commission* (1936), p. 107. The author expressed (p. 126) his

dispelled the legend and it is still said, usually with a tinge of envy, that in European countries all promises are enforced provided they have "sufficient cause."[6]

The traditions inherited from Roman law would have prevented "want of cause" from being translated into anything comparable to our own idea of bargain consideration as a comprehensive test in contract formation. The gratuitous contracts of Roman law—mandate, deposit, money loan— were retained through the centuries on the roster of enforceable contracts. The absence of compensation for the service rendered or advantage conferred reduced to a minimum the liabilities attached, but they were well known, were thought useful, and were left intact, with no disposition shown to eliminate them. As to benefactions of other kinds, the attitude was one of indifference and no controls were imposed unless a transmission of wealth was to occur with two specific consequences, both being needed: a permanent depletion of the estate owned by the giver and a permanent increase in that owned by the taker. This extremely strict and narrow conception was manufactured for a purpose, to pre-

------

agreement "for the most part" with the conclusions reached by E. Lorenzen, "Causa and Consideration in Contracts," 28 *Yale Law Journal* 621 (1919), one of which was (p. 646) that "There is in reality no definable 'doctrine' of *causa*. The term '*causa*' includes a variety of notions which may equally well be derived from the nature of a juristic act and from considerations of equity." M. Mason, "The Utility of Consideration—a Comparative View," 41 *Columbia Law Review* 825, 831 (1941), found that "the doctrine of cause is, from a logical point of view, a reduplication of other elements in the French contract system" but is useful in directing the attention of courts to the purposes of the transaction challenged.

6. Corbin, *Contracts* (1963), vol. 1, sec. 38. Writing in an English journal, a more recent author finds that cause and consideration have brought "parallel" solutions in the treatment of mistake, breach, frustration, and illegality though the French solutions are "invariably neater and more convincing" and have "elegance and consistency." B. Markezinis, "Cause and Consideration: a Study in Parallel," [1978] *Cambridge Law Journal*, pp. 53, 55. No comment seems called for.

vent married persons from making permanent diversions of transmissible wealth from one to the other though leaving them entirely free while the marriage lasted to use and to share their resources and to perform services of all kinds for each other. This distinction in the forms that bounty might take became securely locked in when it came to be used for a different purpose whose priority rose higher as the centuries progressed—protecting guaranteed shares in inheritance against gifts by owners that would permanently deplete the estates they would otherwise leave at death. In the controls set up for this purpose, the narrow Roman definition of "gift" recaptured from donees as much as, but no more than, was needed and performed its function admirably.

The priority of the purpose—protection to forced heirs—still remains as high as ever. The escape from the Code, better described as a disorderly flight, has not been an escape from all its provisions, especially not from the guarantees of inheritance by kindred of the owner's genetic line. The disguises and devices that are used to dispense with the need for notarization are all stripped away when the question raised is whether a gift has exceeded the disposable quotas or has brought undue inequality between heirs of equal rank. And it should be added that there are other provisions in the Code, such as those authorizing donors to revoke, with which the courts have been entirely willing to comply, though with considerably less energy and conviction. In the sector of French law that has been examined here, nullification by the courts has been confined to the Code requirement of notarization. Here their success has been almost complete. One occasionally finds broad statements such as: "all promises seriously intended to be binding are now binding in the Civil Law."[7] This is not true of Germany, as we

7. H. Lawson, *A Common Lawyer Looks at the Civil Law* (Ann Arbor, Mich., 1953), pp. 159–160.

shall see. In France it would be true if corrected to say: "all promises seriously intended to be binding can be made binding by using a well-designed disguise" (unless they encroach on forced heirs' shares). But even such a modified statement should give credit where it is due—to courts for their success in nullifying Code provisions that imposed excessive and burdensome controls inherited from earlier centuries.

The Code provisions on gifts apply, of course, only to those that conform to the ancient tests and diminish one "patrimony" while augmenting another. Where an unnotarized transfer of any interest whatever, of any kind or size, that would have these effects is attempted, the entire transaction is declared by the Code to be wholly and incurably void. And to notarize, it will be remembered, both donor and donee must appear before two notaries (or one plus two other persons); a written document must be acknowledged, read aloud, signed by all present, and copied into a public record. After such a gift has been executed it remains vulnerable to attack on grounds that, with one exception (the nonperformance of an express condition), are entirely unknown in our own law. Some critics, as we shall see, describe our law, for meanness of spirit, as "primitive" and "uncouth." If an important index of superior legal culture were thought to be the facilities it gives the generous for sharing their wealth with others, the design contained in the French Civil Code would have to be described as backward-looking.

Backward-looking it was, in a literal sense. The controls over gifts that were installed in the Code of 1804 had been maintained by the French crown under the old regime for more than 250 years. The reasons for its insistence on these controls were not formally stated, but it is a fair surmise that the high obstacles the government interposed were for the purpose of preventing dispersal of the wealth of the great families, on whose dominant role in society the monarchy conceived that its own stability depended. The Revolution brought a swing in the opposite direction, but its leadership over fierce opposition chose, as its means of promoting equality in inheritance and a wider distribution of family-owned wealth, a severe restriction—almost the removal—of the power to make gifts by will. The restrictions that had been so long maintained on the making and promising of inter vivos gifts were consistent, at least, with these purposes and might, perhaps, promote them. So the comprehensive controls over gifts that the monarchy had devised were transposed to the Code without contest.

A reminder of these events is offered now because, among all the decisions made by the codifiers on the issues here discussed, this was surely to prove the most crucial. Most of the confusion and disarray that have already been described can be traced to a single, overriding impulse in the courts: to open wide the avenues of escape from the Code's requirements of notarization. It took only eleven years after the Code took effect for the high court to invent the "manual gift," a plain evasion of the Code that could at least be explained on the ground of expediency: the lack of means to prevent an owner from surrendering an object that can be readily handed over. Another invention—the disguised gift or sham—was not finally approved until twenty years had gone by and after prolonged strife within the high court; perhaps this invention prevailed because it provided another way of showing disrespect for Napoleon's Code. This much, at least, it surely does. The disguised gift deceives no one, not even the courts, which police it only to ensure that the mask be well designed.

There is more that needs to be said and will later be said about tokens used to symbolize assent, but "simulation" involves much more than the solemn delivery of a peppercorn.

It means outright falsification, the statement of pretended terms to which the parties in fact did not assent, as they and the courts also are fully aware. It is hard to believe that in a mature legal system which otherwise disclaims the use of voodoo, courts, authors, and other spokesmen for the regime accept this use of transparent pretense as fully justified because notarization would otherwise be needed. When it became apparent that the requirements of form in the newly enacted Code were greatly overbuilt and that the historical reasons for them had faded away, there was an alternative available at the time—that the legislature intervene to reduce them to tolerable dimensions. There is no need for this now, since the courts have done their work so well.

The work of French courts has one other aspect that is more directly relevant to the present study, their tests of donors' motives. To decide that a transaction is a gift, it must be found that its effect will be to transfer a "giveable" interest and also to produce the necessary and permanent loss-matched-by-gain. After these elements have been established, however, there still remains one further question—will the one who is to incur the sacrifice receive something in return that he desires and that will make it therefore an exchange, not a gift? To answer this question German law, as we shall soon see, employs the concept of "recompense," which (I will contend) expresses the notion of bargain under a very thin disguise. In the French Code the contrast drawn is between the gift and the "onerous" contract in which each party is to "give or do something," the giving or doing by each being "regarded as the equivalent" for that of the other. The overwhelming majority of consensual transactions no doubt conform well enough to this unvarnished description, which does not suggest any need to inquire into motives—to ask, for example, whether each party's giving or doing was not only "regarded" as an "equivalent" but was for the *pur-*

pose of inducing the other to "give or do." So inquiries of this kind were not made.

Questions as to motives had to be faced, however, in a series of transactions that began to appear quite early. They were mostly in the form of promises in which the "giving or doing" was to be on one side only, pure benefactions for churchly or other worthy purposes that were then attacked as void because not notarized. I have earlier described the means by which French courts managed to escape a conclusion so distasteful as this. They warmed over some laudatory language, drawn from garbled texts of the Corpus Juris, describing the generosity and unselfishness that animate donors. This created a painful necessity, to be somewhat unkind to the donors in the transactions brought before them, to find in their motives some impurities, some traces of selfishness that could be detected after careful search, so that the proposed transfers would not be gifts. This reasoning is now accepted and extolled by French authors as showing the honor and respect that French law has for disinterested generosity, which is so greatly esteemed that it seldom exists in unadulterated form and notarization therefore is seldom needed. This, the trace-of-selfishness test, is the one that is most prominently displayed and widely approved for distinguishing between gifts and "onerous" contracts, at least where notarization is the issue. Whether it will be used for other purposes, who knows? It cannot be said to have displaced, here or elsewhere, the idea of bargained-for exchange; for the idea of bargained-for exchange is one that French courts apparently have not yet discovered. Whether French law is worse or better off on account of this the reader can judge.

III Germany

Crossing from France to Germany will provide some opportunities to glance back and forth across the border to compare the vistas on either side. Comparison will first of all reveal the many similarities that exist in the two countries in this enclave of their private law. The similarities are the product of a common source, most of it an inheritance from Roman law that is remarkably unchanged though now adapted to other purposes. But there are also notable divergences, mostly in the ways in which these ideas have been put to use, with great differences in results. It is the divergences that will have the most interest. An objection may be raised, and it is no doubt valid, that in societies as advanced as the French and German the law of gifts deals with transactions that are off the main track—eccentric—and that to focus on such deviant transactions is to limit oneself to a sideline view. But a sideline can give a good view of many public events, and this may be true of some legal systems. The area observed will be limited, but the differences in the ways the codes have been applied may help at least to correct an impression that is widespread, especially in the United States, that western Europe is one flat plain, blanketed uniformly by "the civil law." My hope will be to give a glimpse of plateaus and valleys, mixed with some rough terrain and at least one swamp with quicksand.

1. The Earlier History of Controls over Gifts

The history of controls over gifts shows many parallels between the German states and France, with some coincidences even in timing. For, as indicated before, the restrictions on gifts (and sales) of inherited land that were taking form in northern and central France in the decades around A.D. 1200 carried forward and defined more precisely the rights of "family communities" among the races of Germanic origin that had occupied France long before. Among those that settled in the more easterly regions of Europe, the controls exercised by family groups took various forms and changed over time. Probably the oldest form was a quota limiting the fraction of family-used assets of which individual members, even elder members, could effectively dispose. The size of the quota could be determined simply by a head count, with all males counting equally; or a fraction could be fixed (one-third or one-fourth) that would apply to all families without regard to their size. To extract some asset from the common fund it might be necessary to have a partition. Somewhat later, in other racial groups, a procedure developed by which the heirs with rights to inherit could express their assent to the alienation of some particular asset, usually in aid of some pious cause fostered by the church, which therefore appeared often in the role of active promoter.[1]

Whichever form the restrictions took they concentrated

1. The available evidence for the period extending roughly from A.D. 500 to 1000 is described by H. Brunner, "Beiträge zur Geschichte des germanischen Warterechts," *Festgabe für Dernburg* (1900), pp. 41–60; idem, *Grundzüge der deutschen Rechtsgeschichte*, 7th ed. (1923), sec. 57; J. Braude, *Die Familiengemeinschaften der Angelsachsen* (Leipzig, 1932); and is summarized by R. Schröder-E. von Künssberg, *Lehrbuch der deutschen Rechtsgeschichte*, 7th ed. (1932), pp. 302–307, 365–367.

more and more on inherited land. By the thirteenth century,
when the customary law adhered to in large areas of German
settlement was described in influential law books written by
private authors, there were many close parallels between the
customs they described and those then taking form in northern and central France.[2] It is not surprising that the response
was similar among peoples whose racial origins had been essentially the same, whose experience had been focused and
whose survival had depended on small cohesive family
groups whose resources did not often exceed by much the
requirements for subsistence.

The rights of heirs to prevent or restrict the disposal of
family-used land extended, as in France, to both sales and
gifts. As to sales, the controls came to require in some places
that the land must be offered first, at the price projected, to
the next heirs whose consent was needed. Or the heirs might
be given instead, as in France, a power to cancel within a
short time limit any sale made or encumbrance imposed after
reimbursing the third-party grantee. Such devices—first options in one form or another—came into use in other situations where mutual interests interlocked and have proved
widely useful in modern German law.[3] But there must have
been many occasions when senior family members sought to
neutralize the claims of expectant heirs, to buy them off with
token payments or use stronger measures to suppress their

2. The medieval German word used to describe the right of an expectant heir in property devoted to family use was *Warterecht,* a term that had
appeared much earlier. It was described quite fully in thirteenth-century
law books, the *Sachsenspiegel, Schwabenspiegel* and others. Good accounts are given by H. Siegel, *Das deutsche Erbrecht nach den Rechts-
quellen des Mittelalters* (1853), pp. 88–111, and J. von Gosen, *Das
Privatrecht nach dem kleinen Kaiserrecht* (1866), pp. 171–177.

3. The derivation of these widely used devices from the "house
community" of the German middle ages is traced in a most interesting way
by O. von Gierke, *Deutsches Privatrecht* (1905), vol. 2, sec. 152.

dissent. This must have been almost equally true when the transfers proposed were to be outright gifts that the elders had been persuaded to make. There could have been little incentive to record the outcome in such disputes. In the German-speaking settlements, furthermore, there were no courts assigned by a central government and empowered, as were the royal courts in France, to ascertain through neighborhood juries (*enquêtes par turbes*) the rules derived from custom that were adhered to in local communities— empowered also to apply the rules in litigation so as to validate and preserve them. In some localities in Germany the customary rules that conferred these rights on expectant heirs fell into disuse during the late Middle Ages or else were much diluted.[4] But the notions they expressed of mutual responsibility within families were rooted deeply in ancient experience, deeply enough to survive in another form when Roman law came flooding in.[5]

4. In many areas the rights of family members were translated into forms of joint ownership that could be dissolved by partition. In some places, especially some cities, rights of family members disappeared entirely (Schröder-von Künssberg, *Lehrbuch*, pp. 791–92). Another author describes their disappearance in the Baltic lands that had been settled by Germans, a process that was well begun before Roman law had acquired much influence, though in its later phases Roman law accelerated the process. A. von Freytagh-Loringhoven, "Beispruchsrecht und Erbenhaftung," 28 *Z.S.S. (germ.)* 69 (1907).

5. By describing the experience as ancient I mean to suggest my own view that despite the extreme skepticism of Maitland (see above, chap. 2, sec. 1), the various medieval forms of control by the kindred over disposal of family land cannot be explained otherwise than by presupposing much closer and more restrictive forms of family interdependence in prehistoric times. This hypothesis is surely common ground now among historians of German law. It seems entirely credible also that these controls maintained by groups were sufficiently central to human experience in those early times so that the family could have served as the source and model of the "corporateness" that pervaded German medieval society and that the great historian of that subject has described. O. von Gierke,

Among the rules derived from German experience that were much revised through the reception of Roman law were those empowering the kindred to prevent sales and gifts of family land. These powers could normally operate only on inter vivos transactions and indeed had originated well before wills had been invented. The *légitime*, the alternative devised in Roman law, had originated as a restriction on gifts by will. As it took form in postclassical Roman law, it aimed to ensure that all the heirs in the protected group would receive, as a minimum, one-fourth of the shares they would have received if there had been no will. In a few isolated instances the protection accorded expectant heirs had been somewhat extended in rescripts of late Roman emperors, preserved in the Corpus Juris, that decreed the annulment of "immense" or "immoderate" lifetime gifts that had depleted the estates the donors left behind for their close blood-relatives.[6] These rescripts had been issued under the prerogative powers of the emperors and had dealt with the particular cases on a strictly individualized basis. They made no attempt to state any generalized tests for defining the "undutiful" gift which, like the "undutiful" will, should be set aside. In a few instances it was intimated that the gifts had been made "in order to evade [or escape]" the controls over undutiful wills, or the gifts were described as "enormous," "immense"—so large a share of the donor's estate as to leave substantially nothing behind and make it difficult to escape the inference that one purpose, at least, was to defeat succession by the donor's heirs. There was also one analogous case in which inter vivos gifts could be attacked for impairing rights of succession at death, though only through affirmative proof that this was the donor's purpose.[7]

Die genossenschafts-theorie und die deutsche Rechtsprechung (1887), pp. 356–435.

    6. References are given above, chapter 2, section 1, note 24.

    7. This was the case of the owner who had freed a slave and thereby

The leading agents and promoters of the reception—Germany's learned men—soon reached agreement that the motives of donors must be disregarded, that what counted was the result. What, for example, if an owner made an inter vivos gift in the erroneous belief that one of his own children was dead? Or what if another child was born to him after the gift had been made? In such cases it would be impossible, in many others it would be difficult, to prove a conscious purpose to exclude the eligible heir from the succession. In any event this purpose soon came to seem irrelevant. The "necessary" heirs (*Noterben*), as they came to be called, were entitled in their own right. And the jurists soon concluded that if the estate did not suffice to fill this quota, the assets given away by lifetime gift must be retrieved. Land (especially inherited land) was no longer singled out as the exclusive target. The extended family, collateral relatives on the lines from which the assets had come, were excluded; the classes of "necessary" heirs whose shares were guaranteed were restricted, as in Roman law, to descendants, ancestors, and in one instance to brothers and sisters of the deceased.[8] There was thus erected on German soil an imposing edifice built out of some scattered leavings found in late Roman law. It anticipated to a remarkable degree the structures that were to be reproduced in modern codifications.[9]

---

became entitled to inherit one-half of his assets on the freedman's death. By the actions *Fabiana* or *Calvisiana* the former owner could cancel gifts made in "fraud" of his rights, *dolo malo* (Buckland, *Textbook*, p. 592). The refusal of German jurists to make use of this analogy, which called for a finding of intentional evasion, is described by W. Francke, *Das Recht der Noterben* (1831), sec. 40.

8. Brothers and sisters would prevail over a "base" (*turpis*) person to whom a gift had been made. Buckland, *Textbook*, p. 325.

9. I confess that I have not attempted to trace these ideas through the glossators and postglossators or to read the German literature which becomes voluminous in the sixteenth century, but have relied on the summaries by Francke, *Das Recht der Noterben*, secs. 40–46, and C. F. Glück, *Ausführliche Erläuterung der Pandecten* (1804), 7: 93–107, 156–179. As

These ideas, formulated by the jurists, were accepted throughout the German-speaking lands from the sixteenth century onward. It was a sign of general acceptance and also of widespread interest that these topics stimulated much special legislation at both state and local levels. There was much tinkering, for example, with the size of the guaranteed shares, which were usually made to vary with the numbers and kinds of "necessary" heirs. The children of the decedent were very commonly awarded one-third of their intestate shares if they numbered three or less and one-half if they were more than three. Parents and grandparents had smaller fractions. In quite a few districts widows were introduced into the protected group, though they might have to prove they were "needy." Considerable imagination was shown in inventing grounds for disinheriting heirs who had misbehaved in various ways. With numerous variations of this kind in detail, the basic system of guaranteed inheritance remained in force through the intervening centuries until it was finally incorporated, not much changed, in the Civil Code of 1900.[10]

Francke points out (sec. 43), four authors (Faber, Thomasius, Kritz, and Mühlenbruch) had required in the donor "an evil purpose," but all the rest considered that this was not needed, and Glück (7: 167) testified that the latter view was followed by the courts. There was a sharp difference of opinion as to whether the "unloving" (*lieblos*) gift was wholly void (as would be true ordinarily of an "undutiful" will) or was merely reduced to the donor's disposable quota, this being the usual solution. My impression is that on most issues involved in forced heirship, disputes among the learned authors were rare. The learning on this subject was of course not restricted to German authors. The sixteenth-century French jurist, Charles Dumoulin, gave quite a full treatment to the subject, in which he disagreed with some of the conclusions accepted in Germany (especially on whether an afterborn child could have a guaranteed share). See Dumoulin, *Tractatus Analyticus de Inofficiosis Testamentis, Donationibus et Dotibus, Opera Quae Extant Omnia* (Paris, 1681), 3: 528.

10. Summaries of the provisions in force in most of the German territories were presented in convenient form by the report of Meyersburg to

The reception of Roman law also brought in most of Germany a widespread adoption of that hesitant and equivocal form of control over gifts that had been devised late in the Roman empire. This was a requirement of public registration for gifts of substantial size. The cut-off point defined in Justinian's legislation was 500 *solidi*; unregistered gifts or promises of gift that attempted to transfer values greater than this were void as to the excess, though in all other respects they were valid. The figure chosen represented a considerable sum, both in Byzantium where it first appeared and in the equivalents into which it was translated in Germany in the sixteenth and later centuries.[11] The interests that could be served by controls in this form are hard to imagine. A wary dictatorship in the Greek east may have wished to be informed of transactions by which the wealthy and powerful gave away large portions of their resources and may have hoped to set some limits to the influence they could thereby exert. However, this would not explain why similar legislation was reenacted in two German states, Saxony and Bavaria, with somewhat lower ceiling figures.[12] The figure fixed in Justinian's legislation was high enough

the 14th Deutscher Juristentag, in its *Verhandlungen* 50 (1878) and the "Motives of the First Drafting Commission for the Preparation of a Civil Code," Mugdan, *Die Gesammte Materialien zum bürgerlichen Gesetzbuch* (1899), 5: 202–206. In the "Motives of the First Drafting Commission," there is a summary of the various means used to determine when inter vivos gifts became "excessive" (Mugdan, 5: 240–241). A full account of forced heirship in Prussia under the Prussian Allgemeines Landrecht (1794), with references to its workings in other German states, is given by H. Dernburg, *Lehrbuch des preussischen Privatrechts,* 2d ed. (1881), 3: secs. 195–212.

11. Translated into gulden, 500 *solidi* became 2,000 gulden in most of the German states. F. von Savigny, *System des heutigen römischen Rechts* (Berlin, 1841), 4: sec. 166. Savigny himself was extremely critical of this form of control and called the monetary limitation "arbitrary and irrelevant."

12. O. von Gierke, *Deutsches Privatrecht* (1917), 3: 422–423.

and the sanction mild enough so that not much inconvenience could have been caused. Nowhere in Germany during the intermediate centuries did there appear the obsession with this topic that was shown by the central government in France, with its insistent commands, five times repeated, that all gifts without exception, of all kinds and sizes, must be publicly registered on pain of nullity. These reiterated efforts have been and probably must be explained, as I have already said, by the desire of French royal officials to deter by publicity and hampering formality transactions that might dissipate "the wealth of families." Political leadership in Germany, if it sympathized with this purpose, must have concluded that any such task was not for them. And in Prussia when (in 1794) the value given was eliminated as a test from legislation requiring registration of gifts, all gifts executed by physical delivery were declared to be valid, so that the power to make them was if anything enlarged and registration was required only for promises of gift.[13]

2. The Solutions of the Civil Code

The preparation of a Civil Code for Germany was long postponed and the work, when it began, proceeded with utmost deliberation. The first important step was the preparation of a commercial code, which was approved in 1861 as uniform legislation and was then adopted by the separate states to apply in their own territories. The same year work began on a general code of obligations. Then came a Code of Civil

13. The Prussian *Allgemeines Landrecht*, part 1, title 11, arts. 1063–1064, required not only a writing, but court registration, for all "gift contracts." But articles 1065, 1066, and 1068 provided that a gift by manual delivery of movables or money would be valid, and so would a written, though unregistered, conveyance of land if possession was also delivered. The Austrian Code of 1811 likewise provided (art. 943) that a manual gift with delivery would be valid as to movables without further formality.

Procedure, adopted in 1879 for all of Germany by the national legislature that was created after national unity had been achieved, in 1871, and the *Reich* established. Planning had already begun for a drafting commission to prepare the text of a Civil Code. Its meetings began in 1881. Its membership was impressive. High government officials and high-court judges took a leading role, prominent lawyers, renowned professors were members—Windscheid himself was one of the most influential. It worked intensively for the next six years, until 1887 when its draft of a Code was presented for public criticism. The criticism was intense and searching and continued for three years, when a Second Drafting Commission was appointed. It then worked for another five years, until 1895, when its own revised draft was published. The Second Drafting Commission made many changes and the legislature made more in its own independent review before it approved the final text in 1896, with an effective date of January 1, 1900. Thus, through a deliberative process as extensive and thorough as it could well be, there was brought to bear in a great collective effort the trained legal intelligence of Germany.[1]

On the issues with which this study has been most concerned the great reappraisal did not reveal any deep divisions of opinion. Objections to forced heirship were raised and debated. It was pointed out that forced heirship cut sharply into the power of owners to dispose of their own property and at times could cause real prejudice by interfering with an informed and disinterested judgment as to how the differing needs of younger dependents could best be

1. The preparation of the German Civil Code was well described by Maitland, "The Making of the German Civil Code," *Collected Papers* (Cambridge, 1911), 3: 474. I have relied here, as for many other purposes, on F. Wieacker, *Die Privatrechtsgeschichte der Neuzeit*, 2d ed. (1967), pp. 468–472.

provided for. It could impair the management or force a disruptive break-up of unitary enterprises in industry or agriculture, and by the very attempt at mathematical precision could provoke dissension and litigation. The First Drafting Commission, reviewing all the objections, concluded nevertheless that the *Pflichtteil* (the German equivalent of *légitime*) was an accepted part of the law of succession in all the German states, that it expressed convictions that had been long and strongly held, and that more persuasive objections than these were needed to eliminate guarantees that had been built so deeply into German experience.[2]

The draftsmen were convinced from the outset that the guarantees, to be effective, must be carried back to restrict the power to make inter vivos gifts.[3] It was harder to decide how far back they should be carried. The Prussian Code of 1794 had fixed a time limit of only three years prior to the donor's death.[4] The First Drafting Commission rejected any time limit, but the Second Commission decided that one was needed, and after prolonged indecision[5] it settled on ten years and this limit was adopted in the Civil Code.[6] There

2. Arguments for and against preserving the *Pflichtteil* had been presented at some length to the 1878 meeting of the Deutscher Juristentag by Meyersburg and Bruns (*Verhandlungen*, pp. 60, 72). But the debates were going on all over Germany. Even Hegel participated, coming out strongly for preserving the *Pflichtteil* on philosophical grounds (Dernburg, *Preussisches Privatrecht*, 2d ed. [1885], vol. 3, secs. 195–196). The conclusions of the First Drafting Commission are summarized in Mugdan, *Materialien*, 5: 202–203.

3. Mugdan, *Materialien*, 5: 239–241 (First Commission); pp. 875–876 (Second Commission).

4. *Allgemeines Landrecht*, arts. 1113 and 1118.

5. Mugdan, *Materialien*, 5: 241–242, gives the reasons that persuaded the First Commission to reject a time limit. The Second, after reaching the opposite conclusion, remained for long undecided on what the limit should be (ibid., p. 791).

6. B.G.B., arts. 2325, 2327. Art. 2329 provided that the gift made latest in time should be cancelled first.

was some debate also as to what classes of surviving relatives should rank as "necessary" heirs with shares in inheritance guaranteed. Brothers and sisters were soon eliminated, but the decedent's surviving spouse was added[7] and these conclusions were adopted in the Code.[8]

The result was a scheme that did not differ much from that set up in the French Civil Code. The groups of heirs with guaranteed shares were almost the same, descendants and ancestors of the decedent, with the German Code adding only the surviving spouse. The shares of each estate that would be guaranteed were calculated somewhat differently. Instead of the French nondisposable "reserve," a percentage of the whole estate that varied with the number and the kinds of forced heirs who survived, the German Code guaranteed to each "necessary" heir one-half the share in the whole estate that he or she would have received through intestacy;[9] these formulas usually brought results that did not differ greatly from those in France. Under both Codes the controls reached back and applied as well to inter vivos gifts, thereby reinforcing the need, for which there were other reasons also, for means to distinguish gifts from consensual transactions of other types. The overhauling of past, supposedly closed transactions was in Germany made less disruptive by the ten-year time limit introduced by the German Code. The Code also simplified somewhat the procedure for retrieving unauthorized gifts by restoring to the heir whose share had been infringed not a share in the particular assets themselves but their money value.[10] The net effect of both

7. These decisions were taken by the First Drafting Commission. Mugdan, *Materialien*, 5: 203–204.

8. B.G.B., art. 2303.

9. B.G.B., art. 2303.

10. This was decided by the First Commission in order to avoid the disruptive effects of partition, with forced sales (Mugdan, *Materialien*, 5: 204–205). Money restitution is called for by B.G.B., arts. 2305, 2311, 2312,

sets of Code provisions, however, was much the same in singling out gifts for very special treatment and making them vulnerable to attack on grounds that did not apply to any other transactions.

The need for means to identify gifts was further confirmed by another decision made by the Code draftsmen. It was made quite early: that an authenticating formality, notarization, should be required, but only for promises of gift. Several reasons were given: the need when gifts were promised to ensure care and deliberation by promisors; the need for better evidence than the informal and ambiguous language often used in spontaneous, one-sided expressions; the unwisdom of allowing the strict requirements of form for testamentary gifts to be bypassed too easily; the need to prevent exploitation of the thoughtless and good-natured and to protect their creditors and heirs.[11] Some, if not most, of these reasons could have been used to justify a requirement of notarization for gifts in every form. But the German states, unlike France, had had no experience with comprehensive schemes of public registration, strongly promoted by political authority. Two more recent codes in German-speaking states, the Prussian (1794) and the Austrian (1811), had exempted executed gifts from registration. The commissions engaged in drafting the German Civil Code decided to fol-

---

and elsewhere. It should be noted also that the claims to equal treatment of heirs of the same rank, leading to enforced return (*rapport*) of any excess gift received, play a much less prominent role in Germany than they do in France. The nearest analogy in Germany is "equalization," which applies only to advances made by a parent to his own child or children to help create a marital establishment or maintain a business enterprise, and the need to account for any extra margin of benefaction received can be dispensed with by the parental donor. T. Kipp-H. Coing, *Erbrecht*, (1955), pp. 416–422, describes this.

11. Some of these reasons had been stated in the official Motives of the First Drafting Commission. The Second Commission adopted them and added some more of its own. Mugdan, *Materialien*, 2: 162, 743.

low this course, after persuading themselves that the acts or expressions needed to transfer ownership by gift would provide all the safeguards needed.[12]

It was taken for granted that the means required to execute a gift would vary with the subject matter given. For land a written conveyance acknowledged before a court or notary would be needed, just as it would be for a transfer made under a contract of sale. For movables physical delivery would suffice; for claims not connected with a physical subject matter (choses in action, we would say) words of present assignment would be enough; not even a writing would be needed.[13] Similarly, a creditor could discharge a debtor either in writing or orally through language of present release, even though it was intended and understood by the parties that nothing was to be given in return.[14] In these and

12. Ibid., p. 163.

13. The Second Drafting Commission, recognizing that oral assignments of intangibles were valid in exchange transactions, expressed some foreboding concerning the lack of formality in gift assignments but concluded that gift assignments should not be marked off from others by a special requirement, such as that of a signed writing. Ibid., p. 743. The foreboding had some basis, for it has been chiefly in assignments of intangibles that trouble has come in drawing the line between promise and presently effective gift. The difficulty has been increased by the willingness of courts to find that a presently operative transfer though the assignee's right to payment was made contingent on an uncertain future event: Warneyer, 1909, no. 33 (R.G., 1908), assignment to take effect if the assignee outlived the assignor; *J.W.*, 1916, 37 (R.G., 1915), assignee to be entitled to collect the balance in a savings bank deposit "if anything happens to me"; Warneyer, 1908, no. 141 (1907), assignment to operate if plaintiff indemnified a third party, with no obligation of the plaintiff to do so.

14. 53 *R.G.Z.* 294 (1903), oral release of principal with interest still due until creditor's death; and 76 *R.G.Z.* 59 (1911), oral statement that debt was discharged accompanied by physical destruction of debtor's promissory note. Again, the release can be a present gift though effective only when a future event occurs, as in Warneyer, 1921, no. 95 (R.G., 1921), oral release by creditor if debtor outlived her; *N.J.W.* 1961, 76 (R.G., 1960), release effective on creditor's death.

other instances wherever the language used did not accomplish an operative transfer or discharge and amounted merely to a promise, a transaction that had not been notarized would be wholly void. But the disability would not be fatal, since the Code itself provides expressly, for all unnotarized promises of gift, that their performance "cures" the defect of form.[15]

There was, however, an antecedent question that had to be answered before these questions of ways and means could arise: was the interest one that could be "given"? In defining the potential subjects of gift the Code followed most of the way a well-trodden path: "A disposition [*Zuwendung*] through which one person out of his property enriches another is a gift, if both parties are agreed that the disposition is to occur without recompense."[16] Thus the result to be achieved by the transaction must include two features, the disposer's impoverishment and the receiver's enrichment; and, as we shall see, both are strictly required. The disposer must be impoverished in a particular way, by a subtraction from ("out of") the disposer's "property." The effect produced by this language will be described in the section that follows. Its evident purpose was to preserve the ancient restrictions on the types of gratuitous transactions that could constitute "gifts."

There was, however, one other feature of the Code definition that was essentially new, contained in the clause requiring (1) that the impoverishment involved be "unrecompensed" and (2) that on this issue, the absence of any recompense, both parties must agree. The word *Entgelt*, which I

15. B.G.B., art. 518(2).
16. B.G.B., art. 516(1). It would be more intelligible English if *Zuwendung* were translated as "transfer," but since a gift can be made in other ways (e.g., by discharge of a duty) and by indirect means, it seems better to preserve the vagueness of the German word.

have translated as "recompense," was a familiar word in common use in many other surroundings. But the Romanesque learning that had lasted late in Germany had put forward, as the principal index of a gift, the generosity and unselfishness of the motives that inspired it, the magnanimous spirit that was summed up as the *animus donandi*. In the great nineteenth-century reconstruction of a "modernized" Roman law—Germany's second reception—these ideas, like all the others that appeared in the Roman sources, had been subjected to intensive scrutiny. Savigny and the later great authors, like Windscheid, had penetrated some of the vaporous clouds that still obscure the landscape in France. They asserted that a transaction could still be a gift though the motives were selfish or even malign—to force the recipient into a higher tax bracket or destroy a lady's reputation. Yet the great Pandectists still insisted that the essential test, marking off gifts from other transactions was the purpose of the donor to enrich.[17] This became the principal test in the definition of gift in the draft prepared by the First Drafting Commission.[18] At a very late stage it was replaced by another test, in a somewhat roundabout way.

In 1889 Otto Lenel, a distinguished historian of Roman

17. F. von Savigny, *System des heutigen römischen Rechts* (Berlin, 1841), vol. 4, sec. 143; Windscheid, *Pandekten*, 9th ed. (1906), vol. 2, sec. 365. The Second Drafting Commission also was clear that a transaction could still be a gift though the motive was predominantly selfish (Mugdan, *Materialien*, 2: 737). A good short account of Pandectist ideas is given by F. Haymann, *Die Schenkung unter einer Auflage* (1905), pp. 1–9. The definitions of gift put forth by authors ranging all the way from the Accursian gloss to Savigny are summarized by H. Burckhart, *Zum Begriff der Schenkung* (1899), pp. 76–91.

18. The language is quoted in Haymann, *Die Schenkung*, p. 2: "A gift is a disposition made to another by which the property (*Vermögen*) of the disposer is diminished and that of the other is enriched, insofar as this occurs with the purpose of [accomplishing] the enrichment and the other accepts it as a gift."

law, published an article in which he referred, quite incidentally, to the tautology involved in the currently accepted definition of gift. Everyone had agreed that one feature was essential, that the net result of the transaction must be to enrich the donee. Then he asked whether anything was added by saying that the purpose of enriching the donee must be to enrich the donee. There were many purposes, he argued, for making gifts—laudable, discreditable, or often mixed—but all so unstructured and subjective that the donor's success or failure in achieving them would seldom have legal consequence. The only significant feature that marked off the gift from other transactions was purely negative, the absence of any element of agreed exchange: "if a gift is to exist the purpose must *not* be directed toward securing a recompense [*Entgelt*]."[19]

The Second Drafting Commission met in 1890, the following year, and promptly showed that it was impressed by Lenel's argument. In its own first draft the "purpose to enrich" was abandoned and it was required instead that the gain to be conferred must be "unrecompensed" (*unentgeltlich*). This was an adjective that was much used in common speech and had even appeared many decades before in definitions of gifts in the codes of Prussia (1794) and Austria (1811).[20] But the new phrasing that was now pro-

19. O. Lenel, "Die Lehre von der Voraussetzung," *Archiv für die zivilistische Praxis* 74 (1889): 213, 230–235, the sentence quoted being on page 232. The discussion of motives in gifts, contained in this short passage, was incidental to an extended discussion of "presuppositions" in contract formation, aiming to broaden and clarify the bases of relief for failure or frustration of purpose in exchange transactions. The strong impact on the Second Drafting Commission of Lenel's "unassailable" argument in this short passage is described by Haymann, *Die Schenkung*, pp. 2–7.

20. Prussian *Allgemeines Landrecht*, I, 11, sec. 1037: "Gifts are contracts by which one obligates himself to transfer to the other without recompense [*unentgeltlich*] the ownership of a thing or of a right." Austrian

posed required, for any transaction to constitute a gift, not only that there be no "recompense," but also that on the absence of all recompense both parties must have agreed. No reasons were given to explain this last refinement but we should be able to guess. In the traditions derived from Roman law the habit was well established of describing gifts as contracts, and the Code draftsmen showed plainly enough their conviction that gifts, like other contracts, were the product of mutual assent.[21] From this premise it must have seemed to follow that the agreement of both parties was needed to establish an attribute that had suddenly been made essential: they must have *agreed* to exclude any recompense for the gain to be conferred.[22]

In a later section we can return to the question whether it ever makes a difference that the requirement of recompense

Code, art. 938: "A contract by which a thing [*Sache*] is turned over to another without recompense [*unentgeltlich*] is called a gift."

21. The Second Drafting Commission was confronted with some alternative proposals on the issues whether acceptance by the donee was essential for a gift to have any legal effect, or whether acceptance should be presumed, or could perhaps be inferred from noncompliance with an imposed time limit. The commission's view, stated emphatically, was that acceptance could not be presumed or inferred, that every gift was composed of two elements, a transfer of ownership by an appropriate means but also—and equally necessary—the subjective, understanding assent of the receiver. It concluded that until this assent was manifested the transfer, though technically completed, would constitute nothing more than an offer. Mugdan, *Materialien*, 2: 735–739.

A helpful discussion of the relations between donee's acceptance and the "contractual" nature of a gift is that of F. Haymann, "Grenzziehung zwischen Schenkung und unentgeltlichem Vertrag," *Jherings Jahrbucher*, 2d ser. 20 (1910): 86, 102–118.

22. The Protocol (report) of the Second Commission indicates that its own draft, which it had already prepared, coincided closely with a proposal later presented to it by which, for a gift, an enrichment was required and also that "both parties are agreed that the enrichment will occur *unentgeltlich*" (Mugdan, *Materialien*, 2: 735–736). Precisely when the Second Commission decided on its new phrasing is not disclosed in any source I have found.

is phrased by the Code in this inverted way, not as an element needed to produce an enforceable exchange but rather as something that the parties must agree to omit in order to have a gift. The new test clearly did not eliminate inquiries into the motives for conferring gains on others. But the initial question now became more specific, whether the producer of the gain aimed to secure compensation in the form of some act or abstention of the other party and thereby meet some need or serve some purpose of his own. If the answer was yes, the transaction was not a gift, no matter how magnanimous his purposes might otherwise have been. If the answer was no, then it probably was a gift.

The German Code listed numerous grounds for special treatment of gifts—more than the French—so the need for means of identifying them was made all the more apparent. Of these only two have been mentioned so far: (1) the requirement of notarization, applying only to promises of gift; and (2) guaranteed shares in inheritance, protected by cancelling or cutting back inter vivos gifts that deplete those shares. To these should be added the power of donors to revoke, on two grounds that are peculiar to gifts—the subsequent "gross ingratitude" of the donee[23] and the subsequent impoverishment of the donor[24]—and also on another

---

23. B.G.B., art. 530(1). The privilege is personal and (except where the donee has murdered the donor or has unlawfully prevented a revocation) is extinguished by the death of either. Ibid., arts. 530(2) and 532. This ground for revocation originated in late Roman law and applied at first only to gifts between certain near relatives (C.8.55.7 and C.8.55.9). It was more broadly phrased by Justinian in A.D. 530 (C.8.55[56].10) so as to include as marks of ingratitude "atrocious injuries," the laying on of "impious" hands, endangering the donor's life, and failure to carry out a charge imposed upon the gift.

24. B.G.B., arts. 519 and 528, the first applying to gifts merely promised and the latter to those already executed. To revoke on this ground, the donor would need to prove inability to support himself in a reasonable manner or to perform duties imposed on him by law for the support of his spouse or near relatives.

ground that is not so peculiar—the donee's failure to perform a condition.[25] In a variety of situations persons empowered to administer property that is owned in whole or in part by others are forbidden to dispose of their shares by gift—that is, without "recompense."[26] Gifts made by one married person for the purpose of defeating the rights of the other can also be set aside.[27] Gifts by insolvent debtors that will defeat or delay their creditors have provoked much litigation in German law, as they have in our own. But there are various disapproved ways of causing prejudice to creditors and from them there is no spill-over to speak of into the general law of gifts, so this topic will be ignored henceforth. The Code tests are sometimes used to identify gifts that are subject to taxation and these instances will be mentioned.

Altogether it would seem too much to expect that the Code definitions of gift could be applied uniformly over the whole broad range of miscellaneous purposes for which "un-recompensed" transactions are marked for special treatment. Some authors claim that it would be a mistake to try.[28] But the draftsmen of the Code were more ambitious. They aimed to provide a single set of all-purpose tests that would be used consistently wherever the Code itself applied.[29] We shall see whether they succeeded.

25. B.G.B., art. 527.

26. B.G.B., art. 1804 (guardian disposing of his ward's estate); art. 2205 (executor disposing of his decedent's estate); art. 1641 (parents administering property of their children); art. 1425 (married person administering assets of the marital community); art. 2113 (owner of limited interest disposing of or burdening his successor's interest).

27. B.G.B., arts. 1375 and 1390. Likewise art. 2287 provides for setting aside gifts that deplete the shares of heirs appointed by contract with another.

28. Burckhardt, *Zum Begriff der Schenkung*, pp. 4–24; A. Liebisch, *Das Wesen der unentgeltlichen Zuwendungen unter Lebenden* (1927), pp. 82–84.

29. Mugdan, *Materialien*, 2: 286.

The protracted efforts that produced the German Code have been given, no doubt, more attention than was needed. This has had, however, an ulterior motive. The provisions in the German Code on the topics here considered resemble closely the Code provisions in France, as should already be apparent. Yet the attitudes adopted toward them were from the outset very different. As a leading French author has put it, the French Code was viewed for decades after it first appeared as though it had suddenly "fallen from the sky."[30] In fact this strange celestial phenomenon had been prepared in four months by a commission of four men who for a connected statement of past and present law had not much more to guide them than the plausible banalities of Pothier.[31] The French Code was then driven through the legislative mill in a short two years by the imperious will of the dictator from whom the Code was named. There could hardly be a contrast more complete than with the prolonged and public process by which the German Code was drafted, rewritten, and searchingly reexamined before it was finally ratified. Even more important was the complete commitment of all those engaged to a grand design—a "modernized" Roman law that had been constructed by the German Pandectists through a century of effort, an intricate structure of legal ideas that the Code expressed in shorthand.

3. What is Giveable

In the critical reappraisal of Roman law that continued through the nineteenth century there had not been much disposition to expand the narrow limits defined in Roman

---

30. Planiol, *Traité élémentaire de droit civil*, 2d ed. (1901), 1: 43.

31. The profusion of sources and absence of structure in French legal literature of the late eighteenth century have been described elsewhere (Dawson, *Oracles of the Law*, pp. 347–350).

law on the interests or advantages that could be subjects of gift. On this issue, as on many others, the influence of Savigny was decisive. He gave a full account of the Roman solutions and applauded them all. He pointed out that the discussion of gifts by the Roman jurists had been centered almost exclusively on gifts between husband and wife, but he urged strongly that the tests they used to enforce the prohibition of such gifts were rational and workable and should be generalized.[1] He did not say, nor did the other authors who adhered to his views, that an additional purpose for controls over gifts had acquired high priority during the centuries intervening—forced heirship that required quotas to be set on inter vivos gifts to prevent depletion of "patrimonies" left at death. This was the effect (and perhaps also an unexpressed purpose) of the Roman law controls over gifts between husband and wife. For nineteenth-century Germans the tests used for this purpose must have had some added attraction because they gave the control needed, and no more than was needed, for the protection of forced heirship.

Savigny therefore required as the first element in a gift that the donor incur a loss through a depletion of his property (*Vermögen*). Equally essential was an enrichment of the donee that produced an increase in the donee's property. He reviewed and approved the standard exclusions—services and human conduct of every kind, deposit of goods, interest-free loans, and the use of assets in other ways. He did dig up one text of the Corpus Juris saying that the use of land could be the subject of a gift if it were shown that similar land was commonly rented, even though the use involved took nothing from its substance.[2] Some other nineteenth-century au-

1. Savigny, *System des heutigen römischen Rechts*, sec. 151. His discussion of the whole topic extends from section 142 to section 176.
2. Savigny, *System*, sec. 146. The Roman law text was D.39.5.9.pr.,

thors followed Savigny in this, though like him they confined
the concession to the rent-free use of land.[3] Before the Second Drafting Commission a group proposed that the Code
describe as a gift any service, facility, or advantage by which
"economic value" was transferred through profit foregone or
expenditure saved. The Commission rejected this proposal,
especially because of the unsettling effects it would have on
the law regulating inheritance and marital property.[4] So the
text of the Code that the Commission proposed and that was
finally adopted defined a gift as consisting, in its primary
elements, of "a disposition through which one person out of
his property enriches another."[5]

It is clear that this language, like that of the French Civil
Code, excludes human action or inaction of every kind as
potential subjects of gift. Mandate, which in Roman law had
been the leading example of the contract for gratuitous services, is listed in the German Code as a fully accredited contract and is defined as "unrecompensed."[6] The liabilities
attached to it are attenuated, since either party can termi-
nate it any time.[7] But it can generate enforceable duties
nevertheless—the principal must reimburse the "agent" for

---

which measured the value of the occupancy by the amount the occupant
saved. In the same passage, Savigny even threw off the suggestion that it
might be possible for services to be subjects of gift if they were of a type
commonly paid for.

3. H. Dernburg, *Pandekten*, 5th ed. (1897), vol. 2, sec. 106, and other
authors referred to by Liebisch, *Unentgeltlichen Zuwendungen* pp. 70–72.

4. Mugdan, *Materialien*, 2: 736–737.

5. B.G.B., art. 516.

6. B.G.B., art. 662. The effect of a finding that there was to be payment
would be, it seems, merely to change the name—to "work-contract,"
perhaps, instead of "mandate" (*Auftrag*).

7. B.G.B., art 671(1), though subsection (2) requires the mandatory
(agent) to give notice of termination "in such a way" that the mandator
(principal) can provide for completion of the task in some other way.

necessary expenses, the "agent" must account for any gains realized and undertakes to perform the mission assigned.[8]

Two other ghostly reminders of the Roman past are mentioned in the German Code, as they are in the French: the loan for use and the deposit, both applicable to movable goods. Though "unrecompensed," they are described as contracts and likewise can generate enforceable, though scaled-down, liabilities.[9] It is not for this reason, however, that the gratuitous use of another's property in these and other instances is not to be viewed as a gift. If the use of the asset was marketable, the owner would sacrifice a realizable profit and the user would usually save a measurable expenditure if no recompense was exacted. If the owner had a claim for restitution—perhaps because the use was from the outset wrongful or had been permitted under a contract that was then cancelled for fraud or mistake—the use would quite surely be an enrichment whose money value could be recovered.[10] But this is clearly not enough. For a gift the donor must be deprived in a particular way, through subtraction from his "property." This conclusion is even more firmly established in German law[11] than it is in the French, since

8. B.G.B., art. 670 (duty to reimburse for necessary expenses), art. 667 (duty to account for profits), 662 (duty to perform without recompense).

9. The Code (art. 598) defines the contract of loan (for use) as "unrecompensed." Article 599 makes the lender liable only for intentional or grossly negligent injuries and Article 601 requires the user to assume the normal costs of preserving the subject matter.

The contract for "custody" (*Verwahrung*) is the modern equivalent of the Roman deposit. A stipend can be expressly provided or can be inferred (B.G.B., art. 689). If it is "unrecompensed," the custodian owes a duty only to exercise the care that he is accustomed to exercise in his own affairs (B.G.B., art. 690).

10. A useful collection of authorities is given by H. Reeb, *Grundprobleme des Bereicherungsrechts* (1975), pp. 91–112.

11. Among the many authors who assert that gratuitous use of property is not a gift: L. Enneccerus-H. Lehmann, *Lehrbuch des bürgerlichen*

German courts have not followed the French example of
exempting from control gifts of "fruits and revenues"—not
merely the use that produces income but the assets that come
from income.

The property "out of" which the gift must come does not
need to have any connection with a physical subject matter.
Rights enforceable against third persons are readily assigned
by way of gift, provided the gifts are "executed" by language
of present transfer,[12] though if nothing more than a promise
to assign at some future time can be extracted from the language used, the promise, being a promise of gift, will be void
if not notarized.[13] Similarly, a release by a creditor of his own
debtor can be a gift to the debtor. Even an oral release will
suffice if the language indicates that immediate legal effect is
intended. But again, a promise of release at some future time,
made without "recompense," will be a promise of gift that
must be notarized, since a release would take the obligation
"out of" the creditor's "property."[14]

Rechts (1954), vol. 2, § 120; Liebisch, *Unentgeltlichen Verwendung*, pp.
68–82; K. Larenz, *Lehrbuch des Schuldrechts*, 7th ed., (1965), 2: 119.

12. *J.W.*, 1916, 37 (R.G., 1915), where a gift assignment was made by a
savings-bank depositor who wrote a letter to his sister: "If anything happens to me you are provided for, see to it that you receive the bankbook";
Warneyer, 1921, no. 123 (R.G., 1921), delivery to donee of a letter addressed to the debtor and instructing it to pay the donee; Warneyer, 1908,
no. 141 (1907), conditional assignment by a writing delivered to the donee.

Written directions to pay donees, delivered to the *debtors*, were held to
be effective assignments in *J.W.*, 1907, 73 (R.G., 1906), and Warneyer 1909,
no. 33 (R.G., 1908).

13. 161 *R.G.Z.* 6 (1939). Similarly, 7 *B.G.H.Z.* 378 (1952), promise to
split the assets of a partnership with no documentation other than recording the promisee's name as partner on the books of the partnership.

14. Releases by creditors, some of them oral and conditioned on some
future event, that were held to be presently operative gifts to the debtors
are referred to above, section 2, note 14. But in Warneyer, 1908, no. 302
(R.G., 1908), the court held that an endorsement by the creditor on the
debtor's promissory note that "this note becomes void on my death" was
merely a promise, not a presently effective release, and void because not

A gift can likewise be made by more indirect means, with third persons serving as intermediaries. It might take the form, for example, of payment of a debt that the intended donee already owes to a third party.[15] Or the benefactor can contract to buy some asset that is owned by a third party and arrange for title to be conveyed directly to the donee.[16] The money payments made in either case would meet the first test, since they would come "out of" the benefactor's own estate. But what if the land conveyed to the donee turned out to be worth either more or less than the sum paid for it; in that case what would the payor have "given," the money he paid or the land that the donee acquired?[17] This kind of question arises where premiums are paid for life insurance whose proceeds are to be paid to a third party. The total sum of premiums paid and the proceeds eventually payable are not at all likely to coincide. Where there is a discrepancy, which of the two sums is "given"? The short answer is: whichever is smaller; for impoverishment of the donor and enrichment of the donee are *both* essential. The beneficiary can collect the proceeds from the insurer in either case, since contracts

notarized. Other cases in which the same conclusion was reached because the creditor's words were construed to be words of promise: *J.W.*, 1911, 37 (R.G., 1910) and Warneyer 1911, no. 12 (R.G., 1910).

15. 167 *R.G.Z.* 199 (1941). The payment of the debt was held to be a gift to the debtor, revocable for the donee's subsequent ingratitude, unless the lower court on remand found that the donee after all had promised some recompense for the payment.

16. *J.W.*, 1928, 894 (R.G., 1927), another action to revoke for the donee's ingratitude.

17. This issue arose in 167 *R.G.Z.* 199, discussed above, note 15. Here the donor's payment of the donee's debt enabled the donee to secure the conveyance to her of a brewery. Revoking for donee's ingratitude, the donor wanted the donee to surrender the brewery, not merely the money the donor had paid. The Reichsgericht had earlier held that a donor in such a case could recover only what had come "out of" his estate, not its product as received by the donee. The court indicated a readiness to abandon this strict view but did not, in the end, answer the question.

for the benefit of third parties are fully enforceable in German law. But if the proceeds exceed the total of the premiums paid and a forced heir sues to set the gift aside, the gift will consist of the premiums paid, since the donor's loss sets a ceiling. The German high court that reached this conclusion also declared in the converse case, where the proceeds were less, that the gift would consist of the proceeds received, since the donee's gain if it is less also serves as a ceiling.[18]

Another proving ground for these ideas has been the promise to provide security for a debt owed to some third person. The usual form would be a promise of guaranty carrying personal liability in the guarantor, but the issue would be the same if he made land or goods available to be used as mortgage or pledge. In Roman law suretyship, well known and much used, was classified as a service, a form of mandate, and was therefore expected normally to be gratuitous. When a promise in either form is made nowadays, with no "recompense" given or promised, is it a promise of gift to either creditor or debtor? The answer in German law is—almost certainly no. If the promise is made directly to the

18. The leading case on the subject is 128 *R.G.Z.* 187 (1930), where the contest was between the beneficiary, widow of the insured, and the daughter of the insured by a former marriage who claimed her share as forced heir of her father. The premiums had totaled 20,823.80 marks and the proceeds of the policy were 83,295.20 marks. The insured had retained power to amend the policy in his lifetime, but the court was clear that on his death the beneficiary's right "vested" and was fully enforceable against the insurer. As against the insured's heir, nevertheless, she was a donee and must surrender the gift, which consisted of the premiums paid by the insured.

The same analysis was applied in 61 *R.G.Z.* 217 (1904) to the claim of an administrator of an insolvent estate to the proceeds of insurance payable to the insolvent's wife; only the premium payments made by the insolvent husband (not the proceeds paid to the wife) constituted a gift that could be set aside.

creditor, it merely adds further assurance that he will receive what he is already entitled to independently, through his debtor's existing debt to him.[19] Some authors have suggested that if the creditor knew his remedy against the debtor to be useless or highly uncertain, then he ought to know that the added security would confer a substantial economic advantage beyond what he had before and this might make a difference.[20] Then could the added security for payment of his debt be construed as a promise of gift to the debtor? The difficulty with this will be the absence of any loss to the guarantor. For if he is eventually forced to pay the debt or if the asset pledged is taken and sold through foreclosure, the principal debtor will be obligated to indemnify him and save him from loss. So the promisor's estate will not be diminished, it will merely have been subjected to risk.[21]

Some qualification is again needed. If the principal debtor expressly contracted away any duty to indemnify or perhaps if he were shown to be clearly judgment-proof, the promise might be construed to be a promise of gift but some such extra twist would be needed.[22] In the usual case, where

19. 90 *R.G.Z.* 177, 181 (1917) and *Rechtsprechung der Oberlandesgerichte* (1903), 8, 75; W. Schütz, "Schenkweise Sicherheiten," *Juristische Rundschau*, 1964, p. 453; Staudinger, *Kommentar zum B.G.B.*, art. 516, secs. 36–37.

20. This suggestion has been made by several authors, including Schütz and Staudinger, cited in the preceding note.

21. *Monatschrift für Deutsches Recht,* 1955, p. 282 (B.G.H., 1955); *Betriebsrater,* 1956, p. 446 (B.G.H., 1956).

22. Schütz, "Schenkweise Sicherheiten." It is more difficult to extract from French decisions any settled principle as to whether a promise to guarantee another's debt is to be construed as a promise of gift requiring notarization. Where the debt guaranteed arose from an exchange transaction in a commercial setting, the promise of guarantee is enforceable and is described as not a promise of gift. D.H. 1931, 531 (Lyon, 1931); D.1916.2.191 (Paris, 1913); D.1872.1.252 (1872); but in all these cases the guarantor had an economic interest in the survival and prosperity of the principal debtor. It has been held that the guarantee "takes color" from the

no such showing could be made, there would remain the risk
that the guarantor might be forced to pay and be unable to
secure indemnity, so as in the end to give something for nothing. But the peculiar feature of this case is that the event
that would cause both loss and gain—the forced payment—
would simultaneously operate to execute the gift; the Code
provides that performance of an unnotarized promise of gift
cures its defect of form. If the spirits of the Code draftsmen
still brood over the scene, they must nod their approval of
these results. An earlier draft of the Code had contained two
clauses stating expressly that the provision of security for
another's debt did not enrich the debtor or cause loss to the
guarantor. These clauses were struck by the Second Drafting
Commission on the ground that the conclusions were so obvious they did not need to be stated.[23]

In other situations it becomes still more clear that the
Code requirements of loss-plus-gain call for appraisal of all
elements of a transaction to determine their net effect. For a
finding that it will entail a loss, it is not enough that a measurable economic sacrifice will be made by the promisor,
even though it comes "out of" his property, if a gain will flow
to him from another direction so that he will end up no
poorer; the gain can even come at a subsequent time if at the
time of the initial transfer it was a highly probable consequence. So an oral promise of a stockholder to pay money to
the corporation will not be a promise of gift if the sum paid,
when used for the purpose specified, will increase the value

principal debt, so that if the principal debt was a promise of gift, the
guarantee will be likewise (S.1872.1.325 [1872]). But it has also been held
that a finding that the surety "intended" a gift (to his son) is decisive.
S.1890.1.206 (1889).

23. Mugdan, *Materialien*, 2: 739–740, discussed by Staudinger, Kommentar zum B.G.B., art. 516, sec. 36. Some members of the Commission
also offered as an additional reason for omitting the clauses that, if the
debtor was already judgment-proof, the promise might be considered a
promise of gift and that it was better to leave this issue open.

of his own shares in at least an equal amount.[24] More commonly the hard questions come at the other end of the equation, in deciding whether the recipient will end up richer as a net result and whether it matters if he does not. These problems we must postpone for the present.

When one compares the conclusions reached in French and German law as to what is giveable, the most remarkable feature, surely, is their extremely close resemblance. They coincide almost completely in their exclusions—the kinds of benefits or advantages that cannot be made into subjects of gift no matter how much fall-out gain they may generate. The main difference, not great, comes from the games the French play with "fruits and revenues," going a considerable distance toward excluding altogether from the controls over gifts the income and the products of income derived from property. The solutions in the two countries also coincide closely in defining the essential elements of gain and loss and the relative weight to be attributed to each. Most remarkable of all are the parallels between the solutions in both countries and those marked out in Roman law, centuries ago, for very different reasons. From this point onward, however, some differences will appear.

4. Forms of Recompense

Though a transaction has the effect, essential for a gift, of producing net loss, a depletion of assets, for one and an in-

24. 59 *R.G.Z.* 423 (1904), promise to corporation having two stockholders to pay organization costs, each stockholder contributing in proportion to his stockholdings. The court was clear that an equivalent increase in the value of the promisor's shares would be a "direct and necessary" result of his payment. Similar analysis is used in *N.J.W.*, 1951, 268 (B.G.H., 1951), where a brother in 1936 promised to make monthly payments to his sister on the "condition" that their father leave his estate equally to them both on his death, which occurred in 1939. The court pointed out that the father was induced by this promise to give his son an inheritance with greater value than the sums the latter had promised to pay his sister.

crease in assets for another, it can be made into an exchange, not a gift, by a recompense to the gain-producer that has no measurable economic value whatever. Thus parents who wish to bring about a marriage that one of their children contemplates may promise that, if the marriage occurs, they will make a payment or transfer to one or both of the newlyweds; the marriage, if it does occur, will be the promisors' recompense.[1] Or if a young woman who is engaged to marry is reluctant to resign a job she holds and thereby lose a pension to which she would otherwise be entitled, her fiancé, who prefers that she spend more time at home, can promise her a substantial sum if on their marriage she resigns; if they marry and she does resign his promise becomes enforceable, since the resignation is the recompense that the promisor desired.[2] The withholding of discreditable information whose disclosure would prevent a projected marriage can provide sufficient return for a promise to pay for silence.[3] If an employer wishes to prevent his retiring employee from disclosing to others manufacturing techniques that are used by the employer, the employee's nondisclosure can be a sufficient recompense for the employer's promise to pay him a lifetime pension.[4] Or where a hard-pressed debtor owes an overdue

1. Seuff. Arch. 62, no. 61 (R.G., 1906); Warneyer, 1908, no. 203 (1907); Gruchot, *Beiträge*, 51, 396 (R.G., 1906); Gruchot, *Beiträge*, 55, 920 (R.G., 1911).

2. *Leipziger Zeitschrift*, 1919, 1135 (R.G., 1919).

3. *M.D.R.*, 1957, 26 (Bundesgerichtshof, hereafter cited as B.G.H., 1955). Here the promisor, intending to marry a married man who was in the process of divorcing his first wife, promised to provide sums adequate to maintain the first wife if the wife's brother did not disclose the husband's past sexual misdeeds whose disclosure would prevent the divorce. Similarly, *Leipziger Zeitschrift*, 1916, 896 (R.G., 1916), where the payment was promised for not disclosing to the promisor's new wife the intimate relations, leading to the birth of an illegitimate child, that had existed between the promisor and a lady friend, the promisee.

4. Warneyer, 1914, no. 317 (R.G., 1914). And compare 94 *R.G.Z.* 157

debt, a well-disposed friend can effectively promise to guarantee the debt through a recompense supplied by the creditor, taking the form of an extension of time by creditor to debtor.[5]

As the last illustration suggests, any advantage that the transaction will produce can accrue, not to the one who is "recompensed," but to some third person who as beneficiary gives nothing. Where this result is reached it is usually accomplished by an exchange of promises, in which each promise entails only sacrifice for the promisor and the gain accrues to the third party. An example would be a case in which three sisters promised each other that each would pay their mother a specified sum of money to be used for the mother's support; each promise was a "recompense" for the others.[6] Performances that benefit third persons can also be purchased by paying cash (for example, in the form of premiums on life insurance made payable to another),[7] through the discharge of an existing debt,[8] or as one of the terms in a contract of sale.[9] If the objection is raised that one party to the

(1918), promise of retiring employee not to compete for a specific time with his employer.

5. 54 *R.G.Z.* 282 (1903).

6. Warneyer, 1914, no. 243 (R.G., 1914).

7. Illustrations appear in chapter 3, section 3, note 18.

8. In 88 *R.G.Z.* 137 (1915) the debtor was a bank. One of its depositors directed it to pay 5,000 marks to a designated Frau W. on the depositor's death and charge his account with that sum. This, the court held, was an exchange of a discharge of the bank's debt for a promise to a third party beneficiary (we might call it a novation), and did not require notarization. A similar case appears in 106 *R.G.Z.* 1 (1923).

Arrangements to benefit third parties are at times more complex. In Gruchot, *Beiträge,* 55, 923 (R.G., 1911) the defendant had promised to pay 100,000 marks to Lieutenant X if (1) X would marry defendant's daughter and (2) the plaintiff, uncle of X, would pay a debt of 19,250 marks that X owed a third person. Both events occurred but defendant did not perform his promise to pay 100,000 marks to X. Plaintiff, the promisee, was held entitled to enforce the promise to pay X 100,000 marks.

9. In 112 *R.G.Z.* 362 (1926) the inventor of a machine usable in au-

purported exchange will receive nothing in return for his own sacrifice, the answer will be familiar to an American reader—he will receive precisely what he sought, a gain for someone else.

For a time, immediately before and after the Code took effect, there were some respectable authors who contended that the "recompense" sufficient to make a promise enforceable must first become the subject of a promise—that an exchange of promises was essential. This was an aberration that may perhaps be explained by the novelty in this context of the *Entgelt* idea.[10] But it was odd that the question should have been raised at all, for the exchange structured as an act for a promise (or a promise for an act) was fully established in late Roman law well before the end of the classical period. It is true that the word *Entgelt* (like "recompense," which I have used to translate it) carries with it a strong implication of reimbursement or return "for" something else. This element of exchange was fairly easy to infer where promises were made at about the same time, each promisor making his promise directly to the other. But if there was only one promise and its recompense would have to be an act (or abstention) that might occur at some other time and could serve purposes that were quite different, a close look at motives might be needed. In order to look closely it would be necessary also to define, as Romanesque sources had not had to do, precisely what one was looking for.

An occasion for defining the test more precisely was pro-

tomobile production assigned his patent and agreed not to manufacture any similar machines, in return for 50,000 marks which the seller directed the buyer to pay to the seller's brother. When sued for an injunction against making any similar machines, the seller's contention that his promise was "unrecompensed" was dismissed abruptly.

10. The almost complete absence of discussion of the *Entgelt* concept in earlier German legal writing is commented on by Haymann, *Die Schenkung*, pp. 5–6.

vided by a case that reached the high court in 1906. Here the
promisor, the defendant, was a married man who had impreg-
nated a female servant. Defendant, before the child was
born, promised to pay another man whom he knew a substantial sum if he would marry the pregnant woman, and also
promised the woman regular payments for the child's support if she would marry his friend. The two then married. An
action brought by the male promisee to enforce the two
promises was dismissed in the lower court because the newlyweds had not exchanged promises to marry. The lower
court concluded that the defendant had therefore received
no recompense and his promises were promises of gift. The
Reichsgericht reversed. It declared that objective tests must
be used to determine whether the payments promised would
enrich the promisees, as in this case they clearly would. But
whether the marriage was a recompense depended on subjective tests of motive. The court said that even though it
appeared that the two promisees before the defendant's
promises were made had already formed a firm purpose to
marry, the critical questions were: (1) whether one of their
motives (though not necessarily a decisive motive) was that
of securing the payments promised; and (2) whether the defendant promisor included among his own motives that of
bringing about the marriage. The latter motive, if it was
found to have existed in fact, would make the marriage when
it occurred a recompense, so that his promises would not be
promises of gift.[11]

These ideas were clarified and developed further by the
authors. The notion that an exchange of promises was
needed was refuted convincingly by a leading scholar, writing in 1912. It was enough, he argued, that the action or inaction of the other party was a "desired counterperformance"

11. 62 *R.G.Z.* 273 (1906).

and its linkage with the promise could be shown by language of condition or any other suitable means.[12] As another author pointed out, in answering the essential question, which was one of psychological fact, it would be important to know whether the performance of the other would promote some interest or meet some need of the one who made the promise. To have a full-scale exchange it was essential, he argued, "that each side conceive its own performance as a means for securing from the other the proposed counterperformance." It would not have to be *the* motive—that is, the sole or even the predominant motive—for there could be various motives, intermingled. It was necessary only to find that in fact the securing of the other's performance was one of the motives included.[13]

There is an air of novelty, almost of new discovery, that surrounds the unveiling, in German, of this conception of the bargained-for exchange, which coincides so closely with our own. The notion of exchange was familiar enough, in Germany too: the notion that act A is to occur "in order to secure" or "in return for" act B. But the problems in identifying exchange transactions were now presented in a new way. In transactions on the fringe between trade and gift, some important legal consequences had been made to depend on the *absence* of any recompense for the gain conferred; the Code also required some kind of showing that the parties had agreed there was none. An explicit agreement on what was *not* included could seldom be expected; ordinarily the most

12. P. Oertmann, *Entgeltliche Geschäfte* (1912), pp. 7–46. He referred (pp. 7–11) to the numerous earlier German writers who had maintained a contrary view and made good use, in support of his argument, of the Roman "innominate" contracts (pp. 23–35). Later German decisions that have found an act sufficient recompense for a promise: Gruchot, *Beiträge*, 55, 923 (R.G., 1911); *J.W.*, 1911, 278 (R.G., 1911); *J.W.*, 1938, 91 (R.G., 1937); *N.J.W.*, 1951, 268 (B.G.H., 1951).
13. Haymann, *Die Schenkung*, pp. 15–21.

that could be shown would be an awareness in both parties that no recompense had been proposed or arranged. But if there was doubt—if the gain-receiver was to take some action or produce some result that the gain-producer *might* have desired—the new test called for an answer to an unfamiliar question that was posed in an awkward way.

On another question that was, in contrast, entirely familiar there was from the outset full agreement. A recompense could suffice though it had no economic value whatever or a value much lower so that the exchange produced was very unequal. Several of the early court decisions already mentioned took this view without hesitation. Authors could cite the consensus reached in nineteenth-century German literature, the strong opposition that had then developed to judicial review to ensure equality in values exchanged.[14] If the excess gain was intended as a gift, some perplexing problems could arise, as the next section will indicate. But the German high court in 1960 seized the occasion to reaffirm its view that the test of recompense did not of itself reopen inquiries into disparities in values in exchange transactions.

The case that provided the occasion was one in which the reason for inquiring was, as the court conceded, as persuasive as it could be. An heir was suing to set aside a sale of land for a price well below its market value, claiming that his guaranteed share in the estate of the seller, since deceased, had thereby been depleted. The court declared that if it were enough to show an inequality in the values exchanged of which the contracting parties were aware, then they would not be free, as they ought to be, to place their own valuations on the performances they exchanged. In the particular case of the forced heir, this would mean that sales made by a decedent in his lifetime would be subject to cancellation for ten

14. Ibid., pp. 12–14 collects references to standard nineteenth-century authors.

years after his death and that purchasers in such sales would be subject for the same length of time to claims for restitution that they had not had reason to anticipate. Furthermore, this would be a misreading of the Civil Code which explicitly required something more—a finding that both parties *agreed* on the omission of any recompense. Their knowledge that the sale price was very low would not be enough to prove this; despite this knowledge there could be an exchange and for each of the parties a recompense.[15]

Another form that an exchange can take is the payment of an existing debt. If the debt is enforceable and the participants have the same conception of its existence and amount, the recompense will be of course the discharge produced by the payment.[16] What if the conceptions of the parties differ, as in a case decided in 1909 where a man performed services, including legal services, for the widow of a friend who had recently died? In rendering the services, the plaintiff at no time intended to charge for them and indeed hoped later to marry the widow himself. The widow, believing throughout that she had been under a legal duty to pay him (and having later rejected his proposal of marriage), promised to pay him a specific sum but then failed to pay. The plaintiff sued for this sum and recovered. Having rendered the services without mistake and with no expectation of payment, the plaintiff clearly could not have recovered at all without the express promise by the widow. But the court concluded that this was not a promise of gift, for the widow-promisor believed that the money was due and that she was to secure a recompense through discharge of this supposed, though nonexistent, debt. It might seem strange that the disagreement between

15. *N.J.W.*, 1961, 604 (B.G.H., 1960).

16. 50 *R.G.Z.* 134 (1902); 88 *R.G.Z.* 137 (1915); 125 *R.G.Z.* 380, 383; Liebisch, *Unentgeltlichen Zuwendungen*, pp. 40–41; *Commentary of Reichsgericht Judges*, (1959), art. 516, n. 21.

the parties as to the existence of a debt—their misunderstanding, one might say—could produce an enforceable promise. But the promise could not be a promise of gift since *both* parties had not agreed that there was to be no recompense. There was no other ground for objecting to the promise and the widow, at least, secured what she wanted, the discharge of a debt that *she* thought she owed.[17]

Divergent views of this kind can also appear in reverse order—the promisor being convinced that his promise was one of gift and the promisee equally convinced that he was entitled to the performance promised. In some promises of pensions to superannuated employees this feature appeared. In a case decided in 1911, a cashier of a business enterprise was notified after twenty-seven years of service that his employment was ended. Accompanying the notice was a statement that he would be paid a pension of 100 marks a year. After paying these sums for a year and half, the employer sued for a declaratory judgment that the promise of a pension, being an unnotarized promise of gift, was void. The Reichsgericht concluded: not so. Defendant, the employee, testified at the trial that he considered the pension payments to be due him for his long service. The court pointed out that if the employer considered its promise to be one of gift, it did not at any time say so and seek to secure the promisee's agreement that no obligation existed.[18]

Where the main object of the transaction was, as in this instance, to reimburse for services or other benefits received

17. 72 *R.G.Z.* 188 (1909). A similar case is 74 *R.G.Z.* 139 (1910), where a sister, out of sisterly affection and without intending to charge, helped her brother, a broker, to sell machinery to the sister's husband and the brother (defendant in the action) believed she had earned half of his broker's commission and signed a note of promising to pay her this. The promise was held to be enforceable, since the parties had not agreed on an absence of recompense.

18. 75 *R.G.Z.* 325 (1911).

in the past, the elements of an exchange might be discovered by another route, by finding that the payment or promise discharged a duty that was strongly felt as morally though not legally binding. The test of recompense, as all now agreed, was subjective in the sense that it must be something that was in fact desired by the one to be "recompensed." Could it be subjective in the different sense of being *felt* to be due though not enforceable by action? For a time it seemed that this was enough. Suppose, for example, a substantial payment made by a corporation to one of its directors as a reward for valuable services in the past; though it was expressly found that no legal duty had existed to pay for them, "a feeling of real obligation on both sides" led the court to conclude that the payment was not a gift.[19] Household services rendered in the past could generate enough impulse to give reimbursement so that promises of future payment should be enforceable.[20] The same could be true of benefits received incidentally through services rendered to third persons under contracts with them.[21] Or the father of an illegitimate child could effectively promise the mother to support it though not himself legally bound to do so.[22]

This small cluster of cases stirred some echoes. In the

19. 94 *R.G.Z.* 332 (1919), the question being whether the 50,000 marks paid were a gift within the gift-tax statute, which had adopted the Civil Code definition of gift. Similarly, 94 *R.G.Z.* 157 (1918) where a promise of a pension to a retired employee was held to be enforceable because it reflected a commendable sense of responsibility in the employer.

20. *J.W.*, 1917, 710 (R.G., 1916); 98 *R.G.Z.* 176 (1920). But the claim of a man that he had given "the best years of his life" and sacrificed opportunities to marry in order to live with the female defendant was dismissed abruptly when presented as a reason for her promise to pay him 5,000 marks.

21. Estate brokers who had been hired but not paid by third persons: *J.W.*, 1911, 94 (R.G., 1910); Seuff. Arch. 70, no. 212 (R.G., 1914). Similarly, *Das Recht*, 1909, no. 1984.

22. *J.W.*, 1917, 103 (R.G., 1916).

Romanesque tradition as it had been transplanted to Germany, natural or moral obligation had continued to play a significant role, as a reason both for the enforcement of promises and for upholding conveyances already made.[23] In the German Code these ideas had reappeared, though only to perform the second function. Where transfers complying with moral duty had already been made, for example, restitution on the ground of unjust enrichment was expressly excluded by the Code.[24] Donors similarly could not revoke them on any one of the three standard grounds for revoking gifts,[25] and—more significant still—transfers in compliance with moral duty could not be cancelled or cut back on the ground that they had encroached on the shares guaranteed to forced heirs.[26] Taken together these measures clearly showed a strong purpose to sustain transfers that had already been made in compliance with moral duty. So German courts faced the kind of question that can arise in reading any legislation, but especially in reading a code. Should these provisions be taken to express a broader purpose that applied as well to promises inspired by similar motives but not yet performed, so that, as in France, such promises would be

23. R. Schmidt, "Die rechtliche Wirkung der Befolgung sittlicher Pflichten," in *Die Reichsgerichtspraxis im deutschen Rechtsleben* (1929), pp. 25–27.

24. B.G.B., art. 814, the description being "transfers that correspond with moral duty or the respect that is due for propriety."

25. B.G.B., art. 534.

26. B.G.B., art. 2330. There are several other Code provisions that give special immunity to gifts inspired by moral duty. All these provisions invalidate gifts of assets belonging in whole or in part to others, made by persons engaged in administering them. These provisions then make exceptions for gifts that "correspond with moral duty." Arts. 1425(2) (married person administering community property); 1641 (parent administering child's property); 1804 (guardian); 2112(3) (heir with interest of limited duration who burdens a successor's interest); 2205 (testamentary executor).

exempt within wide and undefinable limits from the Code requirement of notarization? Or should strict barriers be set to such excursions, so that *expressio unius* or *plurium* should be considered to be an *exclusio alteriorum* that left no doors ajar?

The reaction came in 1929, in a case in which there could hardly have been even a lingering sensation that a contingent or potential legal liability had reinforced the dictates of conscience. For the promise was made by a registered business partnership engaged in the wholesale lumber business. The promise was to pay a sum of money—8,000 marks—to the two illegitimate children of the founder and sole owner of the business, who had died before the promise was made. His heirs were his widow and one legitimate child, who had inherited substantially nothing except their shares in the partnership, so the most direct solution was for the partnership to make the promise, as it did with their full approval. The lower court found that these heirs felt themselves to be morally bound to make this provision for the two illegitimate children, plaintiffs in the action. The Reichsgericht concluded that this attribution to moral duty clinched the matter: if the promise was inspired by moral duty, that meant that it was a promise of gift and, not being notarized, was void. Strangely enough, this conclusion was rested mainly on a Code provision that had usually been read as validating such transactions. This was the clause that excluded revocation by donors of "gifts that correspond with moral duty." By describing the transfers as gifts, the court said, the Code by necessary implication declared that the discharge of moral duty is not and cannot be a recompense for any other purpose. The implication, many argue, was not necessary at all, but the consequence has been sweeping.[27]

27. 125 *R.G.Z.* 380 (1929). The court took the precaution of adding that this conclusion did not apply to promises made in return for the discharge of legally enforceable duties, which would of course be a recompense.

This decision surely came as a sudden shock to the numerous authors who had applauded the willingness previously shown to accept as a sufficient recompense the discharge of moral duty. The results in French law had been well known and greatly praised for the encouragement they were thought to give to the higher impulses in human nature.[28] For a man of honor, it was said, duty resting on conscience could be "more pressing" than any duty that courts could enforce (though it was not explained why, if this were true, enforcement by courts was needed).[29] These authors conceded that some limits must be set, that the moral duties they had in mind must arise out of definable relations, something more than the generalized love of neighbors that religion had prescribed.[30] The limits now set are narrow indeed and have been maintained consistently. Promises to perform moral duties, where nothing more than this is involved, have

28. A very useful survey of the literature up to that time, not only German but French, Italian, and English, is that of Schmidt, "Die rechtliche Wirkung," p. 25. French decisions are discussed on pp. 27–32. The author indicated that preparation of his paper was completed in January 1928, slightly more than a year before the Reichsgericht decision cited in the preceding note.

29. Liebisch, *Unentgeltlichen Zuwendungen*, pp. 43–49. These passages, like the survey of Schmidt, describe much dispute among the authors and some views that were directly contrary to their own. But both are emphatic in insisting that moral obligation *must* be enough; for Liebisch any other view would be a degraded form of materialism. These authors had considered the argument that could be based on B.G.B., art. 534 and that the Reichsgericht made use of in the turning-point decision in 125 *R.G.Z.* 380 (1929) (see above, n. 27). They contended that art. 534 aimed only at *sustaining* transfers that complied with moral duty and did not contain a reverse implication that all transactions complying with moral duty were for that reason gifts. Schmidt, "Die rechtliche Wirkung," pp. 38–40; Liebisch, pp. 43–45.

30. Schmidt, "Die rechtliche Wirkung," pp. 40–45, giving illustrations of the kinds of "special connection" between giver or taker that make the required moral duty into something more definite than a duty to "do good." For Liebisch the test was whether the promisor had the "feeling" that he *must* perform the duty in order to "face his own conscience."

almost disappeared from German law reports. If the parties were shown to have believed in fact (though erroneously) that an enforceable duty had existed, its discharge might be held to be a recompense and make a new promise enforceable.[31] It might even be that a subjective view would be carried one step further, to a situation where the existence of enforceable obligation had been left doubtful or unclear to one or both parties.[32] But if it is understood that the duty was inspired only by conscience, its discharge would now quite surely be considered insufficient as a recompense and a promise to comply would be void unless notarized. Why the sudden shift occurred one can only guess. Though German courts have not developed any catchword comparable to our "detriment" test, there may have been at work some thought that the promisee in such a case would not have given up very much. It is more likely that the terrain already exposed by three decades of experience was found by the court to be so uncharted and befogged that judges were losing their way.

When these clouds that had drifted in from the past were

31. The pre-1929 decision in Seuff. Arch., 70, no. 213 (R.G., 1915) involved a promise by a discharged bankrupt to pay a creditor the whole debt originally due. The court made a point of the fact that the parties both believed the unpaid debt survived the discharge. If a similar showing were made nowadays, it seems a reasonable guess that it would suffice.

The Code (art. 222) provides expressly that an obligation barred by lapse of time can be revived by a written acknowledgement or by giving security. The Reichsgericht has held that one or the other of these requirements must be met: 78 *R.G.Z.* 163 (1911). In *J.W.*, 1928, 1388, the court had been more lenient and invoked moral duty to uphold an informal promise to pay a time-barred obligation.

32. This seems to be the contention of Werner Lorenz, "Entgeltliche und unentgeltliche Geschäfte," *Jus Privatum Gentium* (Festschrift für Max Rheinstein (1969), 2: 547, 554–561. He urged that the reasoning of 125 R.G.Z. 380 (above, note 27) should be confined to situations where the parties are "truly" agreed that the performance promised is required only by moral duty. He urged also that there is no need to safeguard promises in which the parties were content to leave this question unanswered.

stripped away, the meaning of *Entgelt* emerged still more distinctly. *Entgelt*—"recompense"—is that other component in an exchange that is in fact sought by one and rendered in return by the other. As formulated in the German Code, the requirement was that the parties agree on its *absence*. This roundabout mode of expression has not made a difference in any but a few rare cases. Expressions of agreement will ordinarily center on what is to be included, not on the enormously wide range of elements omitted. Seldom will there be divergence in the views of the parties as to the presence or absence of some return for the gain that is to be conferred. If this should occur, the disagreement, it is true, will preclude a finding of gift because one party will then conceive it to be an exchange. But such cases, as one might expect, are exceedingly rare. Most of the time the reason why private transactions fall outside the controls over gifts is that both parties know that each will have a recompense that each has bargained for in fact.

5. *Mixed Gifts*

The real stress comes where the Code's distinctions between gift and exchange must be applied to transactions in which the participants intend to include some elements of both. The combinations can occur in a variety of forms, but the broad distinction commonly drawn is between the gift with charge and the exchange mixed with gift. Though at times it becomes difficult to distinguish between them, they differ enough in external forms to require separate treatment.

A. *The Gift with Charge*

The starting point is that a gift with charge (*Schenkung unter Auflage*) is a gift, not an exchange, though the Code treats it as almost a contract. After the gift has been fully executed by the donor, for example, he can sue to compel performance of the charge.[1] Or if it has not been completed, he can cancel whatever transfer he has made, using the tests provided by the Code for cancellation of contracts on the ground of breach, and can then recover the object given, using the unjust enrichment provisions of the Code.[2] Similar remedies had existed in Roman law where the gift *sub modo*, as it came to be called, was much discussed by the classical jurists.[3] It had such a prominent position, no doubt, because Roman contract law was for so long walled off into separate compartments that it provided not much shelter for transactions like these, far out on the fringe of contract. The gift *sub modo* and the double-barreled remedies provided for it were a familiar part of the legacy from Rome and were incorporated in the Code without contest.[4]

A recurring problem that is relevant here is that of distinguishing such transactions from contracts of exchange. For the purpose in imposing a charge on a gift will normally be to ensure that some act or result desired by the donor will occur. Could this be a "recompense," so as to produce an exchange? For a time a test was urged that would minimize probes into motives, so that an *Auflage*, as its German name suggests, must be a burden that subtracts from the gain trans-

1. B.G.B., art. 525 (1). Subsection (2) provides further that if performance of the charge is "in the public interest," the appropriate public officials after the donor's death can sue to enforce it.

2. Article 527 (1). Restitution is here limited to the portion of the gift that "should have been applied to performance of the charge."

3. Girard, *Manuel élémentaire du droit romain,* 8th ed., (1929), pp. 64, 480, 1002. Through most of the classical period direct enforcement required a formal stipulation by the donee, but late imperial legislation dispensed with this.

4. A full and interesting account of both the Roman solutions and their later reworking is given by F. Haymann, *Die Schenkung unter einer Auflage* (1905), pp. 22–56.

ferred.[5] And it is true that in the gift with charge it would be normal to expect the subject of the gift to supply the resources needed to perform the charge. The Code seemed to assume this by allowing the donee to suspend performance of the charge if the assets given proved insufficient.[6] But this is not the same thing as saying that a charge could not be imposed in such a way as to draw on a donee's other resources.[7] Still less did it answer the essential question, which called inescapably for a probing of motives. This subtraction test is still useful but is no longer thought to be controlling.[8]

Another line of inquiry has proved more productive: for whose advantage was the charge imposed, that of donee, donor, or outsiders? The first of these suggestions might at first sight seem peculiar, that a term introduced as a restriction or burden could be intended to work to the donee's advantage. The Roman sources, however, referred fairly often

5. The leading protagonists of this view were Oertmann, *Entgeltliche Geschäfte,* pp. 52–61 (1912) and Haymann, *Die Schenkung unter einer Auflage,* pp. 56–77.

6. B.G.B., art. 526. In the two cases reported in 112 *R.G.Z.* 210 (1925) and 112 *R.G.Z.* 237 (1928), this provision was extended to relieve churches of charges on gifts requiring them to maintain graves of members of the donors' families. The churches proved that the great inflation after the First World War had wiped out the investments they had acquired with the money originally given. In the case first cited, the Reichsgericht rejected with indignation the conclusion reached by the lower court that the arrangement was a contract of exchange and asserted strongly that a church was not a commercial enterpriser making "work contracts" so that it must have assumed this burden out of piety and honor for the dead. Would the court have said the same if the church had been seeking to enforce an unnotarized promise to contribute money for the same purpose?

7. Liebisch, *Unentgeltliche Zuwendungen,* pp. 30–31, gives a hypothetical example of a gift of money to a university with a charge that it thereafter open to the public a castle garden that the university already owned. Oertmann's thesis required him to say that this must be a contract of exchange. Liebisch insisted that in this and similar cases such an arrangement could be made perfectly well through a gift with charge.

8. Enneccerus-Lehmann, *Lehrbuch,* vol. 2, sec. 125.

to charges on gifts whose principal function was to define the purpose for which the benefaction was to be used—to buy a house, to take a trip, or to carry on a course of study. And benefactions nowadays will often define some specific destination for the resources transferred—funds for a church to repair its chapel, for a town to build a hall or buy a park. It seems that such transactions can fit the tests for gifts with charge and that the remedies provided by the Code—direct enforcement or cancellation—could be used if needed.[9] With this type of charge, however, problems have seldom arisen. The transferees will usually have their own incentives to comply and the activity called for by the charge will promote no interest of the donors, so that it is not likely to be thought of as a "recompense" for them, one side of a two-way exchange.

The inference will be strong the other way, however, where the advantage that the charge will produce will accrue directly to the donor himself. Some problems remain. Even here the transaction will appear to be primarily a gift as the activity called for from the receiver is diminished, so that the charge looks more and more like a mere subtraction from the gift itself. Examples would be a reservation by the transferor of a right to reside for life on land conveyed,[10] or an existing mortgage that the transferee does not assume. But even if the transferee does assume the mortgage, an inquisitive court can ask—was this was something the "donor"-debtor

9. As is pointed out in the excellent account by Haymann, *Die Schenkung*, pp. 22–39, the charge that merely produced or defined the benefits to be received by the donee came to be called the *modus simplex*. It was denied affirmative enforcement in the intermediate centuries, but the Code now makes it enforceable.

10. Held to be merely subtraction from the gift; *N.J.W.*, 1949, p. 260 (*O.G.H.Z.*, 1948); *N.J.W.*, 1949, 788 (Oberlandesgericht, hereafter cited as O.L.G., Bamberg, 1948).

really wanted enough to form part of an agreed exchange?[11] Or if the charge takes the form of periodic payments by the transferee and the amounts are small, the conclusion may be that the payments are not "for," but merely "out of" the asset transferred.[12] As a noted scholar has said, the distinction in such cases between exchange and gift with charge is one that is "often almost impossible" to make.[13] Fortunately not much depends upon it. If the transaction can be attacked on some other ground, such as "ingratitude" of the donee or impairment of a forced heir's guaranteed share, it may be somewhat easier to unwind completely if it has been labeled a gift, but the recovery allowed will be much the same.[14]

11. 60 *R.G.Z.* 238 (1905). Here a house valued at 54,000 marks was conveyed from one sister to another by a document that provided as a "condition" that the transferee assume a 49,000-mark mortgage as well as all other liens on the property. The contention of tax authorities that the gift tax should be based on the 54,000-mark value of the estate without any encumbrance must have been wrong from every point of view, but the court went on to describe at length the vital difference between an exchange and a gift with charge. It concluded that this was not an exchange but a gift with charge, since the donor-sister was about to leave for a long stay in America and must have been wholly indifferent about relief from her liability on the mortgage.

12. 2 *O.G.H.Z.* 289 (High Court for the British Zone, 1948). This case is not quite apposite because the payments called for by the charge were to be made, not to the donor himself, but to two sisters of the transferee-"donee." The action was one by the donor to cancel for the donee's ingratitude. The court conceded that this might be thought of as a gift "mixed" with exchange but concluded that in either case the donor should recover the land conveyed.

13. Professor Helmut Coing, comment on the case cited in the preceding note, in *N.J.W.*, 1949, p. 260. He approved the decision for both its result and its reasoning.

14. It should be noted again (see n. 2, above) that if the ground for the donor's revocation is the donee's nonperformance of a charge, the donor will recover only that portion of the gift that "should have been" expended in performing the charge. The result, seemingly, is an apportionment not much different in result from that achieved in unscrambling mixed gifts (discussed in the next section). Revocation of gifts on other grounds was

The third type of charge, in which the advantage to be conferred will accrue to outsiders, opened an avenue that led in a different direction: toward escape from the Code's whole scheme for control of gifts. The reasoning was simple and all too familiar. If the gain to be received must all be expended for some purpose not connected with either donor or donee, the donee will not be enriched; likewise, if only part must be expended, the donee *to that extent* is not enriched, since for centuries one inescapable test for a gift had been the extent of the donee's enrichment. The case that led the German high court in 1905 to this conclusion presented the issue clearly. It involved a promise to contribute to a registered nonprofit association that had been organized to promote cremation. The association had decided to build a crematorium on land owned by the local city government, and by its own charter the association was required to deposit all extraordinary receipts from outside sources in a fund to be used for that purpose. It secured a promise from a single contributor to pay 50,000 marks in five instalments to cover the whole cost of the project. Construction of the new building was begun and the contributor paid two 10,000-mark instalments but then refused to pay more as a result of disputes with the officers of the association. When sued, he defended on the ground that his promise, not notarized, was a promise of gift and void. Not so, the court held. The money was all to be spent for purposes that were to promote the public good; even the building, if completed, would be located on city-owned land. The association was not enriched so it was not a promise of gift and notarization was not needed.[15]

---

sought in 1 *O.G.H.Z.* 289 (1948) and 2 *O.G.H.Z.* 289 (1949), both of them decisions of the High Court of the British Zone involving gifts with charge. In both cases total cancellation was granted, under tests somewhat less strict than those for unmixing of mixed gifts.

15. 62 *R.G.Z.* 386 (1905).

Some of the implications of this were seen quickly. The very next year the Reichsgericht encountered a case in which a payment had been made to a church corporation, to be used to construct a church building and pastor's house. The question was whether the payment should be taxed as a gift under a tax statute that borrowed verbatim the Civil Code definition of gift. The court concluded that it *must* be taxed, since otherwise payments to incorporated groups, organized to promote altruistic purposes, would all be exempt from taxation. To support its conclusion, the court argued further that a "juristic person" cannot be divorced from the purposes for which it is organized, that since the sums paid to the church corporation in the particular case would have to be spent to achieve one, at least, of the purposes defined by its charter, it was a gift to the church.[16] This conclusion was followed in later tax cases[17] and was then very broadly generalized. It is now part of the common learning that if a benefactor chooses a "juristic person" to distribute his bounty for some socially beneficial purpose to which the "juristic person" is already committed, the transfer will be for all purposes a gift.[18]

The difficulty clearly was that in viewing the transaction through an ancient telescope, the Roman conception of gift,

16. 71 *R.G.Z.* 140 (1906). The court was clear that the definition of gift in article 516 of the Civil Code controlled in applying the gift tax, so its argument dealt with the issue in general terms. The court had a hard time distinguishing its own decision the year before (cited in the preceding note). It said that was a different case but did not indicate why.

17. *J.W.*, 1909, 397 (R.G., 1909), association for the care of ill and frail children; *J.W.*, 1913, 640 (R.G., 1913), home for poor children.

18. Liebisch, *Unentgeltlichen Zuwendungen,* pp. 62–66, 104–108; Commentary on the B.G.B. by Reichsgericht judges, art. 516, n. 4 (11th ed., 1959); Soergel-Siebert, commentary on the B.G.B., art. 516, nn. 27–28 (9th ed., 1962). The great difficulties that French courts have had in discovering solutions for promises of gift to organized charities are referred to above in chapter 2, section 4, note 16.

the court kept it focused on the first receiver, the inter-mediary chosen by the donor to distribute his bounty. If German courts and lawyers had been more accustomed to observing gifts to trustees, which are none the less gifts though the trustees will make no profit, they might have looked beyond the first receiver to view the total effect—pure benefaction through a chosen instrument. But this would have raised another troublesome question: for a gift has it not always been required that there be a donee? Where the directive is to transfer a specified fund to a named indi-vidual on the occurrence of a certain event, it is entirely pos-sible for a German court to disregard the go-between and consider the transaction a gift to the ultimate receiver.[19] But where is the donee if the purpose is to promote an ideal of human betterment, like cremation of the dead, to bring ben-efits to an indefinite or shifting group of persons or perhaps to some segment of the animal kingdom? And from whom would such benefactions be retrieved if their recall was needed? One can at least say that the high court was prompt in its response and did what it could to close off this avenue of escape from the controls over gifts, though the roadblock only reaches "juristic persons."

Where the intermediary chosen to distribute the fund is a natural person who wears no corporate veil, the test of the donee's enrichment is put back to work: there will be no gift to the extent that the resources transferred will be or should be consumed in performing the charge. This does not mean that the charge itself disappears as a limitation. If its purpose fails or cannot be accomplished, the transfer can be cancelled

19. *Deutsche Notar Zeitung*, 1932, 71, no. 19 (R.G. 1932). Here land was transferred to a woman with a directive to transfer a half-interest to her eleven-year-old child if the transferee remarried. This was held to be a gift to the child, accepted on its behalf by the mother.

and the fund recaptured.[20] If the charge can be or has been accomplished, however, the result is an exemption for a wide range of gifts for what we would call charitable purposes, in which an intermediary is used and the ultimate beneficiaries are left undefined. Courts have thereby been enabled to enforce some highly meritorious contributions to the general good. As our own courts have found in similar situations, the desire to sustain them may be further reinforced by reliance placed on assurances given by persons who pose as public benefactors, though it should be noted that German courts do not lay stress on reliance as a separate and sufficient motive for enforcing such transactions.[21]

20. In 105 *R.G.Z.* 305 (1922), the widow of a regimental officer transferred 100,000 marks to an unregistered "foundation" (*Stiftung*) with a direction that the income be paid to any officer of the regiment who had her husband's family name or, if there were none, to any officer who was less well endowed than the rest. The regiment was then disbanded. The court concluded that the foundation was not a juristic person, that the founder's creation of the fund was not a gift since none of its managers were to profit, but that her heirs could recover the unspent balance that remained, since the purpose of the transfer had failed.

21. An example was the case reported in 38 Rechtsprechung der O.L.G. 114 (O.L.G., Koln, 1916). A town community, evidently not a "juristic person" for this purpose, secured from a group of local citizens promises to pay specified sums of money to the town, which it was to turn over to a street railway company to contribute to the cost of extending the street railway to an outlying community. The town then signed a contract with the railway company, which agreed to construct the extension. The extension was built and put into service before the plaintiff refused to perform his promise, claiming that it was a promise of gift, unnotarized. The court concluded that the town was under a duty to turn over to the railway any money paid by the plaintiff, that the town would therefore not be enriched so the promise was not one of gift, adding that it was intended "to accomplish a purpose that was for the common good, beneficial and ideal" so that it should be enforced though not notarized. The town's and the railway's expenditure in reliance was mentioned in one short sentence.

In the crematorium case (above, n. 15) which began this series of cases, the court had laid no stress at all on the fact that after the promise to pay its

Where the charge requires a complex and extended course of action in which the creator of the fund retains an active interest and forced heirs wait in the wings, classifying the transaction almost necessarily involves a conscious choice of the outcome desired. A case that revealed the difficulties in the choice concerned a widow whose husband at the time of his death had been engaged in extensive scientific research.[22] The widow strongly desired that the research continue. Out of her family of eleven children she selected one son as the one most likely to pursue this work with diligence and devotion. She transferred to him money and securities worth 1,750,000 marks, describing the transfer as a "gift." A corporation was then organized for the sole purpose of administering this fund, the mother owning most of the stock and the son being appointed manager. Within three years disputes arose between mother and son, the son was dismissed, and the mother sued him to recover the whole fund as the subject of a conditional gift whose "presupposition" had failed. The son claimed it all as an outright gift. The court below concluded that the transaction was *both* a gift and a contract, through a finding that the son had promised to apply the gift to the conduct of the research enterprise. This reasoning the high court rejected as "impossible under the laws of thought"; the transfer could not simultaneously both have and not have a "recompense."

There were a number of possible ways to diagnose the transaction. The parties themselves had called it a "gift" and, as the court said, they were of a social class that was likely to know what such a word meant, but to have a gift there must be a finding that both parties agreed there was to be no rec-

cost the association-promisee had begun construction of the building. By the time the two instalment payments had been made, construction was presumably well along.

22. Warneyer, 1941, no. 116 (R.G., 1941).

ompense. Furthermore, if it was an unqualified gift the son would be entirely free to spend the fund as he pleased. It could be a bilateral contract with a promise by the son to carry on his father's research. The lower court pointed out that the mother from the outset had been determined to disinherit her other ten children in order to accomplish her overriding purpose of ensuring that her husband's research continued. The lower court's finding of an exchange of promises rested mainly on its belief that this was the surest way of nullifying the claims of the other children. But, the high court asked, was it likely that a promise so unenforceable and lacking in the standards needed to appraise the son's performance would be desired by the mother and considered to be worth the large price she paid? The court then suggested one other way in which the transfer to the son could be found to be not a gift: if there was a charge requiring the son to expend the whole fund. But the high court thought that the facts would not support such a finding. The case was finally sent back to the lower court with instructions to try again. The high court added a strong hint that, after all, the "will of the parties" (on which, the court said, everything depended) might have been to have a gift with charge. This would have the consequence that if the son ("donee") were found to be at fault in the disputes that had occurred, the transfer to him could be cancelled.

To the original parties to such borderland transactions the choice between the two designations—bilateral contract and gift with charge—is not likely to matter greatly. The remedies provided by the Code, as was stated earlier, make the gift with charge into an almost-contract: where the "donor" has already completed his gift he can enforce the charge directly if this is feasible, and if at any stage the donee defaults in performing the charge the donor can secure restitution by the tests that apply to substantial breach of contract. But the choice of labels can make a large difference in other ways, as the widow's case should indicate. For all the various purposes for which gifts are controlled, including the protection of guaranteed inheritance, it will be crucial to know whether there was a "recompense" that precludes a finding of gift. It is true that if expenditures in an ascertainable amount are required by the charge, that amount will be deducted, the enrichment being reduced to that extent (unless the donee is a "juristic person"). But from the fact they are deductible it does not follow that they were conceived as a "recompense," sought for and given as part of an exchange. This is a separate question that in any case of doubt a court must answer—somehow.

B. *The Exchange Mixed with Gift*

It has already been pointed out that the "recompense" that will produce an exchange can be much less (or much more) valuable than the performance for which it is to be traded and indeed that it is possible for it to have no economic value whatever.[23] Does this exclude the possibility, where there is a known discrepancy in values in an authentic exchange, that the margin of gain was intended and understood as gift? This possibility had been mentioned by a Roman law text,[24] had entered into the common learning, and had been much discussed in German Pandectist writing. Nineteenth-century German courts had held in several decisions that such composite transactions could be partially unscrambled so that the gift element would be separated and subjected to the rules for gifts.[25] The Code itself, as finally adopted, contained no

23. Section 4, notes 1–5.
24. D.39.5.18 pr.
25. The nineteenth-century history is reviewed by W. Müller, "Die gemischte Schenkung," *Iherings Jahrbuch* 48:209. A long list of authors, led by Savigny, and a number of court decisions are cited, ibid., p. 216.

provision that dealt directly with this question, but the first of the two Code drafting commissions expressed the same view and described it as "self-evident."[26]

A 1935 decision of the Reichsgericht[27] illustrates the kind of evidence that, when added to a discrepancy in the values exchanged, could lead to a finding of partial gift. The defendant in 1925 had signed a promise to pay his brother Karl 50,000 marks. Karl died in 1932, leaving half of his estate to his fiancée, who then sued the defendant for 25,000 marks, her half of the sum promised. Defendant defended on the ground that his promise was a promise of gift and, not being notarized, was void. The lower court found that defendant had borrowed 3,000 marks from Karl and owed him that amount, that the two brothers were personally close, that defendant had become wealthy operating a factory in which Karl had worked faithfully for years at a low wage, and that defendant's purposes were to reimburse him for these services in the past and divide with Karl some of the wealth that defendant had inherited from their mother. The lower court concluded that the only recompense defendant was to receive for his promise to pay Karl 50,000 marks was the discharge of his existing 3,000-mark debt, that the element of gift preponderated so greatly that the promise must be treated as entirely one of gift which would then be wholly void since it was not notarized.

Müller's own conclusion (pp. 228–240) was that such transactions should be treated differently for different purposes—as sales if defective goods were sold in breach of warranty, as gifts if the "donor" decided to revoke or his creditors complained of prejudice to them.

26. Mugdan, *Materialien* 2:159 (Motives of the First Drafting Commission, p. 287); "It seems self-evident that when in a bilateral contract a performance with a value exceeding that of the counter-performance is agreed to *animo donandi,* this contract is to be considered a gift insofar as the value of the performance is greater than that of the counter-performance."

27. 148 *R.G.Z.* 236.

The Reichsgericht, after reviewing the decisions and the authors both before and after the Code, rebuked the lower court for adopting this approach, though in the end, for a different reason, it agreed that the note was wholly void.[28] The Code said nothing that bore directly on such transactions in which exchange was mixed with gift, but the court was clear that both the Code's general plan and the strong policies that reinforced it required them to be treated, not as entirely gift or entirely exchange but as comprised of separate parts. In the particular case it would be easy enough to divide them, by subtracting a smaller from a larger sum of money.[29] And the court declared that courts had the means and also the duty, when need arose, to dissect other kinds of mixed transactions, such as gifts combined with sales of assets (a building, for example) that could not themselves be physically split. A loss producing gain, agreed by the parties to be unrecompensed, was still a gift even though tangled up with an authentic exchange. The remedy was clear: to disentangle them.

Willingness to use measures like these reflects, one might say, commendable zeal in enforcing the basic plan and policies of the Code. Some might find the zeal excessive.

28. B.G.B., art. 139 provided that if one part of a legal transaction was void, the transaction would be void as a whole unless it could be inferred that it would have been agreed to without the void part. The Reichsgericht concluded that the defendant's overriding purpose was to share his wealth with a brother to whom he was attached and that he would not have signed the note merely to facilitate collection of his 3,000-mark debt.

29. An earlier case in which this kind of operation had been performed was reported in Seufferts Archiv 69, no. 121 (R.G., 1913). Here the defendant while divorce proceedings were pending made a promise, secured by mortgage, to pay his wife 20,000 marks, with a recital that he had received this amount from her dowry. He was allowed to prove that he had received in fact only 16,500 marks and that, as to the 3,500-mark balance, the promise was made and understood as a gift; being unnotarized, it was to that extent void.

French courts when confronted with the same problem have refused altogether to attempt judicial surgery and have held fast to the conviction that the transaction must be viewed as one or the other—exchange or gift (or possibly nothing at all)—but never as a Siamese twin that was headed for the surgical ward.[30] And we should recall at this point the uniform refusal of our own courts to become engaged with such issues. A familiar case will illustrate the result that is to be expected in all our states in applying the test of consideration.[31]

In this case, one William Story promised his nephew and namesake, aged sixteen, that if nephew Willie would abstain from drinking, smoking, swearing, and gambling until he reached the age of twenty-one, Uncle William would pay him $5,000. When he reached twenty-one, nephew Willie informed his uncle that for that long, dreary time—almost five years—he had duly abstained in the four specified ways and was, he believed, entitled to the payment promised. Uncle William promptly wrote back, reaffirming his promise and also disclosing that his promise had had another motive as well, that of giving his nephew-namesake a good start in life, so that he might escape the hardships that Uncle William had suffered in his own youth.

The New York Court of Appeals was ready to infer that the abstentions by Willie were a detriment to him and could also be found to be a benefit to Uncle William—to borrow a word, that they were a "recompense" that the uncle in fact had desired. But these abstentions by Willie were not a commodity that was saleable in any known market. Furthermore, the uncle's later letter (nearly five years later, it is true) was persuasive evidence that for most of his money he

30. See above, chapter 2, section 5B.
31. Hamer v. Sidway, 124 N.Y. 538, 27 N.E. 256 (1891).

sought no return at all. The promise by Uncle William, in other words, was a promise of mixed gift. If made in Germany after 1900, the promise would have been void since it was not notarized, but void only as to the "unrecompensed" portion; Willie could recover the price of his five years of self-denial. How much was that? Indeed, how would one even begin to find out what portion was gift, unrecompensed? But for the New York court Willie's case could not have been more simple. Since one of the motives of the uncle-promisor had been to induce the abstentions that had in fact occurred, so that he had received the consideration he had "bargained for," there was no need to look further. There was consideration for the promise and nephew Willie could collect $5,000.

The first impression given by the reported cases is that the questions German courts have met in their unmixing of gifts have not been quite so unanswerable as those that would have been raised by corrective surgery if it had been tried in Uncle William's case. But a closer look at the German cases leads one to wonder. The problems with mixed gifts that are the most troublesome and also arise the most often are those involving transfers of land, already made or promised, in return for promises of lifetime support. Usually made between near relatives, they may also include other arrangements, such as the assumption of a mortgage on the property conveyed, periodic payments to the transferors or other relatives, cancellation of old debts. The basic element of uncertainty cannot be relieved by mortality tables—how long will the persons entitled to support actually live, how prolonged and how serious will their illnesses be? But the probability of a margin of gain, in excess of the values of performances to be exchanged, will be determined as of the date when the contract or transfer was made.[32] The parties them-

32. The high court emphasized this in *N.J.W.*, 1953, p. 501 (B.G.H.,

selves may place their own estimates of money-value on the performances involved, in order, perhaps, to forestall an attack by some aggrieved heir. But such estimates are in no way controlling, and courts must make their own appraisals. All too often appellate courts send the findings back—more facts must be found, not enough has been taken into account.

One example may suffice, out of a considerable cluster of such cases. In a case decided by the high court in 1972,[33] it appeared that a woman and her second husband owned jointly the house in which they lived with the woman's daughter by an earlier marriage. They contracted to sell this house to the daughter. The price was stated to be 50,000 marks and was to be paid by the daughter in the form of care of the "sellers" for their lives (valued in the contract at 300 marks a month), a right of the "sellers" to live in the house for life (valued in the contract at 100 marks a month), monthly payments to them for life of 100 marks, the assumption by the daughter of a 5,000-mark mortgage, and cancellation of a 6,000-mark debt they owed to her. Subsequently the daughter failed to make the monthly payments and discord intervened so that she left home, though when the "sellers" died the following year they left the house to her in their wills. The daughter was then sued by her two brothers, who contended that the transfer of the house to her infringed their guaranteed shares of inheritance from their mother. In support of this contention they asserted that the value of the building was 72,000 and not the recited 50,000 marks, that the stepfather and mother had been well and needed no care so that 300 marks a month was a purely nominal figure, that the daughter (the "buyer") had no funds of her own so that her promise to pay the old folks 100 marks a month was

---

1952). This is the assumption, most of the time unspoken, of the cases and authors cited below.

33. 59 *B.G.H.Z.* 132.

worthless. The lower court had seemingly accepted the estimate in the contract of a 50,000-mark value for the house and then had come up with a figure on the other side, that the several performances to be rendered by the daughter had a value of 34,800 marks. The high court remanded the case and directed the lower court to examine much more closely the value of the house and also the value of the daughter's performances, with the suggestion that extra care in such findings was needed where the guaranteed shares of heirs might be infringed.

One of the problems that the trial court must then have faced—how to divide a mixed gift that includes some indivisible asset, like a building—has arisen fairly often. The need to divide can arise for various reasons. In one case in which the donor sought to revoke for the donee's ingratitude, the court concluded that the exchange element predominated because the price to be paid was more than half the value of the building conveyed, so the donee was allowed to keep the property and restore the "gift" in the form of a money payment for the difference.[34] In determining which element predominates—exchange or gift—all benefits and burdens on both sides of the mixed transaction must be appraised and brought into the equation. If, for example, a life estate was reserved in property that had been conveyed, the life tenant's prospects for survival must be estimated to determine which party must pay cash and how much.[35] The unreality of

34. 68 *R.G.Z.* 326 (1908).
35. 163 *R.G.Z.* 257 (1940) was another revocation for the donee's ingratitude. The owner had sold land to her son for a price that was found to be slightly more than half its market value after deducting the appraised value of the life estate she had reserved. The land and the parties were in Czechoslovakia, then under German occupation. The transaction was governed by the Austrian Code, whose provisions were similar to those of the German Code. The report did not disclose what methods were used to estimate the prospects for survival of a Czech resident living under the Nazis.

appraisals based on imaginary sales of such interests in nonexistent markets has led to some dissatisfaction, but the high court still insists that the attempt must be made.[36]

Services and other activities that are to extend over time present even greater difficulties of appraisal, and they are not confined to transfers in return for care and support. One more example should suffice, a commercial partnership in which the contribution of one partner was to take the form of service as business manager, for the duration of the partnership with no time limit expressed. A year and four months later disputes led to the decision to dissolve the partnership. Then the other partner contended that the anticipated service of the managing partner had been greatly overvalued, that the 30 percent share of partnership assets assigned to him was excessive, and that the excess constituted a promise of gift, void because not notarized. Unfortunately the report of the case leaves the story unfinished so that there is no way to tell how this particular mixture was unscrambled.[37]

After a measurable discrepancy in the values exchanged has been established, however, there remains one other question that at times must be even harder to answer: was

36. The high court set up by the British military government in the British zone after the Second World War struggled to find another formula. In two cases involving revocations by donors for the donees' "gross ingratitude," they developed a test which was aimed in effect at the importance to the participants of including the gift element; if the finding was that without its inclusion the transaction would not have been agreed to at all, specific restoration to the donor would be ordered. 1 *O.G.H.Z.* 258 (1948); 2 *O.G.H.Z.* 160 (1948). The Bundesgerichtshof in 1952 (*N.J.W.*, 1953, 501) and again in 1959 (30 *B.G.H.Z.* 120) rejected these tests as unusable in practice and likely to undermine the protective purposes of the controls over gifts.

37. The report of the case in 7 *B.G.H.Z.* 174 (1952) ends with a direction to the trial court to find the value that should have been assigned when the partnership was formed to the future services of the managing partner. The other partner's contention that an excessive valuation might make the excess amount to a promise of mixed gift was apparently accepted.

the discrepancy intended and understood as a gift? In the phrasing used by the Code the question would be: did both parties agree that the gain anticipated for one party was to be unrecompensed? For even in transactions between close relatives the high court has continued to insist that the requirement of recompense is not a back-door route to judicial review for adequacy of price, that a transaction does not include an element of gift merely because the exchange it proposes is unequal.[38] In transfers in return for lifetime support it was easier to adhere to this position if there had been in the past no close ties through family or friendship, for then the arrangements would probably rest on unsentimental calculations of mutual advantage, even though one side was to acquire a substantial gain.[39] In the usual case, where such close ties do exist, the high court has been willing lately to concede that a marked discrepancy in the values exchanged makes a donative purpose more likely.[40]

38. This was strongly stated in 163 *R.G.Z.* 25 (1940), the mother-son case referred to in note 35 above. Similarly, *J.W.*, 1935, 275 (R.G. 1934), a sale to a son by a father at a price claimed by another son to be unduly low.

39. In the case reported in *Zeitschrift für das gesamte Familienrecht* (1964), p. 729 (B.G.H., 1963) the court first let off a salvo proclaiming the freedom of contracting parties to enter into unequal exchanges and sell land at a "friendship price." It then pointed out that in the particular case there had been no evidence of "love and affection" between the two parties at any time before the contract for lifetime support was made and that the failure of the "seller's" own alternative plans and the opening up of space in the "buyer's" establishment had happened to coincide. So the inference was strong that no gift was intended, even though the discrepancy in values might turn out to be large.

40. 59 *B.G.H.Z.* 132 (1972). A case the next year that seems to follow these ideas is reported in *N.J.W.*, 1973, p. 995 (B.G.H., 1973). Here a half-interest in land had been conveyed by a father to his son in return for a promise to support the father and the defendant's sister for their lives, to pay the sister 100 marks a month, and to assume mortgages in the amount of 50,000 marks. The lower court had found the estate conveyed was worth 260,939 marks, and by means not explained found that the defendant's performances were worth only 28,253.31 marks, so that the parties "could not"

It should be said again that these efforts to split up into separate parts elements that the parties did their best to commingle were not required by anything said in the Code. As the preceding section indicated, the Code does provide means for enforcing charges on gifts but has nothing to say about composite transactions in which gift and exchange have been mixed. The only language that does apply is the Code definition of gift as a transaction in which the parties agree that the performance will be "without recompense." It would be enough to say in these transactions that the parties have agreed, on the contrary, that the transaction is to be *with* recompense. But the motive of courts in intervening is evident enough. If the inclusion of an element of exchange provided exemption from the controls over gifts, the controls could be circumvented by the same means by which American promisors can readily comply with the requirement of consideration ("circumvent" would be for us too harsh a word).

So it seems safe to conclude that German courts have been convinced that the policies served by the controls over gifts are important enough to call on them for some strenuous effort—the kind of effort that American courts would surely not undertake in support of—to reinforce—the requirement of consideration. The surgery undertaken by German courts in dissecting mixed gifts is difficult in itself, it inevitably has had only partial success and, in order to promote the policies of the Code, goes well beyond any duty the Code defines.

---

have conceived them to be an exchange and the sister was entitled to set aside the transaction to the extent necessary to restore her guaranteed share in her father's estate.

A very good review of recent decisions, especially as they relate to the protection of heirs against exchanges mixed with gifts, is that of U. Spellenberg, "Schenkungen und unentgeltliche Verfügungen zum Nachteil des Erben oder Pflichtteilsberechtigten," *Zeitschrift für das gesamte Familienrecht* (1974), p. 350.

6. A Well-Tended Enclave

The account just given would mislead if it left the impression that courts have maintained over the whole range of German private law the posture here described of strict adherence and dutiful submission to the Code. For this account does not mention the extensive areas of German private law that have been transformed by innovations made through judicial decision. For the most part these innovations have been ascribed to three general clauses contained in the Code, which thus provide a formal sanction: all obligations must be performed in "good faith" (article 242), violation of "good morals" can invalidate a transaction (article 138) or lead to liability if harm to others is thereby intentionally caused (article 826). These clauses were resorted to quite soon after the Code took effect, and then on a greatly increased scale after the First World War produced economic dislocations that were wholly unforeseen, in unimaginable variety, and on an expanding scale. There is no need to describe again the far-reaching network of judge-made rules that German courts and scholars, working in a remarkable partnership, have striven to assimilate and organize into newly built structures of order.[1] So if there is any problem at all it is to explain why the small enclave in German law that has been examined here has not been extensively redesigned from the high vantage points—good faith and good morals—from which German judges have maintained their vigil over German law.

The possibilities are suggested by another strict requirement of form, that imposed on contracts for the sale of inter-

1. The richest and most illuminating account is that of Wieacker, *Privatrechtsgeschichte,* pp. 514–625. I have attempted to summarize the main course of events in the *Oracles of the Law,* pp. 461–502 and to comment further on some of the consequences in "The General Clauses, Viewed from a Distance," 41 *Rabels Zeitschrift* 441 (1977).

ests in land. Like promises of gift, the Code makes them void
unless notarized.[2] Misgivings began to be felt when there
was ground to suspect that defects of form were brought
about deliberately, as by falsifying contract terms in the
document recorded,[3] by assurances (known to be false) given
by one party to the other that no formalities were needed,[4] by
part performance conferring a substantial advantage that
could not be readily restored.[5] The Code provision they
used, the "good faith" clause, seemed to call for some finding
of moral fault or shortcoming in the one who asserted the
defect of form. But, as in the "part performance" doctrine as
it emerged from the fogs of English equity, there was often
mixed in some element of prejudice to the other party,
through being induced by the unnotarized promise to take or
refrain from action. In the more recent German decisions that
use the "good faith" clause to give dispensations from re-

2. B.G.B., article 313, requiring notarization; article 125, providing
that any transaction that lacks a formality required by law is void. Article
313, however, does go on to say that if a conveyance is later made and
recorded at the land-title registry, the nullity is cured.

3. 107 *R.G.Z.* 351 (1923) was such a case.

4. A useful short summary of the course of decision between the
1920s and the 1950s is given by W. Lorenz, "Das Problem der Auf-
rechterhaltung formnichtiger Verträge," 156 *Archiv für die civilistische
Praxis* 381, 398–405 (1957).

5. 153 *R.G.Z.* 59 (1936). Here the plaintiff in 1930 had leased a bakery
to the defendant for five years, with a clause precluding the defendant,
after termination of the lease, from selling bakery goods in the town in
which the leased bakery was located. The lease agreement also contained
an option in the lessee, defendant, to purchase the bakery, an option that
he did not exercise. The lease was terminated in 1935. Plaintiff resumed
operation of the leased building as a bakery and then defendant opened
another bakery in the town, selling to the same clientele with whom he
had become acquainted. When plaintiff sued for an injunction, defendant
contended that all provisions in the lease were void because it contained a
conditional promise of plaintiff to sell land and was not notarized. The
court conceded that the absence of notarization was not premeditated on
the part of the defendant, but nevertheless concluded that his conduct
could not be reconciled with the "general conscience of the people."

quirements of form, the promisee's reliance can at times appear as the predominant reason[6] and may now be almost a requirement.[7]

If German courts had felt any impulse to redesign the Code law on gifts, the notion of reliance should have been one of the first to be incorporated in any new design. Certainly in our own experience it was with promises of gift, especially charitable gifts, that the need was demonstrated early for the idea that we have subsequently generalized and have come to call promissory estoppel. German authors who are familiar with it have urged its adoption in Germany, especially to deal with promises that fall in the borderland between exchange and gift. For this, in their view, no legislation would be needed.[8] And indeed the essential elements of estoppel have been well known in Europe for a very long time, ever since they first appeared in Roman law. They came to be expressed in a slogan—that no one is permitted

6. 12 *B.G.H.Z.* 286 (1954), a case in which a son lived on and managed the family farm for eighteen years, had married and had five children while being repeatedly assured that he would inherit the farm on his parents' death. Specific enforcement was ordered. Among those who praise the result in this case are G. and D. Reinecke, "Formvorschrift, Treu and Glauben und Schadenersatz," *M.D.R.*, 1954, p. 641. It is sharply criticized by Lorenz in the article cited above, note 4, and F. Wieacker, "Stillschweigende Hoferbenbestimmung?," *Deutsche Notar Zeitung*, 1956, p. 115.

7. The Bundesgerichtshof in 1965 (*N.J.W.*, 1965, p. 812) declared in strong language that for purchasers to enforce unnotarized contracts to sell land it must appear that they would otherwise incur harmful consequences that would be not only "harsh" but "unbearable." Perhaps the court did not mean all of this, for in the end their reason for enforcing by an award of damages was that the seller, a large land development corporation, must have known that notarization was needed and the purchasers were legally "uninformed."

8. K. Zweigert, "Seriositätsindizien," *Juristen Zeitung*, 1964, pp. 349, 354; Lorenz, "Entgeltliche und unentgeltliche Geschäfte," pp. 547, 567–568. Gino Gorla, writing with a still broader perspective, has urged widespread adoption of this idea. *Il Contratto*, pp. 356–365.

"to contradict his own act" (*venire contra factum proprium*). In most of its applications this idea performed the function of our old-fashioned estoppel: after an assertion had been made that a certain fact presently existed, reliance on the assertion would preclude proof that the assertion was false.[9] There were also some traces, even in classical sources, of reliance as a ground for limited enforcement of promises of gift.[10] In the intermediate centuries the essential idea—excluding proof of the falsity of assertions that had been relied on—was accepted without question as an expression of elementary fairness.[11] It has become one of the familiar and much-used precepts, at an intermediate level of generality, that derive operative force from the "good faith" clause and that aid in the continuing effort to restructure and maintain coherence in the case law ascribed to that source.[12]

The idea of reliance thus lies within easy reach. Nevertheless, it has been in effect excluded from the whole area of gifts, including promises of gift, where for us it has become an indispensable aid. In trying to speculate why this could have occurred it seems best to start with a concrete example. For this purpose I would take the crematorium case, described in the previous section, in which a promise had been

9. E. Riezler, *Venire Contra Factum Proprium* (1912), pp. 4–32.

10. D.12.4.5. pr. gives an example. Here the promisee was promised a sum of money if he took a trip. After he had taken the trip the promisor sued, for a reason not stated, to recover the money, which he had in the meantime paid the promisee. The promisee was given a deduction for his expenditures from the payor's recovery of the money paid but was not allowed to recover damages in excess of that sum. Riezler (ibid., pp. 32–35) gives other examples.

11. Riezler, *Venire Contra Factum Proprium,* pp. 43–53.

12. The numerous situations in which the result is attributed to this precept, made operative by article 242, are described in Soergel-Siebert, commentary on the B.G.B., article 242, paragraphs 228–244 (10th ed., 1967). The importance and usefulness of such subordinate propositions are described by F. Wieacker, "Zur rechtstheoretischen Präzisierung des 242, B.G.B.," (1956), pp. 20–44.

made to contribute 50,000 marks, to be paid in five instalments, toward the cost of building a crematorium.[13] Construction of the building was well advanced and two instalments had been paid when the contributor refused to pay more. The promise, though not notarized, was held to be enforceable for a reason that would not be acceptable now—that the registered association which was to receive the money would not be enriched because it had been organized for the purposes of constructing and maintaining a crematorium and in this instance would be required to spend all the money in building the building. The promise, being to a "legal entity" to serve its announced purposes, would in Germany now be considered a promise of gift.

Our own approach to such a case would first of all emphasize the substantial and foreseeable reliance that had already occurred. But in Germany would this reliance by the donee-promisee exempt the transaction from the controls over gifts? No one, presumably, would feel the earth quiver if notarization were held not to be needed or even if the donor, after reliance by the donee that he should have foreseen, were precluded from revoking the gift when all the payments had been made and the building built. But what reaction could be expected if a son of the donor-promisor came forward in the crematorium case and showed that payments either made or promised would so deplete the father's estate as to dissipate all or part of the son's guaranteed share? The question, phrased in general terms, would then be whether a donee's reliance, costly to him and foreseeable by the donor, will validate a gift that exceeds the donor's disposable quota and encroaches on the share guaranteed to an heir. To a question so framed the answer, I think, would almost surely be a reluctant no.

13. The case is discussed in chapter 3, section 5A, p. 170, in connection with note 15.

One other choice remains: to follow French courts in a selective approach. One could say that for the purpose of protecting the shares guaranteed to forced heirs, the transaction is a gift, despite the donee's reliance, but for all or most other purposes it is not. So in the crematorium case the promise would not have to be notarized, any payments made could not be recovered through revocation on one of the grounds authorized for revoking gifts, and so on through the list of vulnerabilities that are attached to gifts. So one must ask, why are courts in Germany not as free as courts in France to read words in a code in opposite ways, so that their meaning will in large part depend on the question that is being asked? The contrast between the two countries suggested by this contrast is one that cuts deeply and reaches in all directions. The contrast goes to central problems of legal method in administering codes, problems that can arise in many different ways. They often have the initial appearance of purely semantic problems: when the primary source of most private law is the condensed language of a comprehensive code, how much effort should be spent and how high a price should be paid in order to maintain coherence and internal consistency in the meanings attached to the code's vocabulary? I venture the opinion that German courts and legal scholars have continued to make a strenuous effort and are willing to pay a considerable price.

One of the advantages of codification has been thought to be that it forces the draftsmen to clarify the central store of essential ideas and define both their limits and their numerous interconnections before projecting them forth and assigning them to work. They will be strewn all over the code and perform different functions in different places, but the hope is that the core of meaning will not be thereby changed or shaded. The precision and care with which the network is contrived will largely determine how much later users will be willing to invest to keep it intact. In Germany, as I have said, the Civil Code was drafted with painstaking care to express in condensed form an intricate system of legal ideas to which all trained lawyers of the time gave allegiance. So the users of the Code after it came into force were not only ready but fully determined to maintain its order and internal cohesion. Was the "flight into the general clauses" a sign that this purpose has been greatly weakened or even, perhaps, turned into reverse?

By their resort to the general clauses courts have opened the way for an influx—one could almost call it a flood—of new ideas, new standards of fairness and of ethical conduct that are highly individualized in their application, in ways that Code rules often did not permit. So the results have been new legal formulas in great abundance and new ways of thinking that the nineteenth-century Pandectists could not have imagined. Heavy deposits of new legal ideas, generated by new experience, have added complications of many kinds that are spread over large areas of German private law. They are not found everywhere. They are found in those areas where new needs were discovered, areas not provided for or not adequately provided for by the Code. Where they do exist, the effort to assimilate and to combine old and new continues unabated, with an energy at least as great as before.

In trying to discover why the Code controls over gifts, including promises of gift, are one of the areas that have been left undisturbed, one should again recall that the area policed is confined within narrow limits. The ancient restrictions are firmly maintained. To be a gift the transaction must accomplish both a permanent subtraction from the donor's capital resources and a permanent increase in those of the donee. All other forms of generosity or aid, whether com-

pleted or promised, are disregarded. The transfers of wealth
that are included are precisely the kind that could diminish
the estate transmissible at death and thus jeopardize the
prospects of inheritance that are assured to the donor's heirs.
One of the theses I have advanced is that safeguards for inheritance by the nearest of kin have been and remain a compelling reason, much the strongest reason, for the controls
over gifts as they now exist.

There can be many other reasons for policing transactions
that produce unrecompensed gains: to discourage the brib-
ery of public officials, to prevent harm to their creditors by
insolvent debtors, to recapture profits obtained by fiduciaries
through misuse of their powers. In our own law each special
purpose for reviewing or undoing such transactions will have
its own rationale and its own separate tests which can vary in
rigor and in the means employed. So it was an ambitious
project for the German Code to set up a comprehensive
scheme whose coverage was wide and whose application
was supposedly uniform. To me it seems unlikely that the
controls would have been retained in their present form or
would have been adhered to so consistently if they had not
served so well one leading purpose—a purpose, it should be
added, that is not aimed merely at freakish people like "un-
grateful" donees but is pervasive in its consequences. It
applies to every owner of disposable property who might at
his death leave as survivors either a widow or heirs of his
own genetic line—ancestors or descendants. The purpose is
to ensure to each one of this protected group a substantial,
predetermined share of all assets that the decedent owned at
his death and also of those he once owned and gave away
(without "recompense") during the ten years before his
death. These guarantees, it seems, are widely believed to be
the minimum required of every owner by loyalty and responsibility to his kindred. German courts surely have given

every sign, by the vigor they show in enforcing these controls, that this is a conviction they share.

The restrictions on gifts had been narrowed by the Code in one other way, by requiring notarization only for promises of gift. Toward this provision the attitude seems to be one of general acquiescence, with no audible expressions of discontent. Among the authors it is difficult to find any comment on them at all, though one can occasionally find an expression of mild approval.[14] And the courts, as I have said, have made no use at all of the avenues of escape through the general clauses that they have used to travel far and wide on voyages of discovery that led in other directions.

It is the concept of recompense, I suggest, that has proved the most useful in reaching an accommodation of conflicting interests involved. Not part of the legacy from Rome, this concept was discovered very late, just in time to be included in the German Code. It was introduced into the law of contract by a back-door route. This may have helped to delay recognition by German lawyers of the idea of bargained-for exchange which they had unexpectedly acquired under another name and found in a strange location. Only two German authors that I have read have noted that *Entgelt* and bargain consideration are very much alike.[15] That they are

14. Lorenz, "Entgeltliche und unentgeltliche Geschäfte," pp. 547–567: "for pure liberalities a requirement of form makes good sense." In this passage the author is expressing his agreement with Max Rheinstein, who had made a similar comment.

15. M. Rheinstein, *Die Struktur des Vertragsverhältnisses in Anglo-Amerikanischen Recht* (1932), p. 100. The discussion by W. Lorenz of the German meanings of *Entgelt* (see ibid.) clearly shows his awareness of the similarities.

One noted German comparatist has flatly rejected the suggestion that continental countries could make any use of the requirement of consideration, pointing out that it has been condemned for such good reason in its countries of origin. Zweigert, "Seriositätsindizien," p. 349. The author, however, may have had in mind only the preexisting duty rule, which he

indeed so much alike should occasion no surprise. These ideas perform functions which are essentially the same in societies that give the same high priority to private consent as the means of organizing the exchange of goods and services. The premise, which German courts had accepted long before the Code, was that those who engaged in such exchanges are best qualified to estimate their own wants and needs and to secure by agreement with others the advantages and satisfactions that each desires. After the Code took effect and courts were called on to construe a word well known in common speech but to which a crucial role had suddenly been assigned, they gave "recompense" from the outset an expanded meaning. The essential question became one of psychological fact: did the person whose performance would produce gain for another in fact desire to secure in return some action or abstention of the other? If the performances were connected by this psychological link, there was an exchange and that was enough. And the readiness of courts to enforce unequal exchanges, despite evident disparities in the values exchanged, was consistent with attitudes that were already well established and with the basic solutions of the Code itself. This readiness also meant that the area within which the controls over gifts could operate would be sharply reduced, though for at least one of the purposes served by the controls (protection of forced heirship) the courts had shown their own strong support.

So the idea of "recompense" has become a familiar and most useful instrument that German courts have used to preserve a wide-ranging regime of free contract, surrounding and containing within narrow limits the area policed by the law of gifts. As a test it is by no means easy to apply, for it

then went on to criticize. As the next chapter will suggest, there should be worldwide agreement on the disutility of the preexisting duty rule.

calls for appraisals of human motives which the participants themselves have often not clearly defined. Yet on these appraisals more may depend than the validity of an informal promise. There are a number of purposes for which it is necessary to decide whether some action or inaction of the other party was actually sought and given in exchange ("bargained for in fact," we would say). In their ability to find answers to this question the courts seem entirely confident, even overconfident at times. This appeared particularly in mixed transactions, exchanges mixed with gift. Here one must add to mixed motives in the parties a degree of ambivalence in the judges themselves. For to exempt such mixed transactions from all review, where the margin of gain was a planned benefaction, might make it too easy to escape controls whose policies the judges too supported; but to treat them therefore as exclusively gifts would be to restrict the power to trade resources through what was in part an authentic exchange. So in order that both sets of purposes be achieved, German courts assigned to themselves the immensely difficult task of determining not only whether there was a recompense but *how much* in fact was bargained for.

We can be grateful that our own courts have not felt called upon to apply the concept of bargained-for exchange with such extreme thoroughness and vigor.

IV   The Sources of Our Own Discontent

A remarkable feature of the extensive literature on the requirement of consideration is the intensity and depth of the hostility it has inspired. It has been seriously urged that it should be abolished altogether.[1] Writers have expressed scorn for this "enormous and shapeless grab-bag"[2] or described it as "primitive" and "uncouth."[3] It is more common to explain it through historical accident—that the tyranny exercised in English law by the medieval forms of action was just beginning to fade at the crucial time, the sixteenth century, when a law of contract was emerging from the shadows cast by the law of tort.[4] A more recent account has proposed a different timing. It postpones the emergence of a law of contract until the nineteenth century and makes consideration a "revolutionary" invention of Mr. Justice Holmes which he

1. Wright, "Should the Doctrine of Consideration Be Abolished?" 49 *Harvard Law Review* 1225 (1936). An American author had made the same proposal in the same periodical: C. Ashley, "The Doctrine of Consideration," 26 *Harvard Law Review* 429 (1913).

2. F. Rodell, *Woe Unto You Lawyers* (1939), p. 59.

3. H. Havighurst, "Consideration, Ethics and Administration," 42 *Columbia Law Review* 1 (1942), the term "primitive" being quoted by that author from an article by Malcolm Sharp, cited in the next note.

4. Holdsworth, *History of English Law,* 8:7 ff. A similar suggestion that rules as to consideration are "the vestigial survivals of procedural evolution—the product of the peculiar and unsystematic history of the writ of assumpsit"—appears in M. Sharp, "Pacta Sunt Servanda," 41 *Columbia Law Review* 777, 785 (1941).

first disclosed in 1881. This news, however, is meant to reassure, for it is accompanied by the forecast that the law of contract, including especially the consideration test, will again be swallowed up by the law of tort.[5] We thus can hope for an early return to the state of peace and piety that prevailed in medieval times, before contracts were invented.

For English law my own estimate of the timing is different. Among the odds and ends that are assembled under the heading of consideration the one central and essential idea is that of exchange, the product of a bargain. In the chapter on German law I have tried to show that in Germany this idea, under the name of "recompense," actually was invented in 1889, ninety years ago, by a noted scholar, that it was then promptly incorporated in the German Civil Code and put to intensive use. In France the idea was also discovered by a solitary author but no one else noticed, so that those in a position to use it have not discovered it at all.[6] The purpose of the discussion that follows will be to show that the concept of bargained-for exchange became an established feature of the English law of contract in the decades when English lawyers were first becoming aware that a law of contract existed. What happened about a century ago, when Holmes was "inventing" bargain consideration, was that this central idea, which had been familiar in England for more than three hundred years, was overloaded with additional tasks for which it was wholly unsuited. The distortions and evasions that the added functions produced have brought them all into disrepute. The reassuring news is that we have made a good start toward removing these excrescences and could

5. G. Gilmore, *The Death of Contract* (1974).
6. The publication by Lenel in 1889 of his conception of "recompense" is discussed in chapter 3, section 2, in the text connected with note 19. The argument in France of Dupeyroux is discussed in chapter 2, section 4, in text connected with note 20.

succeed before long in eliminating them altogether. They never were needed, as the experience of France and Germany should indicate.

The next section will aim, first, to locate the time when *consideration,* a word borrowed from common speech, first acquired a technical meaning in English law, and second, to describe the much later stages when its functions were made to proliferate. Thereafter there will be some brief comments addressed to the general question: does the account already given of the solutions found in French and German law reveal other features that we should envy and emulate?

1. The Functions of Consideration

A. The Enforcement of Bargains

When in England in the 1530s and 1540s the mere nonperformance of a promise began to be recognized as sufficient ground for an award of damages, the common lawyers had a very small vocabulary with which to describe the elements needed to make a promise enforceable. They had a few phrases that had been used for other purposes and that must have helped to precipitate thought in these new directions. "Consideration," the term that in the end was to acquire a prominent place, was at the outset the most pallid and least meaningful of them all. It had been much used in preliminary recitals to describe the motives ("for these considerations" or "considering that . . .") that had inspired legislators in drafting statutes or grantors in making conveyances.[1]

---

1. A. Simpson, *History of the Common Law of Contract,* (1975), pp. 329–332. St. Germain, in *Doctor and Student,* Vol. 2, chap. 24, could not have meant more than this when he said that a promise to pay £20 to one who had built the promisor a house should be enforced, but "if his promise be so naked that there is no manner of consideration why it should be made, then I think him not bound to perform it." Simpson, p. 322.

In the few early Chancery cases that were reported by common lawyers, the Chancellors were described as searching for some "consideration" in deciding whether to enforce a use of land; after the Statute of Uses in 1535, the common-law judges also used the word to mean not much more than the grantor's purpose or motive.[2] In the earlier Chancery tradition the phrase "bargain and sale" had become a familiar formula to describe those contracts for the sale of land that the Chancellor would enforce; after the Statute of Uses, when such arrangements became enforceable at law, the common-law judges took over this phrasing.[3] The requirement of the much older action of debt that something must have been given "for" something else, a quid *pro* quo, made extremely familiar the notion of exchange, half completed. So one does not need to follow Holmes in tracing consideration back to the action of debt in order to say that pleaders were at least following a well-beaten track when they urged as a good reason for enforcing a promise the existence of an agreement that this would be given "for" that.[4]

In the 1530s the King's Bench took a strong lead in extending the action of trespass on the case as a damage remedy for mere nonfeasance in not-performing promises. In one of its earliest decisions—the first reported action of this kind that succeeded—the court confirmed a final judgment in favor of a buyer of malt whose allegations were that the defendant had "for" two payments (one made and one promised) "bargained and sold" forty quarters of malt and had failed to deliver, so that the plaintiff had had to buy malt

---

2. Simpson, *Common Law of Contract,* pp. 340–346, 359–374. His later passages attribute to "consideration" in equity a much greater influence on the common law than seems to me likely.

3. Ibid. pp. 346–353.

4. C. Fifoot, *History and Sources of the Common Law: Tort and Contract* (1949), pp. 395–396, has pointed remarks to make about this.

elsewhere at a higher price.[5] Very soon thereafter, the King's Bench extended a money judgment remedy over a wide range of promissory transactions. The main directions that the extensions would follow were fixed not by any theory preordained at the outset but by the reasons urged by lawyers and pleaders for court intervention. As a recent and excellent study has put it, "the classical doctrine of consideration was formulated in the course of discussing those facts which were laid in bills and declarations as the 'consideration' for which the promise was made."[6] More and more it became standard form to allege that the promise had been given "for" some asset or act that the pleader proceeded to specify, and if this kind of connection was not shown, the action was likely to fail.[7] As time went on, the something "for" which the promise was made was described increasingly as "the consideration," though the word still carried a load of vaguer meanings, suggesting other motives for promising that might or might not be good enough.[8]

5. Pykeryng v. Thurgoode (motion in arrest of judgment denied), *Reports of Sir John Spelman* (Selden Society, 1978), 1:4–6. The case is discussed by the editor, J. H. Baker, in his introduction, 2:283–285, and also by Simpson, *Common Law of Contract*, pp. 289–290.

6. Baker, introduction to *Reports of Sir John Spelman,* pp. 285–288, the quoted language appearing on page 287.

7. Ibid., pp. 289–290 surmises that in a case decided as early as 1538 the action failed because the promise to deliver herrings was not shown to have been "linked" to a promise to pay "for" them. In the passages that follow, the author describes the strong emphasis placed, both in pleadings and decisions, on showing that the promise whose enforcement was sought was made "for" (*pro*) some specified advantage.

8. Ibid., pp. 291–292. In a most interesting passage, the author then goes on (pp. 292–297) to discuss the question whether *causa*, a word that was occasionally mentioned, might also have expressed the idea of bargain. He concludes that, despite its occasional appearance, any direct borrowing from canon law was extremely unlikely and, on the other hand, a direct tracking back to the quid pro quo of the action of debt is not necessary, since "the notion of reciprocity was a principle of contemporary morality, part of the common stock of ideas of medieval Western Europe."

There is no need to repeat here the story that has been so often told: how most of these vaguer meanings were stripped away and "consideration" was made over, from an amorphous word drawn from common speech, into a technical requirement for contract formation. As an exclusionary rule preventing enforcement of promises that did not comply, it still had gaps; but its function as an excluder began early. A well-known case decided in 1568 will serve as an example. In this case the defendant's servant had been arrested for trespass. Two citizens of London, by going surety, secured his release. Their reason for doing so was stated to be "in consideration that the business of the master should not go undone." The master, when informed of this, promised one of the guarantors "upon the same friendly consideration" to save him harmless if the guarantor himself was arrested, as he soon was. The action of this guarantor-promisee to recover on the master's promise failed for want of consideration, the reason being that the guarantor had not been requested by the master to procure the release of the servant, "but he did it out of his own head."[9]

During the next decades the courts struggled to define the "request" that would transform into a present exchange some action by another that had produced a result desired by the promisor.[10] That their success in these efforts was far

9. Hunt v. Bate, Dyer 272a (1568).

10. In Lord Grey's case (reproduced by Simpson, *Common Law of Contract*, appendix, p. 633), the court in 1567 had struggled with this question in a case in which a son promised to pay his father's debt and the "consideration" might have been the creditor's abstention from suit. "Past consideration" through benefits received or relations arising in the past also caused much trouble. Marsh v. Rainsford (1587), reproduced by Simpson, appendix, pp. 633–637, involved marriage after a secret elopement with the promisor's daughter, but the relationship thereby produced was held to be a sufficient reason to enforce the promise. Cases involving more standard "past consideration" are discussed by Simpson, pp. 452–459.

from complete matters not at all for the present purpose. It became abundantly clear as the sixteenth century progressed that common-law courts had created the means for enforcing, and were prepared to enforce, a great variety of exchange transactions. In the transactions that were enforced there was one recurring element which provided the reason why they were enforced: each party had in fact desired some act or abstention of the other in return for which he had agreed to perform his own.[11]

All this has made more than somewhat surprising the suggestion that bargain consideration was a "revolutionary" invention by Justice Holmes which he first disclosed to the world in 1881.[12] And the truly astonishing feature is that the revolution was accomplished in two sentences, whose essential message is concentrated in one cryptic phrase—that between the promise and the consideration there must be "the relation of reciprocal conventional inducement each for the other."[13] Whatever else Holmes may have invented, we can be sure, at least, that he invented this phrase. Its novelty becomes apparent when it is contrasted with what had been said before. Chancellor Kent, writing in 1827, could serve as an example. He described consideration as "something given in exchange, something that is mutual, or something which is the inducement to the contract."[14] Holmes seemed

11. A brief but very good account is given by Fifoot, *History and Sources,* pp. 397–402, of events up to the early seventeenth century. The account in Simpson, pp. 416–437, 458–470, gives all the references one could need.

12. Gilmore, *The Death of Contract,* pp. 19–21.

13. The two sentences, quoted by Gilmore, p. 20: "It is the essence of a consideration, that, by the terms of the agreement, it [the promise] is given and accepted as the motive or inducement for furnishing the consideration. The root of the whole matter is the relation of reciprocal conventional inducement, each for the other, between consideration and promise." *The Common Law* (Howe ed., 1963), p. 230.

14. James Kent, *Commentaries on American Law,* 1st ed. (1827), 2:364.

to be requiring much more than this. He seemed to say that both parties must *agree* that each was induced to promise or to act by the promise or act of the other. Perhaps he derived this from the requirement of mutual assent, so that the parties must agree not only on what was to be exchanged but also why; this would mean that the why—the inducement—for each must be disclosed and agreed to by the other.

The same kind of logic, working in reverse, was soon to lead the draftsmen of the German Code to provide that a transaction could not constitute a gift unless both parties had affirmatively agreed that there was to be *no* recompense.[15] But if, as I surmise, by requiring "reciprocal conventional inducement" Holmes meant to say that the parties must both agree that they were "reciprocally induced," this was not a revolution but a flight of fancy. It was already clear then and is more clear now that agreement by each as to what "induced" the other has never been required. Indeed, securing the other party's promise or performance can be for each the highest or the lowest on the scale of motives. It does not need to be a "material" motive, provided that it is in fact one motive.[16] The cryptic phrase that supposedly inspired a revo-

---

This formulation was surely known to Holmes, for it appeared unchanged in his edition of Kent's *Commentaries*, 12th ed. (1873), 2:164.

15. See above, chapter 3, section 2, n. 22.

16. Actually, Holmes in the same passage had been careful to say that consideration should not be confused with "the prevailing or dominant motive in actual fact," giving as an illustration a promise to paint a picture for $500 when the painter's chief motive might be a desire for fame. But he then shifted to "inducement" as the test and made it "the root of the whole matter."

As early as 1833, in Williams v. Carwardine, 4 Barnewall & Adolphus 621 (1833) it had been made clear that an act could be consideration though not "induced" by the promise, in the sense that the act would have been done in any event. Even in the first Restatement of Contracts, section 82 provided that consideration was not insufficient because "obtaining it was not the motive or a material cause inducing the promisor to make the promise." The topic is discussed by Corbin, *Contracts*, vol. 1, sec. 118; Williston, *Contracts*, 3d ed. (1957), vol. 1, Sec. 111.

lution never found a place in our vocabulary and has long since been deservedly forgotten.[17]

There is, however, one central question that has lingered over from earlier times. Is it true, as I have just asserted, that for a promise to become part of a bargain there must in fact exist in the promisor's assortment of motives a desire to receive the recompense that is to be given or promised by the promisee? Or will a tomtit, a peppercorn, or a hairpin suffice? Still more to the point, is it enough, as in France, to describe an exchange of valuable assets, partly completed or merely promised, with the participants understanding clearly that the recitals are on one side, at least, entirely false? One noted English author has urged that by taking the trouble to describe a transaction in the form of a bargain the participants give persuasive evidence of their serious intent.[18] But fortunately there is as yet no reason to think that in the formation of contracts, simulation—the outright sham with falsified terms—will have the success in our law that it has had in France.[19] Simulation through the use of token payments was approved for a time by the Restatement of Contracts, though this suggestion has since been abandoned.[20]

17. One does still occasionally encounter a greatly diluted version of the same idea, tossed off by Holmes in Wisconsin & Michigan Ry. v. Powers, 191 U.S. 379, 386, 24 S. Ct. 107 (1903): ". . . the promise and the consideration must purport to be the motive each for the other, in whole or at least in part. It is not enough that the promise induces the detriment or that the detriment induces the promise if the other half is wanting."

18. C. J. Hamsun, "The Reform of Consideration," 54 *Law Quarterly Review* 233, 242–244 (1938): "Now bargain, or the form of bargain, is an extremely good practical test. . . . Where the promise is gratuitous, the fact that the promisor has been willing to take pains to state his promise in the form of bargain or in that special way which we term a deed is equally conclusive of the intention of that promisor to assume a special obligation with reference to the promise so stated."

19. Corbin, *Contracts,* vol. 1, sec. 130; Williston, *Contracts,* 3d ed., vol. 1, sec. 115B.

20. To the First Restatement, sec. 82, there is appended Illustration 1, in which a father writes his son promising to convey Blackacre (worth

Certainly in transactions that purport to be exchanges the disparity in values can be so extreme that the performance on one side seems hardly more than symbolic. In determining whether it was bargained for in fact the question will be whether the promisor in making the promise had as one of his motives, however low on the scale, a desire to elicit from the promisee the act or abstention that was specified. After motives have been fully probed, the answer must often be nothing more than a guess.[21] Then, if the performance promised will promote some commendable cause, this may inspire an intensive search for some hidden, self-serving motive that will make a gift look like an exchange.[22]

$5,000) if the son will promise to pay him $1. The conclusion given is that if the son accepts, his promise of $1 is consideration. In the Second Restatement, sec. 82, this illustration disappears.

21. The classic case is Thomas v. Thomas, L. J. (N.S.) 11 C.L. 104 (1842), where executors, in compliance with the dying wishes of the deceased owner, promised to convey a house to the latter's widow in return for one pound to be paid yearly and a promise to repair. Was either form of "recompense" from the widow one of the objects of the executors' desire? It seems most unlikely, though court said they both were.

It seems strange indeed that one of the leading advocates of tokenism should have been Professor Williston (*Contracts,* 2d ed. [1936], vol. 1, sec. 115). He justified a refusal to inquire into promisors' motives by invoking the leading principle that the adequacy of consideration should not be examined. These are, of course, entirely separate issues. Of the cases cited, many did not involve formation of contract but token payments for options or discharges of existing duties, and I suggest that this is the main source of confusion. A valuable comment is "The Form of Bargain as Consideration," 24 *Columbia Law Review* 896 (1924).

22. At this point it is compulsory to city Allegheny College v. National Chautauqua County Bank, 246 N.Y. 369, 159 N.E. 173 (1927) where the donor, in fostering education for the Christian ministry, had a hidden motive, unearthed by Judge Cardozo: to be commemorated after her death.

This technique has a certain resemblance to the means used by French courts to find onerosity in charitable gifts (see above, chapter 2, sec. 4), but there is a difference. In Allegheny, the reward to the ego comes through action that the promisee must take, whereas in the French charity cases it is generated by the gift itself.

Questions like these, framed as questions of psychological fact, arise, of course, in innumerable ways. They present wide space for maneuver and for appraising much more in borderline transactions than the narrow issues of fact that are supposedly raised. But I venture the opinion that, on the whole, our courts have not undermined but have sought to preserve the essential elements of the bargain idea. I venture to say further that they *have* preserved it and that still serves us well in the one central role in which it is needed, the formation of contracts.

We have had much loose talk—that for consideration a peppercorn will do, that "consideration is as much a form as the seal." Such statements are true, but only partially true. I call them loose because they do not draw the essential distinction between contract formation and the other functions that have been brought under the rubric "consideration." It is in the performance of these extraneous functions that it has become a scrap-collector.

B. *Discharge or Modification of Obligations*

In the early history of the remedy that came to be called special assumpsit, the question that generated most public debate was whether the remedy could be used to enforce a new promise to pay an existing debt. On this question, as everyone knows, there was a protracted contest between the two central courts of common law, the King's Bench and Common Pleas. The Common Pleas, which resisted the displacement of the action of debt, was willing to concede that some slight variation in the arrangements for payment—place or date or medium used—could make trespass on the case available to enforce a new promise. This problem in due course disappeared with Slade's Case (decided in 1602).[23]

23. 4 Coke Rep. 92 (1602), discussed by many but with most illumina-

But before that date a related problem had appeared: could part payment of a money debt, accepted by the creditor as a full discharge, actually accomplish a full discharge? As will be mentioned in a moment, this question threw the courts into disarray and they were unable at this early stage to agree on a final answer. But it was conceded by all that the method used in expanding assumpsit could be used here too; part payment would suffice if it was accompanied by something extra, "be it never so small." It was enough to exhibit a deed to the opposite party, to take an oath before the mayor of London,[24] to hand over instead of money a hawk or a tomtit, to pay one day early or in another place.[25] When these assertions were made they were usually linked with an effort to define what would be consideration, a word that by the late 1500s had already become a term of art. These assertions have been repeated ever since, hundreds of times, as unassailable expressions of ancient wisdom but without noting the context in which they were made, when permitting the discharge of debts by part payment through slight variations from the payment due. These variations enabled the courts to skirt around and postpone an issue on which opinions at the time were sharply divided and their experience had not yet provided a clear guide.

Conflict in court decisions appeared in the 1580s and continued for thirty years, though the last case in the series

---

tion by J. H. Baker, "New Light on Slade's Case," [1971] *Cambridge Law Journal*, p. 213. The intermediate solution, allowing assumpsit to be used if there were minor variations in arrangements for payment, is discussed by Baker on pp. 218–222.

24. Sturlyn v. Albany, Croke Eliz. 67 (1587), exhibiting a deed; Knight v. Rushworth, Croke Eliz. 469 (1596), the oath. The latter case has often been quoted for its statement that "the smallness of the consideration is not material if there be any."

25. Pinnel's Case, 5 Coke 117a (1602), with Coke, C. J., quoting himself.

strongly affirmed that part payment, if accepted as a complete discharge, supplied whatever consideration was needed.[26] The issue was not resolved thereafter for nearly three hundred years. In 1884 the English House of Lords held that part payment could not accomplish a complete discharge, and most American courts meekly followed.[27] In a few earlier cases a consideration test had been invoked to preclude modifications that would produce the opposite effect, not scaling down or discharging a duty in return for part performance but increasing the sum that the other party must pay to secure a performance already due. These cases mostly arose in a maritime setting—sailors striking to secure higher pay—and it was far from clear how far they could be generalized.[28]

26. Holding part payment ineffective as a discharge: Richards v. Bartlet, 1 Leonard 19 (1584); Greenleaf v. Barker, 1 Leonard 238, Croke Eliz. 193 (1589); Pinnel's case, 5 Coke 117a (1602).

Holding part payment effective as a discharge: Gill v. Harewood, 1 Leonard 61 (1886); Reynolds v. Pinhowe, Croke Eliz. 429 (1595); Bagge v. Slade, 3 Bulstrode 162 (1614). In the case last cited, the latest in date of the series, the language attributed to Coke, C. J. is particularly emphatic: "I have never seen it otherwise, but when one draws money from another that this should be a good consideration to raise a promise" and goes on with an illustration: the "good consideration" there would be for discharging a £1,000 debt by paying £500.

27. It seems hardly necessary to cite Foakes v. Beer, 9 App. Cas. 605 (1884) and the classic article of Dean Ames, "Two Theories of Consideration," *Harvard Law Review* 12 (1899): 515, 522–530. He cited a few American decisions that had anticipated the conclusion of Foakes v. Beer and some that had rejected it. Foakes v. Beer and related themes are discussed extensively by Gilmore, *Death of Contract*, pp. 22–33.

28. Stilk v. Myrick, 2 Camp. 317 (1809) was the famous case, but there were others like it: Bartlett v. Wyman, 14 Johns. (N.Y.) 260 (1817); Harris v. Carter, 3 Ellis and Blackburn, 559 (1854); Frazer v. Hatton, 2 C.B. (N.S.) 512 (1857). The recurring theme, stated in Harris v. Carter, was that it would be "mischievous to commerce" if such wage increases were allowed.

Festerman v. Parker, 32 N.C. (10 Iredell) 474 (1879) extends the reasoning of the sailor cases to a contract to build a sawmill.

After the House of Lords had spoken in 1884, the generalization swept all before it and became an immutable principle of the common law, engraved on a tablet. Any performance that was already due under an existing obligation was erased—deleted—as a permissible subject of new agreement, unless it was modified in some minor way. Otherwise, in any dealings with the person to whom the performance was due it could not form part of an agreed exchange, no matter how convincing the evidence might be that the exchange was desired—bargained for—by both. Thus, within the limits of the obligation their agreement had created, the parties had destroyed their own power to contract. The logic that produced this contradiction could have been refuted, but it seemed easier to find a way around it. The old evasive formulas showed the way. Introduce some slight deviations, small additions, changes in time or place of the performance due—transparent pretexts that nullified whatever protective function the rule might have had.

Fortunately there is reason to hope that before long legislation will eliminate this misconceived aberration.[29] We should then have greater incentive to deal with the real problems that lie behind. We need to do this in any event. Some demands for readjustment of terms represent efforts to exploit necessities or disadvantages that restrict choice severely for the one on whom the demands are made. In both

29. The Uniform Commercial Code, sec. 209(1) has helped greatly: "An agreement modifying a sales contract needs no consideration to be binding." Statutes in twelve states that go varying distances in this direction are described by Dawson and Harvey, *Cases on Contracts,* 3d ed. (1977), pp. 252–254. Among authors, the proposal to abolish the preexisting duty rule altogether has had the support of E. W. Patterson, "An Apology for Consideration," 58 *Columbia Law Review* 929, 936–939 (1958), and F. Kessler, "Einige Betrachtungen zur Lehre von der Consideration," *Festschrift für Ernst Rabel,* pp. 251, 261–262 (1954). But it was believed to be still useful by Havighurst, "Consideration, Ethics and Administration," pp. 1, 25–30 (see n. 3 above).

France and Germany, which have fortunately escaped any such formal restraints on the renegotiation of contract terms, there are remedial doctrines available that open such transactions to review. They rely first of all on the notion of economic duress, as we do. Germany has gone still further in developing means and standards that should be useful to us.[30]

C. The Reinforcement of Offers

Until the nineteenth century was well advanced there seems to have been no serious concern over means for making offers "firm." This was partly, no doubt, because in English sources before that time the whole topic of offer and acceptance had hardly been mentioned.[31] Shortly before 1800 one case had raised the question whether offers could be revoked before acceptance. The answer had come without hesitation that of course they could, that if the offeree was still free to accept or reject, the offeror likewise could not be bound.[32] But what if the offeror himself had fixed a period of time during which the offer would endure, could he revoke before the time limit had expired? One strange English case and dicta in two American cases said that to prevent revocation it would be necessary to have some consideration.[33]

30. Dawson, "Unconscionable Coercion: The German Version," 89 *Harvard Law Review* 1041 (1976). The remedies for duress were discussed earlier by the same author, "Economic Duress and the Fair Exchange in French and German Law," 11 *Tulane Law Review* 345 (1937).

31. The silence of common-law sources on the topic of offer and acceptance until the nineteenth century was well advanced was commented on by A. W. B. Simpson, "Innovation in Nineteenth Century Contract Law," 91 *Law Quarterly Review* 247, 258–262 (1975).

32. Payne v. Cave, 3 Term Rep. 148 (1789); Best, C.J., in Routledge v. Grant, 4 Bing. 653 (1828); McCullough v. Eagle Ins. Co., 1 Pick. (Mass.) 278 (1822).

33. In the mysterious case of Cooke v. Oxley, 3 Term Rep. 635 (1790) there had been a duration fixed for the offer (until 4 P.M.), and it appeared

And this was really all there was until 1876 when an English court concluded with great confidence that a time limit fixed by the offeror could not prevent revocation before the time limit had expired, for in the absence of consideration any restriction on the power to revoke was simply *nudum pactum.*[34] American decisions have dutifully followed this line ever since and thereby made the consideration test a still more prominent target of public ridicule. For making an offer irrevocable the usual price is a dollar, though 25 cents will do.[35] In no reported case as yet has a hairpin been tried. The Second Restatement of Contracts at this point adopts a French form of simulation, with only the slightest support in American cases, and makes it enough to recite a "purported consideration."[36] The Uniform Commercial Code has helped somewhat, but it is amazing how little legislation has done to eliminate this Victorian relic.[37]

---

that he had accepted before that hour, but the court nevertheless concluded that in the absence of consideration the offeror could change his mind. In Boston and Maine R.R. v. Bartlett, 3 Cush. 224 (1849) and Perkins v. Haskell, 50 Ill. 216 (1869), the offers had been duly accepted, but both courts in dicta stated that before this occurred the offers, lacking consideration, could have been revoked.

The opinion strongly asserted by Best, C. J., in Routledge v. Grant, 4 Bing. 653 (1828) should also be mentioned. In the case presented, the offer was declared by the offeror to be effective for six weeks but the offeror revoked before that period had expired. Three judges sitting in the case held the acceptance of the offeree ineffective because it varied from the terms of the offer, but Best, C. J., without mentioning consideration, asserted as an additional ground that the offer had been effectively revoked because it was entirely inadmissible that one party could be bound while the other was free.

34. Dickinson v. Dodds, 2 Ch. Div. 463 (1876).

35. Corbin, *Contracts,* vol. 1A, sec. 263 collects the cases.

36. Restatement of Contracts Second, sec. 89B(1).

37. The U.C.C., sec. 2–205 applies only between merchants, and the assurance that the offer will remain unrevoked cannot be for more than three months. The New York Personal Property Law, sec. 33, which re-

The difficulties were all manufactured by treating offers as a subordinate form of promise.[38] An offer can of course be accompanied by a promise. Of itself it is not a promise but a proposal. Still less is it a gift, as was evident at once to Europeans who had inherited from Roman law their conception of gifts and were also accustomed to one-sided commitments. Normally the offeror's own purpose of providing the offeree time to deliberate could best be accomplished if the offer remained in force for the time that the offeror expressly defined or, if none was defined, for the period that the offeree could be expected to need for decision. This is what the German Code expressly provides unless the offeror has expressly reserved a power to revoke.[39] In France the Code has no provision on the subject, but in modern decisions French courts have concluded that the offeror's manifested intent to have the offer endure for a designated time must be given effect.[40] Any American court could now do the same without appealing to peppercorns or tomtits for help.

---

quires only a signed writing for offers of all kinds, could well be taken as a model.

38. A proposition strongly asserted by Williston, *Contracts,* vol. 1, secs. 24A and 25. The difficulty is that the only way to refute this is to assert the opposite.

39. B.G.B. arts. 145, 148, discussed by Williston, *Contracts,* vol. 1, sec. 63A, with references to other codes that have similar provisions. The arguments for this solution, which was a departure from earlier Pandectist views, were presented in the Motives of the First Drafting Commission, quoted in von Mehren and Gordley, *Civil Law System,* pp. 877–878. They mostly emphasized the need of offerees for a firm basis for their decisions, the likelihood that offerees would rely by foregoing other opportunities, and the service that a binding effect would render in promoting the interests of the offerors themselves.

40. Von Mehren and Gordley, *Civil Law System,* pp. 873–876, collect materials. This is a reversal of the position that was usually taken in earlier decisions. Among the authors there is still dispute as to whether the liability for premature revocation should be described as resting on contract or tort. Planiol et Ripert, *Traité pratique,* vol. 6, secs. 131–132.

214 *Gifts and Promises*

D. *Mutuality of Obligation*

The third overload that has been imposed has been the task of ensuring that in contracts formed through promises exchanged, the restrictions imposed by the obligations on each side are not unduly unbalanced. In this instance it is harder than it was with the other superfluous functions of the consideration test to identify the time when this task was undertaken as a special mission. One can find scattered through nineteenth-century court opinions statements to the effect that where promises are the consideration for each other, they must be "concurrent and obligatory upon both at the same time."[41] It was common to say that to have consideration the obligations must be "mutual" or that "for one to be bound both must be bound," in situations where there had been no exchange of promises at all.[42] The turning point came when language of promise had been used on both sides, but courts undertook to estimate the *degree* of restriction that the promises would produce for either side. An illustration would be a Minnesota case in 1873 involving sale to an iron foundry of all the pig iron it would "want" in the next four months. This was held to be, in effect, an illusory promise, and thus not to be consideration because the buyer had not also promised to have "wants."[43] Thereafter, in the

41. An early example is Tucker v. Woods, 12 Johnson (N.Y.) 190 (1815), where the document presented was described by the court as at most an offer "without mutuality," though the offeror-vendor's title was in any case defective.

After its first edition was published in 1852, the treatise by T. Parsons, *The Law of Contracts,* 1:448–451, was much quoted. After saying that a promise could be good consideration for another promise, the author continued: "but not unless there is an absolute mutuality of engagement, so that each has the right at once to hold the other to a positive agreement."

42. Lester v. Jewett, 12 Barb. (N.Y.) (1849); McKinley v. Watkins, 13 Ill. 141 (1851); Dorsey v. Packwood, 12 How. (U.S.) 126 (1851); Corbitt v. Salem Gaslight Co., 6 Ore. 405 (1877). Similarly in the dicta concerning revocability of offers, see above, note 33.

43. Bailey v. Austrian, 19 Minn. 535 (1873). This was an unsuccessful

last two decades of the century and continuing ever since have come long strings of decisions on whether an option in any one of various forms, retained by one promisor, would destroy "mutuality" so that there would be no consideration and both promises would be void.

Any comments here on this extensive output of case law can only be in the most general terms, but a few seem worth making. First, no one surely would suggest that such transactions should fail because they are conceived on either side as promises of gift. The purpose clearly is to effect an exchange that both parties desire. If enforcement is denied, this will be because a court substitutes its judgment for that of the parties and considers the assurances from one side insufficient. This judgment may be imposed even although the limited commitment on one side signified nothing more than prudence in a promisor who, facing uncertainty and risk, was unwilling to commit himself further and although his limited commitment had produced no disadvantage for the other side. So courts become involved in calculating the effects of promisors' options in the form of alternatives left open, powers to cancel with much or little notice, or other qualifying terms. In such appraisals the verbal formulas that consideration supplies—detriment and benefit—provide no guide to discriminating thought. Still less do they cast light on those one-sided transactions that *do* produce real disadvantage, where existing relations of economic superiority and dependency are preserved and often aggravated. As a guarantor of "mutuality," consideration provides no insight into the origins and effects of such transactions or the standards by

action by the buyer for the seller's refusal to deliver. The case has been severely and justly criticized by T. C. Lavery, "The Doctrine of Bailey v. Austrian," *Minnesota Law Review* 10 (1926): 584, who urged that this should have been read as a requirements contract but conceded that enforcement might be denied if the buyer were a jobber who had complete control over his own requirements.

which they should be judged. On the whole we would do much better without it.[44] Like consideration as a restriction on alterations of preexisting duty, it has served to distract attention and to disguise the hard problems where they do exist.

The experience of France and Germany certainly suggests that we could manage very well without this version of consideration, but it also suggests that other problems would then be exposed to view. In dealing with open-ended promises, both France and Germany started at the other end, with what amounts to a platitude: that a promise in which the promisor was left entirely free to perform or not as he chose was not a promise at all. This idea had surfaced in Roman law[45] and was expressed in the French Code by declaring void any promise with a *condition potestative* (a condition wholly subject to the promisor's control).[46] This provision, read strictly, only meant that there would be no remedy against the promisor. Did it also mean that he was precluded from enforcing the promise of the other that had been made in exchange for his? There would be no difficulty if by the time he sought to enforce the other's promise his own avenues of escape had been cut off.[47] In decisions around 1900, French courts were prepared to go considerably further and award damages for breach of promise to one who had reserved and still retained wide avenues of escape from his

44. The discussion by Corbin of the whole subject is, as always, to be greatly admired, especially his conclusion, announced at the outset, that despite what hundreds of cases have said, a requirement of mutuality of obligation probably does not exist. Corbin, *Contracts*, vol. 1A, sec. 152.

45. D.45.1.108.1: No promise can exist whose effect depends on the promisor's will.

46. Civil Code, art. 1174. French decisions on *conditions potestatives* are discussed by von Mehren, "Civil Law Analogues to Consideration," 72 *Harvard Law Review* 1009, 1024–1026 (1959).

47. D.1873.1.467 (Cass. 1873); D.1881.1.34 (Cass. 1879); D.1897.1. 34 (Cass. 1896).

own undertaking.[48] More recent decisions have found means
to relieve obligors in one type of case—where their performances came first and they were then left suspended in a
state of prolonged uncertainty by the wide choice left to the
other party whether or not to supply the intended return.[49]
And where arrangements that were extremely open-ended
on one side have been upheld, courts have issued warnings
that they would find means to intervene if one party was left
"at the mercy" of the other or subject to a purely "arbitrary"
will. Despite the absence of any relevant provisions in the
Code, some residual controls, phrased in these vague terms,
seem likely to persist.[50]

48. D.1897.1.76 (Cass. 1896); D.1899.1.360 (Cass. 1899); D.1900.1.
392 (Cass. 1900); and other cases cited by W. Brown, "Potestative Conditions and Illusory Promises," 5 *Tulane Law Review* 395, 408 (1931). In
some of these cases the employer's cancellation was effective only after
short periods of notice, so that an American court could find a little detriment in his being bound for short periods of time (eight days, etc.).

But the court refused in S.1906.2.299 (Aix, 1905) to enjoin an apprentice
from practicing as a veterinary on termination of his employment, where
negotiations to continue his employment had broken down through the
employer's wide power to dictate terms. The relations between the parties
were described as unequal and the apprentice was said to have had "no
free choice."

49. Several cases involved policies of liability insurance, in which
premiums were to be paid for protection against liability for lawyers' fees
or other costs of litigation but only if the insurer concluded that the insured's defenses had merit. Cancellation was awarded with restitution of
premiums already paid in D.H. 1951, 101 (Lyon, 1950): Gazette du Palais
1951.2.41 (Tribunal de la Seine, 1951); D.H. 1952, 103 (Tribunal de la
Seine, 1951). Only the first of these cases mentions a reason: want of *cause*
for the promise to pay premiums.

The Court of Cassation likewise refused to award damages against
owners who conferred long-term exclusive rights (1) to extract building
materials from a quarry and (2) to market a patented product, when they
repudiated arrangements by which the "buyers" assumed no obligation
until they had decided that the products were marketable, as they had until
then refused to do. *Bulletin des Arrêts de la Cour de Cassation Civile* 1,
no. 110 (April 7, 1967): 80, and 1, no. 405 (June 28, 1965): 370.

50. They are strongly supported, with a review of recent case law and

German courts have carried such controls considerably further—again, without explicit authority from the Code. The Code draftsmen decided to say nothing about open-ended promises or "potestative" conditions. They explained their two main reasons: (1) they had decided to recognize, as enforceable, sales of goods that were subject to the condition of buyer's approval;[51] and (2) in any event they could see no good reason why contracting parties, if they agreed, should be precluded from making a contract in which one of the promises exchanged contained a condition controlled entirely by the promisor.[52] They assumed that a reservation of this kind would be given full effect, so that until the condition occurred the promise would produce no liability at all.[53] But when it had occurred and the promisor had announced his decision and readiness to perform, his promise would become enforceable in all respects. The operation of this machinery was exemplified by two cases decided in 1922, involving sales of goods in which the sellers had at the outset disclaimed any obligation to deliver but had then declared their readiness to perform and had tendered delivery. In both cases they were allowed to collect the contract price.[54]

---

of comment by the authors, in the survey by J. Ghestin, "L'Indétermination du prix de vente et la condition potestative," Receuil Dalloz Sirey, 1973, Chronique, p. 293. As the title indicates, the author also discusses sales in which the price is left open and is to be fixed by one of the parties, where article 1591 (requiring that in a sale the parties designate a price) can be invoked.

51. As now provided in B.G.B., art. 495. Although it is assumed that the buyer in a sale "on approval" is entirely free to accept or reject, a resale to another before he has had an opportunity to inspect makes the seller liable in damages for breach of contract. *J.W.*, 1923, 605 (Berlin, 1922).

52. Excerpts from the comments on these issues by the two German drafting commissions are quoted in von Mehren and Gordley, *Civil Law System*, pp. 921–923.

53. This was asserted also in an opinion by the Combined Civil Senates of the Reichsgericht in 72 *R.G.Z.* 385 (1910).

54. 104 *R.G.Z.* 98 and 104 *R.G.Z.* 306. In both transactions there was

Actually, this result should not be very startling. If no other complications appeared, an American court might come out the same way.[55]

In these two sales cases, however, other complications did appear. The sales had been made in troubled times, immediately after the First World War. The shortages and dislocations produced by the war were aggravated by a rapid and eventually disastrous inflation of the currency. The buyers contended that these one-sided arrangements reflected and reinforced the economic ascendancy of the sellers, who through combination with other sellers had acquired control over the supply of the commodities sold and were thus enabled to exploit the buyers' necessities. The high court considered these to be justiciable issues. It examined evidence as to market organization and sources of supply for the commodities involved, the relations between the immediate parties, and the nature and extent of the buyers' needs before it concluded that the contention of the buyers

---

the additional feature that no price was fixed and the buyers in each instance were to pay the price that was current (*gültig*) at the time of delivery. In the second of the two cases, the court was more troubled by this feature than by the seller's disclaimer of any duty to deliver, but resolved its doubts by concluding that only price rises that were "fair" would be authorized by this clause.

Another type of transaction that was wide open on one side and that in Germany inspired a brief debate was the right of first refusal (if the owner contracts to sell to another, a right to buy on the same terms). The conclusion was that from its inception such an arrangement was a full-scale contract and not merely an option, even though the one entitled had as yet not decided whether to exercise his right. 72 *R.G.Z.* 385 (1910); 67 *R.G.Z.* 42 (1907).

55. For example, in Obering v. Swain-Roach Lumber Co., 86 Ind. App. 632, 155 N.E. 712 (1927), the vendor agreed that "in the event" that it bought a described tract of land, it would sell the land to the vendee at a designated price. The vendor then bought the land. Since its option (not to buy) had disappeared, it was given specific performance of the vendee's promise to buy. Similar cases are cited and discussed by Corbin, *Contracts*, vol. 1A, sec. 160.

had no basis in fact.[56] Such inquiries were not new. Very soon after the German Code took effect in 1900, the German high court had begun to formulate tests by which limits could be set where the forms of contract were used to consolidate and extend economic power over enterprises that were already heavily dependent. They had as their mandate nothing more precise than article 138 of the Civil Code, which declared void all contracts that offended "good morals." The controls that have since been developed by German case law extend over a wide range of transactions.[57] In arrangements that are found to be oppressive and therefore to need correction, a common feature is an absence or dilution of commitments on the side of the dominant party. But it is only as they contribute to this form of imbalance that the open-ended, even what we would call the illusory, promise has been in Germany a source of concern.

The first object of this section has been to show that the English law of contract discovered very early the idea of bargained-for exchange and has ever since preserved in good working order this extremely useful and—to us—essential instrument. The second object has been to explain the disrepute into which the whole idea has fallen through the acquisition about a century ago of three superfluous functions, excluding as elements in any agreed exchange performances

56. The buyer's claim of monopoly control by the seller was most strongly asserted in the case reported in 104 *R.G.Z.* 306 (1922), involving a sale of four clocks by a wholesaler of clocks. The court examined the record of the Economic Union of Clock Manufacturers, of which the seller was a member, and found that it had not misused its control of the clock trade and that the buyer had not in fact been faced with "economic ruin." In 104 *R.G.Z.* 98 (1922) the court seemed to be persuaded mostly by the absence of any compulsion working on the buyer, a dealer who had bought for resale.

57. Dawson, "Unconscionable Coercion—The German Version," 89 *Harvard Law Review* 1041, 1071–1103 (1976).

that are the subject of preexisting duty, reinforcing offers, and promoting "mutuality." In discussing these themes the hope was expressed that these useless appendages would soon be stripped away. If this occurs, consideration will cease to be, as one author put it, a deficiency of our law for which "apology" is needed.[58] It would then express more clearly an idea that has been accepted for centuries in Anglo-American law: that a sufficient reason for enforcing a promise is that it is part of an agreed exchange which would enable each party to secure from the other an act or result that he sought. There are other exceptional reasons for enforcing promises, but this is overwhelmingly the normal one. Have we sacrificed much by turning it around and making it into a requirement, so that (subject to these few exceptions) it has become the only recognized reason?

2. *The Balance of Disadvantage*

Up to this point attention has been mainly directed toward showing the very considerable differences between France and Germany in their treatment of gift transactions, despite the strong and continuing influence exercised on both by the inheritance from Roman law. The differences between these two legal systems and our own are obviously also wide and call, I think, for some brief additional comment. Some of the differences result from decisions made in the distant past and some reflect value judgments that are beyond the reach of argument. But one can at least look for disadvantages that have resulted—disadvantages that can be identified and to some extent appraised.

One basic difference that has often been mentioned is that in the tradition derived from Roman law a gratuity is not

58. Patterson, "An Apology for Consideration" (see n. 29). This article I describe as superb and agree with completely.

a gift unless it permanently diminishes the estate owned by the giver and permanently adds to that owned by the receiver. So the divergence begins where promises are used, promises made without recompense, to render a service, permit the use of physical property or of an idea, to act or abstain in some other way. In France or Germany they will be exempt from all restrictions and may be enforceable to some extent, whereas in our law they will all be void for want of consideration (in the absence of reliance, antecedent moral duty, or some other special feature). If the index of a superior civilization is taken to be the number or percentage of promises enforced, our own society could be regarded as backward.

In France and Germany, however, where such promises are gratuitous, it is seldom that much is invested in such arrangements, either by the participants themselves or by legal agencies when called on to enforce them. If in a particular case substantial reliance has occurred and was justified, stronger measures than usual may be employed.[1] But ordinarily such arrangements are readily dissolved at the will of either party and the care and diligence required of the promisor in his own performance are much reduced.[2] In most of the situations that have led to litigation (promises to supply free transportation or medical care), a promise would usually add little to the duties that the enterprise itself would gener-

1. This was true, for example, in the early French case discussed in chapter 2, section 2, note 7, in which the defendant, owner of a hotel, promised to permit occupation of some assigned space in his hotel for the reception and use of passengers if the plaintiff would sever his connection with the postal service and reinstate a transportation service that he had previously operated in the district. After the plaintiff had done both, the defendant refused to perform. The court authorized specific performance. It seems hard to believe that the court was not influenced by the plaintiff's shift of occupation and resumption of the transportation service, though this was not mentioned as a reason.

2. Chapter 2, section 2, especially notes 4 and 5.

ate. So I conclude that our law has suffered no real loss by withholding from ties that bind so lightly the descriptive title contract and in attributing to the law of tort whatever redress is needed.

This serves as a reminder that while we too mark off gifts for separate treatment, both the treatment itself and our reasons for it are entirely different. In the history of the common law it would be hard to find any evidence of suspicion or hostility directed toward gifts, either gifts in general or those of some particular form or type. It is true that those made for certain objectionable purposes—for example, to defeat the claims of creditors or bribe public officials—would be set aside because of their purpose. But without the prospect of some specific harm of this kind there would be no occasion for calling them in question. As to promises, I have argued, those forming part of an agreed exchange were early recognized as having strong claims for enforcement and their enforcement soon became a well-settled habit. Within extreme outside limits the content of the performances to be exchanged made no difference, for this was left for the parties to decide.

Among those in charge of administering English law, not many could have heard of the Roman classification of contract-types, with its small subgroup of contracts by which small-scale gratuities could be conferred. So when English judges confronted promises that lacked any element of exchange, their reluctance to intervene may have been due in part to uncertainty and doubt (where does this lead, where could we stop?), but in any event they must have remained unconvinced that there were serious reasons to bestir themselves. Toward gift transactions generally the net result was an attitude of indifference, expressed by almost total abstention. If bounty was promised, the promisor was left free to confer it and no one was likely to interfere; if he decided not to confer it after all, courts would not step in to compel him to give up something for nothing. The presence or absence of an element of exchange provided a relatively simplified test that cut across all varieties of promises. During the period of nearly three hundred years when English contract law was managed without any critical or expository literature, it is unlikely that much connected thought was given to these themes by anyone. Yet even in the last hundred years little disposition has appeared to change the solutions in a basic way. Foreseeable reliance of the promisee has come to be an alternative ground for enforcement, one that we nowadays could not do without. But even in the literature of protest, denouncing the doctrine of consideration, a deeper involvement in gift transactions, either to enforce or undo them, has not been strongly urged.

In the tradition derived from Roman law, the special handling provided for gifts subjects a carefully defined and limited group to direct control, one of whose aims is to deter or prevent, even to the extent of cancelling transfers that have already been executed. The pattern of control as originally devised in Roman law was extremely limited in both content and purpose: (1) it was confined to transactions that transferred ownership of what can be called capital assets; and (2) its only purpose was to prevent such transfers between husband and wife. This purpose was replaced in late medieval and early modern Europe as the conviction grew that the near relatives of every owner of property should be ensured a predetermined and substantial share of the estate that he left at his death. In order to make this guarantee more effective, his "estate" was then conceived as reaching back to include all property that he had at one time owned and had given to others in his lifetime. As the rights of heirs, defined in this way, acquired widespread and deeply rooted support, France and Germany became more and more committed to the monitoring of gifts in order to scale down or cancel all those that had depleted the shares guaranteed to the nearest of kin. This function for the regulation of gifts is now made mandatory by the codes and effectuates policies that clearly seem to have unchallenged support in public opinion.

Controls over gifts can have a broader purpose, not merely to protect some specific third-party interest, but more generally to interpose obstacles, aiming to deter. The French monarchy under the ancien régime must surely have had such a purpose for its legislation, repeatedly reenacted, that imposed stringent requirements of form for all promises or transfers that conformed to the Roman concept of gift: a net subtraction from the donor's "patrimony." There is good reason to believe that the monarchy's main concern was to prevent unproductive transfers that would deplete the wealth of the leading families. It was almost an accident and was to be a misfortune that the leaders of the French Revolution, for different reasons of their own, were strongly disposed to maintain these controls, which survived the revolution and were transferred intact into the Civil Code. The central requirement, notarization, was preserved in a comprehensive and most burdensome form. There ensued a disorderly flight through the manual gift, through "simulation" (that is, deliberate falsification) of terms, through requiring for a finding of gift a generous motive so pure and undefiled that a promise of gift is almost never encountered and notarization therefore is almost never needed. But none of these transparent evasions and distortions are allowed to disguise or protect from revocation the gift that depletes an heir's "legitimate part." So French law on this topic is divided down the middle and as a result is thrown into disarray. To one unsympathetic observer, at least, it seems clear enough that in the whole French experience here described there was nothing that we should either envy or emulate.

In Germany the basic scheme for the monitoring of gifts is essentially the same as that set up in France, though it has been administered very differently. The only gratuities that can constitute gifts and that therefore call for special attention are those that will transfer capital assets. The German Code has a much longer list of grounds for their reduction or recall, but the most prominent, again, is the need to protect the guaranteed shares of the donor's heirs. There were two main differences in the German scheme: (1) insistence on formality was much diminished by requiring notarization only for promises of gift; and (2) a new formula was added that explicitly required agreement of the parties that the gain was to be one-sided, that nothing had been or would be given in exchange.

The response in Germany to the scaled-down requirement of notarization has not been, as in France, disorderly flight but willing compliance, and this despite the fact that notarization procedure in Germany does not differ in significant ways from the procedure in France. The aim is to ensure deliberation, informed assent, and a full public record through active participation by a trained public official. There have been statements made in English that countries governed by "the civil law" will freely enforce all promises, including promises of gift. For France such a statement has become almost true, but in Germany a promise to transfer "without recompense" any "property" owned by the promisor will be void unless verified and recorded through this formal ceremony before a public official.

There would be some advantage in our law, too, if persons who had determined to confer benefactions but were not yet ready to do so were enabled to commit themselves by promise. The advantage would have to be described as highly abstract, the enlargement of their freedom of "contract."[3] In twenty-three of our states they now have this power if their promises are in writing and under seal. But the seal has so completely lost meaning that as a safe-guarding formality it performs no function at all. We surely will not invent another. So notarization as it is used in Germany is a facility that we have some reason to envy but are not likely to emulate. It is, however, worth noting that this "civil law" country, after most extensive deliberation and with a general concurrence that still persists, has imposed on promises of gift, as the Code defines them, a requirement of form that is far more strict than any known to the common law.

The requirement expressed in the German Code that for a gift the transfer must be without "recompense" was introduced at the last minute and in a roundabout way, but to an American it looks just as familiar when seen through a back door. I have argued earlier that if bargain consideration is a blight, as some contend, then in Germany the malady is virulent and deep-seated. This appears particularly in various kinds of mixed transactions, in which elements of both gift and exchange are combined. In dealing with such transactions German courts have undertaken an extraordinarily difficult task—judicial surgery that dissects a fused transaction into separate parts with no ray of light to guide the surgeon's knife. The consideration test as we apply it calls for nothing like this. It is enough, we say, if one of the motives of

3. It is occasionally mentioned as a reproach that the requirement of consideration is a restriction on "freedom of contract," as it plainly is (Kessler, "Einige Betrachtungen," pp. 251, 266–268). That a "net increase in social welfare" can result from making gratuitous promises enforceable is argued by R. Posner, "Gratuitous Promises in Economics and Law," 6 *Journal of Legal Studies* 411 (1977).

the promisor—perhaps the lowest on the scale of his motives—is to secure the act, abstention, or result that is to be supplied by the promisee; all the rest can be gift. Our courts, fortunately, are not likely to engage in the searching inquiries that German courts feel called on to conduct.

Why do they feel called on to conduct them? The German Code gives miscellaneous purposes for its controls over gifts, but it has seemed to me that both the basic scheme and the ways in which it is managed have been shaped most of all by one—that of protecting the shares in inheritance that are guaranteed to near relatives of every owner. The scheme itself operates only on transfers that permanently deprive the owner of some part of his transmissible assets. The zeal shown by courts in penetrating disguises would seem excessive if the object were merely to preserve a donor's powers to revoke or to ensure that promises containing an element of gift were at least partially notarized. I have ventured the guess that the priority of rights guaranteed to forced heirs may explain why foreseeable reliance by donees has not become an accepted reason, as it has with us, for enforcing promises of gift; still more, it may explain why justified reliance by donees is never mentioned as a reason for refusing to cancel or scale down a gift already completed. The argument could be put in various ways, but one might be that reliance on a gift is never justified if it turns out to have encroached on the share guaranteed by law and through an overriding family loyalty to the donor's nearest of kin. The severe cutting back in Germany of moral obligation as an independent ground for enforcing promises may have been another symptom; for a moral obligation owed to a promisee would be at least matched by the obligation, both moral and legal, that the promisor would owe to his own immediate family. And if it were objected that the arguments just presented exaggerate the influence of forced heirship on the reading given by the courts to the Code provisions as a whole, one can only say—perhaps. But consistency and uniformity in the use of the Code's central ideas are still highly prized in Germany, so one can be fairly sure that the content assigned to the concept of gift in contests with forced heirs will be carried over and become part of the tests that are used for all the other purposes that make gifts vulnerable to attack.

If I am wrong and the purpose of protecting guaranteed shares in inheritance has not had as pervasive an influence as all this suggests, it has at any rate remained a prominent feature, a theme that often reappears. There seems to be no room to doubt that it has come to stay, not only in German and French law, but in most of the legal systems throughout the Western world that have followed the Romanesque tradition. It is a theme that is hardly worth debating since reasoned argument does not persuade. Where there actually has been active debate on the issue whether forced heirship should be retained or abolished, as in Louisiana very recently,[4] one can expect each side at the end to reaffirm the view that was held at the outset: forced heirship either is or is not worth the price it exacts. I will do the same and reaffirm the view, held at the outset, that it cannot be worth the price it exacts. I count as part of the price that we, fortunately, do *not* have to pay a set of controls over gift transactions that in France proved so strict as to be both destructive and self-

4. Complications in Louisiana have been magnified because the guarantees can be readily evaded by determined donors (by buying land in another state or buying life insurance, by creation of express trusts) but the state constitution still forbids the abolition of forced heirship and efforts in 1974 to repeal this provision met strong resistance and were abandoned. The arguments for the abolition of forced heirship are presented strongly by M. Nathan, "An Assault on the Citadel," 52 *Tulane Law Review* 5 (1977); the arguments for retention, by T. B. Lemann, "In Defense of Forced Heirship," ibid., p. 20; and further commentary by J. Le Van, "Alternatives to Forced Heirship," ibid., p. 29.

defeating, and that in Germany has been made far more searching and intensive than any for which we have found any need.

This survey leads me to only one conclusion: that our disadvantages, the main sources of our own discontent, are those of our own creation, are not found elsewhere and cannot be removed by borrowings from Europe. But this very fact, that they are strictly our own, offers the hopeful prospect that we should be able to eliminate them and set our own house in order.

Appendix

The tabular view presented here has been prepared with two purposes in mind: to persuade the skeptical reader (1) that guaranteed shares in inheritance for close relatives are very common in countries that follow the Western legal tradition and (2) that the restrictions on gifts to persons outside the donor's own genetic line are often severe.

The division between the two tables is dictated only by geography. In the first table the restrictions in France and Germany, which have been referred to often in the text, are listed for comparison with those now in effect in ten other countries of Western Europe. The second table summarizes the disposable quotas in the twelve Latin American countries (out of nineteen) in which forced heirship is recognized.

In the twenty-four countries whose forced heirship provisions are summarized here the procedure for enforcement is essentially the same as that described in France and Germany. Inter vivos gifts are left undisturbed until the donor's death. At that point the disposable assets left in the decedent's estate are appraised, and to them are "fictively" added gifts made in his or her lifetime, usually appraised as of the time they were made. Of the countries listed only three fix a time limit for this retrospective roundup (ten years in Germany and Venezuela, two years in Austria). When the value of the assets thus disposed of by gift has been totaled up, the number and types of forced heirs who survive the decedent

1. In Denmark, Norway, and Sweden, however, the quotas apply only to the estate left at death plus assets given in anticipation of imminent death or with the effect of the gift postponed until death.

will determine the quota of which he or she had had power to dispose. If the total value of all gifts, by will and inter vivos, exceeds the disposable quota, those in excess of the quota are canceled or scaled down, starting with those made in the decedent's will then moving back, the inter vivos gifts that are latest in time being canceled first.

These tables do not reflect several variables that appear in many of the codes. Illegitimate children, for example, are often included among the forced heirs but under restrictions that vary widely. The codes often announce the principle that heirs of the same rank should be treated alike and provide means for equalizing their shares on complaint of the heirs who had been disfavored; variation comes in the extent to which and the means by which owners who are determined to discriminate can succeed in doing so by declaring this purpose expressly.

In all the legislative systems, priority is given to descendants of the decedent, with those further down in the line of descent taking the shares of their parents. If no descendants survive, ascendants (parents and more remote ancestors in the direct line) usually take their place, though the shares guaranteed to ascendants are smaller. Siblings of the decedent are altogether omitted, except in Switzerland. The surviving spouse is often omitted also and the provisions for the marriage partner, if any are made, vary widely. They may perhaps have some interest, so they are summarized separately.

I emphasize again, though it may by now be obvious enough, that the fractions listed below represent the portions of "giveable" property that the owner is permitted to give for purposes or to persons outside his own genetic line. All the rest—in most countries, the designated fraction of all that he or she *ever* owned—is "reserved" for the decedent's direct descendants or ancestors, with an occasional allowance for a surviving husband or wife.

Disposable Quota
Where Decedent Leaves:

		Descendants		Ascendants Only
Austria		1/2		2/3
Belgium	1	1/2	of two lines	1/2
	2	1/3	of one line	3/4
	3 or more	1/4		
Denmark		1/2		
France	1	1/2	of two lines	1/2
	2	1/3	of one line	3/4
	3 or more	1/4		
Germany		1/2		1/2
Italy	1	1/2		2/3
	2	1/3		
	3 or more	1/4		
Netherlands	1	1/2		1/2
	2	1/3		
	3 or more	1/4		
Norway		1/3		
Portugal	1	1/2	if parent survives	1/2
	2 or more	1/3	if grandparent survives	2/3
Spain		1/3		1/2
			in spouse survives	2/3
Sweden		1/2		
Switzerland		1/4		1/2
Argentina		1/5		1/3
Bolivia		1/5		1/3
Chile		1/4		1/2
Colombia		1/4		1/2
Cuba		1/3		2/3
Brazil		1/2		1/2
Dominican Republic	1	1/2	of two lines	1/2
	2	1/3	of one line	3/4
	3 or more	1/4		
Ecuador		1/4		1/2
Haiti	1	1/2	of two lines	1/2
	2	1/3	of one line	3/4
	3	1/4		
Peru		1/3		1/2
Uruguay	1	1/2		1/2
	2	1/3		
	3	1/4		
Venezuela		1/2		3/4

Note: I found no provisions for forced heirship in Costa Rica, Guatemala, Hon-

The Code provisions on these topics in the countries listed are contained in the following articles:

Austria	762–766, 785
Belgium	913–930
Denmark	Inheritance Law, art. 1, pars. 6–7
France	913–930
Germany	2303–2313, 2325–2329
Italy	536–552
Netherlands	960–962, 967–971
Norway	Inheritance Law, art. 29
Portugal	2156–2173
Spain	806–809, 818–820
Sweden	Inheritance Code, chap. 2, art. 1
Switzerland	471–475, 522–532

Argentina	1832, 3593–3595, 3602
Bolivia	1059–1063, 1066–1069
Brazil	1.721, 1.726–728, 1.176
Chile	1182–1187
Colombia	1240–1245
Cuba	806–809, 819–821
Dominican Republic	913–915, 920–923
Ecuador	1231, 1235–1240
Haiti	741–747
Peru	700–701
Uruguay	885–889, 1640
Venezuela	883–889

The Surviving Spouse

The object here will be merely to describe the extent to which forced heirship is extended beyond the two primary groups, descendants and ascendants of the decedent, to include the surviving spouse. Obviously this tabulation will give only a partial view of the provisions made for marital partners, since it omits all the rights arising out of community property and similar arrangements. Tabulated here are the rights to which the surviving spouse becomes entitled under the regime of forced heirship. Of the countries on the previous list, about half include no provision for the surviving spouse, and they are omitted here.

Denmark	Shares Guaranteed
	(1) 1/2 of estate if no descendants survive
	(2) 1/6 of estate if descendants survive
Germany	1/8 of estate
Italy	usufruct in
	1/3 if one child survives
	1/4 if two children survive
	5/12 if only ascendants survive
	1/3 if a child and ascendants survive
Spain	usufruct in 1/3;
	but if no descendants or ascendants survive, then 2/3
Switzerland	1/4 of estate;
	if sole heir 1/2

Argentina	(1) 1/2 of estate if there are no descendants or ascendants
	(2) a widow takes a child's share if descendants survive
Bolivia	(1) 2/3 if no descendants or ascendants survive
	(2) if descendants survive, a child's share
Chile	twice a child's share if a descendant survives
Colombia	1/4 of estate; but if descendants survive, takes a child's share
Cuba	usufruct in 1/3, 1/2, or 2/3 of estate, depending on whether descendants or ascendants or none survive
Ecuador	if children survive, spouse takes a child's share
Peru	if descendants survive, spouse takes a child's share
Venezuela	1/4 of estate; but if descendants survive, takes a child's share

Germany	2203 and 1371	Argentina	3595, 3570
Italy	540, 542–544	Bolivia	1061, 1062
Spain	834	Chile	1178
Switzerland	471 and 462	Colombia	1236
		Cuba	834–837
		Ecuador	1231
		Peru	704
		Venezuela	883

Index

237